S-£8.
Old edition

CRIME IN EARLY MODERN ENGLAND 1550-1750

D0956927

THEMES IN BRITISH SOCIAL HISTORY

edited by Dr J. Stevenson

This series covers the most important aspects of British social history from the Renaissance to the present day. Topics include education, poverty, health, religion, leisure, crime and popular protest, some of which are treated in more than one volume. The books are written for undergraduates, postgraduates and the general reader, and each volume combines a general approach to the subject with the primary research of the author.

CRIME IN EARLY MODERN ENGLAND 1550–1750

J. A. Sharpe

LONGMAN
London and New York

Addison Wesley Longman Limited
Edinburgh Gate, Harlow
Essex CM20 2JE, England
and Associated Companies throughout the world

*Published in the United States of America
by Addison Wesley Longman Publishing, New York*

© Longman Group Limited 1984

All rights reserved; no part of this publication may be
reproduced, stored in a retrieval system, or transmitted
in any form or by any means, electronic, mechanical,
photocopying, recording, or otherwise, without either
the prior written permission of the Publishers or a
licence permitting restricted copying in the United
Kingdom issued by the Copyright Licensing Agency Ltd,
90 Tottenham Court Road, London, W1P 9HE.

First published 1984
Eighth impression 1996

BRITISH LIBRARY CATALOGUING IN PUBLICATION DATA

Sharpe, J.A.
    Crime in early modern England 1550–1750.
    1. Crime and criminals—England—History
    2. Punishment—England—History
    I. Title
    364'.942 HV6949.E5
ISBN 0-582-48994-6

LIBRARY OF CONGRESS CATALOGING IN PUBLICATION DATA

Sharpe, J.A.
Crime in early modern England, 1550-1750

(Themes in British Social history)
Bibliography: P.
Includes index.
1. Crime and criminals—England—History—16th
century. 2. Crime and criminals—England—History—17th
century. 3. Crime and criminals—England—History—18th
century. I. Title. II. Series.
HV6949.E5S53 1984   364'.942   82-7128
ISBN 0-582-48994-6 (pbk.)

Set in 10/11 pt Linotron Times
Produced by Longman Singapore Publishers (Pte) Ltd
Printed in Singapore.

CONTENTS

LIST OF TABLES AND FIGURES

PREFACE AND ACKNOWLEDGEMENTS

What might be termed the 'intellectual origins' of this book date back some fourteen years, to the period when I was beginning detailed work on my doctoral thesis on crime in seventeenth-century Essex. I was, and remain, convinced of the value of the detailed local study to the history of early modern crime. Similarly, I was, and remain, convinced of the excellence of the facilities of the Essex Record Office. Even at that early stage of my studies around the subject, however, it became obvious to me that it involved issues which stretched far beyond Essex, that much studied corner of Elizabethan and Stuart England, and far beyond the sixty-year period covered by my doctorate. This book is the product of my desire to come to grips with some of those wider issues. Even so, the initial debt I must acknowledge is to two men whose influence on me while I was involved in the earlier exercise still affects my work: Mr Keith Thomas, under whose supervision I learnt how to conduct historical research; and Mr Arthur Searle, from whom I learnt a great deal about how to approach local archives.

In the process of researching this present book my intellectual indebtedness has increased enormously. I have consulted printed primary materials and secondary works in the Bodleian Library, the British Library, the Brotherton Library, Leeds, the Guildhall Library, the Institute of Historical Research, and the J. B. Morrell Library, York. I am grateful to the staff of all these institutions for their assistance. I am also grateful for permission to consult and cite manuscript materials in the Borthwick Institute of Historical Research, York, the Corporation of London Record Office, the Doncaster Metropolitan Borough Archive Service, the Durham University Department of Palaeography and Diplomatic, the Essex Record Office, the Greater London Record Office, the North Humberside Record Office, Sheffield City Libraries, and, above all, the Public Record Office in London. The Crown-copyright records in the Public Record Office and the Greater London Record Office are cited by kind permission of Her Majesty's Stationery Office.

The services of these institutions have been supplemented by assistance from a number of individuals. I should like to thank all those who have given me permission to cite their dissertations or other unpublished materials. More specifically, Dr Tim Curtis, Dr M. J. Ingram, Dr John Stevenson, and Dr Keith Wrightson were all kind enough to read earlier drafts of sections of this book, and the final version has been considerably strengthened by their comments and criticisms. I have also been aided by conversations and correspondence with Ms Joanna Innes, Dr J. B. Post, and Mr John Styles, while my awareness of the wider geographical and chronological issues involved in my chosen subject has been sharpened by debate with continental and transatlantic scholars at the colloquia organised in Paris by the International Association for the History of Crime and Criminal Justice. I am grateful to John Stevenson in his editorial capacity and to Mrs Julie Eastwood for preparing the final typescript with her accustomed speed and accuracy.

I also owe much to having worked for nearly a decade in what is probably one of the best and certainly one of the liveliest history departments in the country, during which time I have learnt much through having to refine my ideas in argument with my colleagues and students. Of the former, Dr Jonathan Powis and Dr Dwyryd Jones have perhaps done most to deepen my understanding of the early modern period. Of the latter, my special subject group of the autumn of 1980 were especially noteworthy for taking nothing that I said on trust, and for voicing their criticism in forthright terms: I hope to see their like again.

Bishophill, York
August 1983

Chapter 1

DEFINITIONS, METHODS AND OBJECTIVES

It is currently becoming a commonplace among professional historians that the history of crime is a major growth area of historical research. It is generally regarded as one of a number of subjects to which serious attention has only recently been turned by historians, and which are frequently described by those working on more familiar themes as fashionable: the family, leisure, childhood and death, for example. Certainly, even though the existence of a number of important earlier studies should not be overlooked, it has been the last decade or so that has witnessed a rapid expansion of scholarly investigation of the history of crime, law and order, and related topics. Nevertheless, much remains to be done, and those working in the field are acutely conscious that if the history of crime is a growth area, it is one which still has considerable growing to do. So far as early modern England is concerned, serious writing on the subject is hardly overwhelming in volume: a handful of monographs; a similar number of collections of essays; less than ten unpublished doctoral theses; and little over twenty isolated articles and essays.[1] The historian of crime, reminded by his colleagues working in more established fields that his subject is fashionable and expanding, is forced to reflect on one of the basic truisms of crime studies: the reaction to deviants is usually far greater than their activities would justify.

That the history of crime is a growing subject is largely the outcome of the neglect with which it has hitherto been treated. The last generation of textbooks, for the most part, makes only passing reference to it. J. B. Black's account of the reign of Elizabeth I in the Oxford History of England series makes a few generalized remarks on lawlessness, mentions highwaymen briefly, and devotes the obligatory few paragraphs to vagabonds. Sir George Clark's account of the later Stuarts, in the same series, restricts itself to a brief and not entirely accurate commentary on witchcraft and duelling. One of the best known general histories of the eighteenth century, by J. H. Plumb, mentions crime and the criminal law as one element in the supposed brutality of the age. A familiar picture is conjured up of gin-drinking, ineffective parish constables, the London slums, and Tyburn, while 'the brutality and ferocity of life . . . prevalence of dirt, disease and poverty' is commented upon. In such a world, it is little wonder that 'angry mobs, burning and looting' were as 'prevalent as disease'. Even books claiming to deal with economic and social history have had little to say about crime. Apart from some problems in London, the 'apprenticeship' which England experienced, according to Charles Wilson, included little schooling in illegality.[2] Indeed, economic historians in general have been content to supply us with accounts of the laudable achievements of the industrious apprentices: the less edifying exploits of the idle ones, it would seem, are best left to William Hogarth.

In large measure, this neglect of crime as an historical phenomenon is just one aspect of a much wider tendency, still with us, to treat social history as the Cinderella of the historical sciences. Since the late nineteenth century, the main thrust of English historical writing has been towards the study of past politics. Social history, when studied on a level above the purely anecdotal, has been approached largely in terms of the history of social policy. Even labour history, potentially an exciting subject, is only just beginning to emerge from its preoccupation with the early prefigurations of the modern labour party and trade union movement. Only recently has much serious attention been paid to those aspects of life which are outside the ken of such political institutions. This past neglect has led to two problems. The first, to use the words of Keith Thomas, is that social history has usually been treated as an 'undemanding subsidiary', something that at best deserves only brief mention before the historian passes on to his central concerns, politics and the constitution. Secondly, as Edward Thompson has put it, to the mainstream historian 'the people of this island (see under Poor Law, Sanitary Reform, Wages Policy) appear as one of the problems which the government has to handle'. Thomas's argument that 'the social history of the future will . . . not be a residual subject, but a central one, around which all other branches of history are likely to be organized',[3] has not been fulfilled in Britain, least of all in the undergraduate syllabus. Nevertheless, important advances have been made.

These advances are the outcome of a number of factors. One of them is the influence of foreign historians, not least French proponents of the *Annales* school. Another is the contribution made to the study of history by the social sciences, of which social anthropology is probably of the most use to the early modernist.[4] Both of these influences have done much to encourage historians of Tudor and Stuart England to approach their subject in new ways. But what is arguably the most important contribution to this rewriting of the history of early modern England has come from the massive growth in what might be best described as archive-consciousness: documentary sources are more widely available than ever before, and historians are becoming increasingly imaginative in their ideas of how to use them.[5] Many sources which were undiscovered, unavailable, or whose usefulness was unappreciated twenty years ago, are now readily on hand at the Public Record Office in London, or in local or specialist record offices. Research on these documentary riches is made easier by the way in which many of them have been repaired, cleaned, catalogued and indexed in such a fashion as to facilitate their use. In 1848 Macaulay, at the beginning of the famous third chapter of his *History of England*, lamented the fact that he was forced to base his account upon 'scanty and dispersed materials'. Most later political historians, in their brief accounts of English society in the past, have used a similarly anecdotal approach, although few have matched Macaulay's vividness of writing. Now, thanks to the labours of the archivist, those embarking on the writing of English social history frequently find an embarrassment of primary materials upon which to base their researches.

In particular, this extensive documentation makes it possible to treat crime as something more than an aspect of an undemanding and subsidiary area of history, capable of and deserving only anecdotal treatment. Recent work in the field has confirmed the suspicion that arises from reading a few of the older studies of the subject[6]: abundant materials await the historian willing to go out and find them, and important results await those willing to show diligence in reading these materials and ingenuity in using them. Court archives, although nowhere near complete, survive in large numbers, and reveal the business of tribunals as disparate as the Star Chamber and King's Bench at Westminster, and the local manorial court in the darkest corner of the realm. Such archives form the basis of the most important research on crime, the actuality of the prosecution of offences and their punishment. Other sources, many of them as yet relatively unexploited, provide insights into other important if ancillary facets of crime in the past. Popular literature, almost since its inception, has been full of accounts of spectacular crimes, accounts which provide some factual evidence as well as information on attitudes towards illegal behaviour. By the early eighteenth century, newspapers were regularly reporting crime, while additional information on the phenomenon is provided by advertisements concerning stolen goods. The statute book and parliamentary diaries can be used to give evidence on official attitudes and preoccupations, while there are also frequent if scattered references to crime in a wide variety of private documents, among them diaries, letters, and estate papers. There is certainly no shortage of material and, as we shall see, this is already reflected in a diversity of approaches to the subject.

This variety of materials relating to the history of crime, and mention of the diversity of ways in which the subject can be approached, serve to introduce a fundamental problem: how 'crime' is to be defined. Our starting-point must be that the word crime is a general blanket term rather than a precise analytical or descriptive category. The term can be used to describe an accident; an incidental and unpremeditated explosion of passion or despair; a behaviour pattern expressive of emotional or mental instability or frustration; something akin to business activity; or even a chosen way of life. Defining behaviour as 'criminal' varies according to different circumstances or social conventions, and there is a constantly moving frontier of what is, and what is not, acceptable conduct in any given society. Crime thus includes not only those acts which most human beings would regard as intrinsically wicked but whose motivation can vary enormously (theft and murder, for example); it also comprehends behaviour which can be newly classified as criminal by a specific society and can therefore be created by legislators or law-enforcement agencies. As criminologists have recently reminded us, there is a need to distinguish between crime waves and 'enforcement waves' when analysing criminal statistics.[7]

Moreover, definition of behaviour as 'criminal' can vary according to social status or class, and is also prone to change over time: what a workforce might regard simply as taking traditional perquisites might be regarded as pilfering by employers, while types of violence which are acceptable in some periods might be less so in others. 'Crime', therefore, covers a wide range of activities, and is likely to be defined differently by different people at different times.[8] For most of our purposes, however, since the early modern historian's concern must be mainly with *recorded* crimes, an effective (if by no means exclusive) working definition of the word must be that crime is behaviour which is regarded as illegal and which, if detected, would lead to prosecution in a court of law or summarily before an accredited agent of law enforcement. Above all, such a definition, allied to good court records, allows us to understand how crime was defined by the relevant institutions of the society experiencing it. Overcoming modern preconceptions on this point is a major obstacle.

The sort of problem which historians encounter when they fail to interpret crime in the past in the terms in which it was understood at the time is clearly demonstrated in G. R. Elton's introductory essay, 'Crime and the historian', in the collection of essays edited by J. S. Cockburn under the title *Crime in England 1550–1800*. Elton, for example, has difficulties with the notion that the historian of crime should concern himself with church courts and thus 'throw theft and adultery into one bag', since 'contemporaries did not regard them as of one kind at all'.[9] This is largely true, although we must bear in mind a number of Puritan writers who did put the two activities on a roughly equal moral plane.[10] Neither, one suspects, did contemporaries regard theft and treason as the same thing: but Elton, a little later, puts these two offences into one bag when he speaks of 'the real crimes as it were . . . treasons and felonies'.[11] The use of the phrase 'the real crimes' betrays the writer's line of thought. His definition of crime, despite his willingness to accuse another contributor to the volume of 'mildly anachronistic confusion',[12] is evidently based on what is perhaps the modern layman's definition of 'serious crime': burglary, robbery, rape and murder. To restrict a study of crime in early modern England to these offences simply will not do.

The first objection to equating 'real crime' with the serious offences, treason and felony, must be that in early modern England, as in modern British society (and, one suspects, all others), petty crime was more common, more typical, and in many ways more entitled to be described as 'real' crime than was the serious offence.[13] In the crisis years of 1629–31, for example, 93 thefts were prosecuted at the Essex quarter sessions. The same years saw the prosecution of 698 individuals for defaulting on their statutory obligation to work on the highways, and of 652 persons for various offences connected with the drink trade.[14] Ignoring petty crime not only obscures the reality of the pattern of prosecutions but also loses sight of one or two important points about the objectives of central and local government. One of the distinctive features of law enforcement in the first half of the period covered by this book was the prosecution of regulative offences, of which infractions of the drink laws perhaps loom largest in the archives of the criminal courts. To ignore this phenomenon is to ignore much of what the authorities of the period would have regarded as the essence of crime control, but to understand its full dimensions the historian must extend his researches into the records of local and minor tribunals, not least the ecclesiastical and manorial courts. The parish constable sending the unlicensed alehouse-keeper to the quarter sessions and the churchwarden sending the adulterer to the church courts would have regarded themselves as participants in the same struggle: disorder and ungodliness were not readily separable entities.

Mention of parish constable and churchwarden introduces another difficulty touched on by Professor Elton, namely that of distinguishing between crime and sin. The inhabitants of Tudor, Stuart, and Hanovarian England were, to say the least, a little unclear on this matter. Even at the end of the eighteenth century, contemporary opinion held crime to be little different from immorality. At earlier moments in time this was probably even more true. Adultery, indeed, is a case in point: in 1650 this sin, hitherto a church court offence, was turned into a crime when it was made felony without benefit of clergy by Act of Parliament. Puritan and other writers, citing both Mosaic law and the example of contemporary societies where such matters were better ordered than England, had been advocating this step for some time. Examination of the intellectual background to the Act provides a neat demonstration not so much of a willingness to criminalize sin as of a widespread inability to comprehend a distinction between the two.[15] Other documentation provides further evidence on this point. When, for example, the Court of Great Sessions at Chester issued an order against unlicensed alehouses in 1654, it justified its action by claiming that alehouses and the disorders found in them were 'to the great dishonour of Almighty God, scandall of all good government, hardening and encouragem[en]t of wicked and licentious p[er]sons in their vicious courses and endangeringe the publique peace'.[16] This criminal court, therefore, obviously held that certain forms of wrongdoing offended God's laws as much as man's: contemporary perceptions, we might therefore suspect, were unused to the idea of any clear-cut division between sin and crime.

This suspicion is strengthened by the way in which contemporary commentators were addicted to the idea that minor sins and vices, if uncorrected, might lead all too easily to major crimes. The highly conventionalized biographies of convicted criminals, as presented in popular literature, abound with illustrations of this notion. Thus we find Edmund Kirk, executed in London in 1684 for murdering his wife, reportedly emphasizing to the crowd how his downfall was in large measure attributable to a youthful indifference to God's commands. He told how

> Time was when I had as great a delight in vanity, as the most debauched among you. The day was lost in my apprehension, in which I met no jovial companion to drink or carouse away my hours; the night misspent, that was not improved in the embraces and dalliances of some Dahlila. The sentence came dully and insipidly from my lips that was not graced with an oath . . .[17]

When dealing with a society which regarded such conduct as the usual first step towards a career of serious crime, historians are obviously obliged to attempt to fit contemporary ideas on sin and its correction into their terms of reference.

If sin and crime were often conflated in the early modern period, a similar if less marked lack of clarity underlay the distinction between crime and what would be regarded currently as tort. A number of offences might be dealt with either by criminal prosecution or a civil action. Hence defamation, although most often remedied through launching a suit at the common law or ecclesiastical courts, might also be prosecuted as a crime, since defamatory language was thought to be conducive to a breach of the peace.[18] Similarly assault, itself a very widely defined offence in this period, could lead to either indictment at a criminal court or the launching of a suit at the court of Common Pleas.[19] Behind such examples, which could be multiplied, there lies a more general problem. The age was a deeply litigious one, and people were apparently very willing to resolve conflicts and settle disputes by going to law. This willingness to use the law imposes a different perspective on prosecuted crime from that familiar to the modern observer. In the absence of a modern police force, most prosecutions of crime, and the overwhelming majority of prosecutions of felony in particular, were brought either by the victim or by local officers or individuals offended at what they regarded as deviant behaviour. Crime control, at this level, was therefore very dependent upon private initiative, and prosecution throughout the court system was essentially the outcome of a series of personal decisions. The prosecution of even serious crime, therefore, derived something of the flavour of a civil action from the social interactions which so often preceded it. With many petty offences, for example if a tenant confronted by a neighbour who damaged his fence sought remedy by presentment at the manorial court, the practical differences between the criminal and civil aspects of a case could be almost non-existent.

Our aim when studying crime in the past, therefore, must be to take as wide a view of the phenomenon as possible. Serious crime is, of course, a subject which demands serious attention, and much of our argument over developments in the period 1550–1750 will revolve around an analysis of recorded changes in the level of serious crime, combined with changes in its punishment and in attitudes towards it. Statistically, however, most crime is petty crime, and it would thus be idle to ignore the less serious offence. From the viewpoint of the authorities, the essential objective of law enforcement was the control, or at least curbing, of all forms of criminal and delinquent behaviour. If the state saw fit to attempt to regulate certain forms of behaviour through courts operated by the state church, it would be illogical to disregard cases tried before such courts. Similarly, if attempts were made to curb delinquencies through the manorial courts, these too should be numbered among our concerns. An exception must be made for such religious offences as heresy, recusancy, and failure to attend church. These are best studied within the context of religious history, and will receive attention in W. J. Sheils' forthcoming volume in this series on religion and society in early modern England. These offences apart, our intention in this book is to come to grips with past definitions and to leave the modern layman's definition of 'real' crime as far away as possible.

Having discussed definitions, we must now turn to examine the various methodologies which might be adopted in studying our subject. Traditionally, the greatest contribution has been made by legal historians.[20] Legal history is still a lively branch of both legal and historical studies,[21] and to study the history of crimes without some prior acquaintance with the basics of legal history is akin to making bricks without straw. Nevertheless, studying crime purely through legal history is an activity which is vulnerable to a number of objections. The first of these is that the practise of both courts and law enforcement officers was often at variance with legal theory. According to this, if we may take the most striking example, the indictment should have been a document so accurate as to constitute an impeccable source upon which the historian might construct a number of conclusions, most of them statistical. Examination of Elizabethan and Jacobean indictments, on the other hand, has shown that they were frequently inaccurate, and that such matters as the occupation or status of offenders, their parish of origin, and even the date of the offence, cannot be derived from them with any reliability.[22] Secondly, one of the hallmarks of the law enforcement system in this period was its flexibility, an attribute which included the correction of a wide variety of conduct which might have defied the precise definitions of the statute book. This flexibility was perhaps most marked in the manorial courts, which were local, decentralized, and to a large extent bound by local custom.[23] It is also evident, however, in the practices of tribunals dealing with serious crime. In particular, the power to bind persons over to be of good behaviour or to keep the peace, and the custom of sending petty offenders to the house of correction, gave the authorities almost unlimited discretion in what was, and what was not, illegal or dangerous behaviour.[24] Such cases as the Cheshire man indicted at the Court of Great Sessions in 1617 for drinking healths in his own blood[25] obviously take us a little beyond the legal historian's ken. Moreover, legal theory can tell us little about another major characteristic of early modern crime, the essentially personal or parochial circumstances which so often formed its context. Prosecution, it must be reiterated, was usually the outcome of choices made by the person offended against, or by village officers or village opinion, and often followed a lengthy period of interaction between them and the offender. This process, almost invisible to the legal historian, is crucial to the understanding of law enforcement in the early modern era.

A second approach, and one which has enjoyed much favour, is to write the history of crime from literary sources. This approach has appealed above all to the writers of textbooks on political history when constructing their brief descriptions of English society. Any social theme, after all, can be illustrated by a brief quote from Chaucer, Shakespeare, or the Paston Letters. Once more we are confronted with a refusal to take social history seriously, and the limitations of what might be termed the *Belles-Lettres* approach to the study of the subject are all too apparent. It is indicative of the priorities of English historical writing that historians who would otherwise have prided themselves on their scholarship, intellectual rigour, and talent for source-criticism should become slack, lazy, and uncritical when using literary sources to discuss social historical topics, crime included. J. B. Black, for example, concludes his brief discussion of highwaymen in Elizabethan England by commenting that 'Falstaff's disgraceful exploit at Gadshill was probably a not uncommon occurrence'.[26] This exploit, of course, never took place outside the playhouse, and cannot be used as evidence of reality. Imaginative literature is imaginative literature: it can be used to illustrate past attitudes or preoccupations, but it should not be confused with historical fact. Unfortunately, the familiarity, vividness, and accessibility of literary sources makes them very attractive, and a number of writers, professional English scholars among them, have thrown these sources together to form easily palatable if hopelessly inadequate books. The reviewer of one such, commenting that its author had simply assembled 'the detritus of some Eng. Lit. lectures and shovelled it lazily behind a catchpenny title', has provided us with an epitaph for a whole approach to the history of crime.[27]

As long as a century ago, however, scholars were already beginning to suggest an alternative body of source material and, by extension, a more systematic approach to the subject. As has been suggested, the historian owes a great deal to the modern archives profession, who have done so much to help him come into contact with primary materials. He also owes a substantial debt of gratitude to those scholars who, from the middle years of Victoria's reign onwards, took an active role in setting up societies for the publication of local history records. By the end of the nineteenth century, most English counties possessed both a local history journal and a series of publications of local records. The rise of this enthusiasm for local history is an interesting phenomenon, which awaits fuller investigation. Its immediate relevance to our argument is that a number of early publications in these records series consisted of editions of court, and especially quarter sessions, records. The standards of editing of these records varies, although some are excellent, and most of the editors were simply content with a brief and relatively uncritical introduction. Already, however, the enthusiasts editing their county's quarter sessions records were beginning to explore what is the most useful initial approach to the history of crime, the systematic study of court archives, usually with some notion of statistical analysis in mind. In particular, the work of J. C. Jeaffreson on the Middlesex sessions records provided a number of pointers as to how much sources might be used.[28]

It is only in recent years, despite an excellent and neglected early study by C. L. Ewen of witch trials,[29] that such an approach has gained much currency. The 1970s, however, were to see the appearance of a number of studies which adopted it. The methodology seemed simple enough: find a good court archive, master the contemporary law relating to the court and the offences tried before it, work through the archive systematically, and produce a statistically-based study. These statistics could then be related to other socio-economic factors, notably grain prices and other economic variables, and important conclusions derived from such correlations as emerged about the nature of crime and punishment in the past. Such a methodology formed the basis of a monograph by Joel Samaha, important essays by J. S. Cockburn and J. M. Beattie, constituted a starting point for Alan Macfarlane's book on witchcraft, and was a major feature of the first two doctoral theses to be completed on seventeenth-century crime, the first by T. C. Curtis, the second by the present writer.[30] Statistically-based studies have also appeared on crime in periods outside the early modern, and it is now possible to gain insights into patterns of and fluctuations in prosecuted crime for periods as far apart as the thirteenth and early twentieth centuries.[31]

The pitfalls involved in attempting to understand any set of criminal statistics are obvious enough, and, since the problems of a statistical approach to the history of crime are discussed in chapter 3, there is little point in rehearsing them here. Whatever their limitations, these statistically-based studies have made a number of important contributions to our understanding of the history of crime and punishment. Not least, such studies have indicated that it is possible to go far beyond that uncritical and anecdotal approach which has so impeded the serious study of the history of crime. Quantification must be limited in its ambitions, extremely cautious in its methods, and its results must be presented and explained with painstaking care. This is not to say that, where appropriate and possible, it is not an essential exercise, and that it cannot yield some important conclusions.

It rapidly became apparent, however, that counting was not the only thing that could be done with court archives. With some archives, of course, it was possible to do little else: the records of the Home circuit of the assizes, for example, although the only assize material which survives in any bulk between the starting point of our study and 1650, are limited mainly to indictments, whose value consists largely in the quantitative insights they provide into law enforcement in the past. Other records provide us with evidence of a qualitative type, and the intrinsically fascinating nature of much of this evidence soon distracted all but the most dedicated or unimaginative quantifier away from the calculator and the computer. Many court archives contain occasional letters, petitions, and other informal documents on a haphazard basis, and these often provide invaluable insights into the enforcement of the law at a grass-roots level. Moreover, and perhaps more importantly, historians began to appreciate the riches of those depositions, examinations, informations, and confessions which survive for some courts, and which contain the evidence of witnesses and the statement of the accused. Unfortunately for the historian, although fortunately for everyone else, England has never been a police state, and has never possessed an inquisitorial system of criminal justice. For this reason, the historian of crime in England will only rarely have access to records comparable to those which Richard Cobb, for example, has turned to such good use in his studies of crime and related topics in late eighteenth-century France.[32] Nevertheless, it became evident that materials existed upon which some impression of the social context of crime in early modern England could be founded: a third approach was thus added to the legal-historical and statistical ones.

Although it was realized that even the isolated documents might furnish telling insights into the social background to the commission and prosecution of crime, it rapidly became apparent that a more systematic study of this problem could be gained from examining crime, those committing it, and those prosecuting it, through the medium of the village or community study.[33] Given adequate sources, such studies have shown how crime can be placed in a wider context. Court records are combined with other forms of documentation to provide detailed profiles of offenders, their victims, and the local officers of law enforcement. Under ideal circumstances, the documentation available can be adequate for the reconstruction of quite detailed biographies of even very lowly villagers, while it can also give a full impression of the nature of the socio-economic power-structure within the village, a subject of vital importance to study of the history of crime at its most local level. My early investigation of crime and delinquency in Kelvedon in Essex, although intended merely as an exploration of what was then an untested methodology for studying the history of crime, did at least demonstrate the potential usefulness of such an approach.[34] Deeper research over a longer timespan on another Essex village, Terling, has allowed Keith Wrightson and David Levine to examine petty crime in its village context, and relate fluctuations in it to wider socio-economic change.[35] Doubtlessly the researches carried out by Alan Macfarlane and his team on Earls Colne and Kirkby Lonsdale, the fruits of which are only just beginning to appear in print,[36] will provide yet more insights into the local context of crime. Arguably, therefore, the village study offers one of the most exciting ways of understanding crime in the past, and there is an urgent need for more studies of this kind, especially for communities outside Essex. Nevertheless, this approach, like all the others, is subject to a number of criticisms, of which the most telling is perhaps the problem of the implications for those embarking on community studies of the high geographical mobility enjoyed in early modern England. Most settlements experienced a high rate of turnover of population, and it seems likely that at least some types of criminal would be drawn from that most mobile sector of all, the rootless and marginal poor. Moreover, there is the objection, evident among even those historians willing to accept the usefulness of detailed village studies, that these must, perforce, be limited in their scope: parish studies are, after all, essentially parochial. Should not the historian be addressing somewhat larger issues?

So far, the most stimulating work in this direction has been carried out by a group formed by E. P. Thompson and a number of younger scholars, most of whom worked under Thompson before his resignation from the academic world.[37] All of them have completed detailed local studies, mostly dealing with the later eighteenth century. Their greatest contribution, however, is the way in which they have raised some far wider issues about the history of crime, and done much to fetch the topic much nearer to the more central concerns of mainstream historical enquiry. The contributors to *Albion's Fatal Tree*, whose lead has already been followed by another important collection of essays,[38] have constructed a wider conceptual framework within which the study of crime in the past might operate. Above all, they show that the law, even though being what, in plain terms, might be described as an instrument of class oppression, was infinitely subtle in the ways in which it oppressed. Douglas Hay's discussion of 'Property, authority and the criminal law', and Thompson's *tour de force* on the significance of the rule of law in *Whigs and Hunters* are of particular importance.[39] Their arguments show how the law in eighteenth century England played a crucial role in maintaining the credibility of the rulers among the ruled. Law, it might be argued, was coming to replace religion as the ideological cement which held society together, but this was a cement which would only prove effective as long as the masses believed in the rule of law, that is to say, the law's equality and the fairness of its operation. Addressing this problem brings the historian into contact with some of the central issues of social history: how the rulers legitimate their authority; why the ruled obey this authority; how the operation of authority is perceived; the way in which different social classes interact; and, ultimately, why and how it is that society coheres.

Thompson and his colleagues have isolated a number of other issues of considerable significance. Hay's emphasis on the flexibility of the application of the criminal law, and of its selective application to suit the circumstances of individual offenders, is a theme of central importance, and one to which we will return in due course. More important, however, is the way in which they have emphasized how different social groups had different perceptions of the law: members of different social strata, they argue, had different assumptions about what constituted 'legal' and hence 'criminal' behaviour. An underlying theme of *Albion's Fatal Tree*, *Whigs and Hunters*, and a later collection, *An Ungovernable People*, is that a number of types of behaviour regarded as illegal by the authorities were thought of as legal, or at least justifiable on quasi-legal grounds, by certain sections of the ruled. Hence poachers, wreckers, coiners, rioters and smugglers are all shown to be operating within a system of popular ideas on legality, or at least of popular legitimizing notions. The emphasis is on 'social crime', illegal behaviour which many of its perpetrators, and large sections of the populace, did not regard as criminal.

The concept of social crime, and the whole idea of differing perceptions of illegal behaviour by differing groups in society, will be discussed at greater length in chapter 6. For the present, it should be reiterated that the great contribution of the approach favoured in *Albion's Fatal Tree* and *An Ungovernable People* is the way in which it reminds us that crime and punishment in the past operated within an ideological framework, as well as the more obvious socio-economic one. The arguments of the contributors to these volumes throw light upon a number of topics, among them, for example, the limited and often legalistic demands which have characterized popular uprisings in England from at least 1381. More importantly, however, they remind us that crime, punishment, and the law did not exist in some sort of vacuum. As we have seen, concentration on the county or the parish can provide one way around this vacuum, by providing a geographical context. Arguably, the sorts of arguments advanced by Hay, Thompson, and others provide an equally valid ideological context. Blackstone, Paley, and other eighteenth-century commentators demonstrate that respect for the common law of England, as successfully defended by the Glorious Revolution, was part of the basic political and social assumptions of most contemporary Englishmen of property. This is familiar enough, but it is evident that we must now consider two further problems: the role of law as an ideological force among people of little or no property; and the way in which the criminal law actually operated.

   Legal history; the use of literary materials; the formulation of criminal statistics; study of crime in the context of the county or village community; social crime and legitimizing notions; the role of the law as an ideological cement in society: all of these are important themes, each of them important enough to provide the basis for a number of monographs. Even after more than a decade of research by scholars in Great Britain and the United States, the history of crime in early modern England remains a relatively undeveloped and extremely problematic field. As we have implied, all of the approaches mentioned in this chapter have their peculiar strengths and weaknesses, and it is doubtful if any of them will prove to be of unique value. There is no single avenue along which the historian of crime might pursue knowledge. At times, this can be infuriating and frustrating: few of those working in the field can not, at some point or other, have been tempted to more familiar topics, where the guidelines are established and the secondary literature extensive. Conversely, historians of crime do have the compensation of labouring in an exciting and expanding area of intellectual endeavour. As has been suggested, much of this excitement lies in the opening up of new approaches, none of which has yet been fully explored. Even more stimulating, in a sense, is the constant discovery (or, indeed, rediscovery) of fresh source material. There is still much to be done, in terms of both empirical research and conceptualization. Above all, we are unsure of where all this will lead us, although the work of Thompson and others examining the questions he addresses has provided a reassuring example of how work on the history of crime can illuminate some of those issues which most historians would consider to be important.

The history of crime in early England thus constitutes a subject where methodologies are not fully established, where the exact extent and nature of the relevant source material is still obscure, and whose ultimate intellectual destination is uncertain. Writing a general book on this subject might, therefore, be regarded as a risky enterprise, not least because earlier essays in this direction have proved unsatisfactory.[40] The exercise can, however, be justified on a number of grounds. First, the initial wave of the new investigation of the history of crime has broken. As was pointed out in the opening paragraph, the bulk of writing it has thrown up is not overwhelming. On the other hand, enough has appeared to justify a work of synthesis summarizing what has been written. The state of the art is not unlike that described about a century ago by F. W. Maitland, in an essay on the then state of research into legal history: further specialized studies are needed, but enough are in existence to justify a general book in the field; while the ideas that are likely to appear in such a work are likely to provoke, or at least inform, further detailed studies.[41] As J. H. Hexter reminded us some years ago, they also serve who sometimes sit and think.[42] This book, however, will attempt more than a synthesis of existing work in the field, necessary though it is. It will also contain much unpublished material, and, it is to be hoped, a number of original ideas. Furthermore, it will suggest a number of future lines of investigation which the historian of crime might follow: given the protean nature of the subject, and the early stage of its development, signposts to what might usefully be studied in the next stage of research have an important part to play.

In particular, argument in this book will revolve around three main themes. The first of these is the quantification of data dealing with crime in the past, and the derivation of conclusions from statistics relating to crime and punishment. Naive quantification is, of course, one of the pitfalls into which the historian of crime can fall all too easily, and any criminal statistics drawn from early modern materials must be treated with extreme caution. Nevertheless, counting offences and offenders is an important initial step in attempting to understand crime in any past society. Since, as one student of the subject has commented, 'most often, the history of crime is the history of what got recorded',[43] counting recorded crime is frequently all that the historian can do with the materials at his disposal. The relationship between actual and recorded crime is always problematic: however, delineating trends in prosecution does at least give the historian a starting-point from which further discussion, however speculative, might develop, as well as providing a framework within which it can take place. Even if we conclude that crime statistics are merely about enforcement, changes in the rate and pattern of prosecuted crime can be used to inform argument about the preoccupations of law-enforcement agencies. Moreover, even if prosecutions give us only an imperfect impression of crime, they do give us hard information on changes in patterns of punishment: knowledge of, for example, what proportion of convicted felons were executed in the late sixteenth rather than in the early eighteenth century is of central importance for a study of this type.

A second major theme of this book is that crime is a phenomenon which must be understood in its social context. This contention can be demonstrated on a number of levels. On a macro-level, it should be remembered that the years covered by this book form the bulk of a period which is thought, by Marxists and others, to have witnessed one of the major transformations in European history: the transition from feudalism to capitalism. It might be logical to expect such a transition to generate changes in crime and punishment, and a number of books have attempted to examine such connections.[44] These studies have not been entirely successful, but the problem is obviously worth serious consideration, and will be returned to at various points in the present work. Of more immediate importance, perhaps, are the implications of the use of the village study, and of qualitative materials in general. These help to provide information on the social context of crime and punishment on a micro-level, and also allow the formulation of ideas on another important issue – which sections of society provided the criminals of the time. Such materials also permit investigation of a matter of central importance which we have already touched upon, the flexibility of the application of the criminal law and its adjustment to the particular circumstances of individual crimes and criminals. This flexibility operated, for the most part, in two contexts. Firstly, in the village, where the decision to prosecute was essentially a local one, and where a number of alternatives to prosecution might operate.[45] Secondly, once the offender was in court, the decision about how he or she was to be punished was often the result of choices made by the judge, as informed by the prosecutor, witnesses, interested parties, or even the jury, rather than according to the strict letter of the law.[46] Such matters, although capable of being informed by statistical evidence, must obviously rest heavily upon qualitative materials and impressionistic sources.

Thirdly, the importance of the short-term objectives and long-term ideologies of groups in positions of authority and power will be a recurrent theme. Crime has been characterized as an excellent vehicle for writing 'history from below', and much of its attraction lies in the way in which the subject can be slanted to explore both popular mentalities and the impact of the state at its most intimate level. This should not obscure the significance of those powerful members of society upon whose decisions a large measure of what happened 'below' depended. The next chapter, describing the actual machinery of law enforcement, provides a basic analysis of the channels through which such decisions were directed, and shows how the decisions of the Privy Council or parliament might actually be brought to impinge upon the locality. Other problems are relevant, however: the history of the legal profession is of central importance, and there are encouraging signs that a number of scholars are turning their attention to this subject.[47] More work needs to be done on the justices of the peace. These have been counted and categorized by students of local politics or local adminstration, but little has been written about their ideological viewpoints. We know how likely a justice in any given period was to have received an Oxbridge degree, but we know little about how he felt when confronted by a habitual thief or regular drunkard. Moreover, given the importance of legislation, the attitudes and aspirations of the peerage and those members of the upper strata of the gentry gathered in the Commons demands at least passing attention. Concentration on parliament as an arena of constitutional conflict has tended to obscure the point that the institution's main business was passing laws. These laws were the outcome of decisions by groups of MPs, and the thinking that lay behind their decisions is a matter worth pondering. The history of crime, therefore, must include some discussion of the attitudes and objectives of the ruling strata in society.

These, then, are the main issues with which this book will be concerned. One further point remains to be explained: the timespan it covers, 1550–1750. Obviously, social history is as unamenable as most other divisions of the discipline to the constraints of dates, and setting up strict time-limits to the type of study envisaged here is especially questionable. The period 1550–1750 does, however, lend itself to coherent treatment, not least because its opening and terminating points seem to coincide with periods which witnessed important shifts in English society. Around 1550, the effects of that great population increase which was to be the underlying force in English life until the Civil Wars were first beginning to become felt. Inflation, pressure on food resources and pressure on land combined to produce a mass of proletarianized poor. The most familiar symbol of official reaction to what was rapidly conceived of as a major threat was the vagrancy legislation of the period, but historians have discerned changes dating from about the same time which might be interpreted as evidence of a wider growth of 'law and order consciousness'. J. H. Langbein has argued that the reign of Mary Tudor saw a number of important steps towards more efficient pre-trial procedure towards criminals.[48] Joel Samaha, in his study of law and order in Elizabethan Essex, claimed to have discovered the emergence of a modern court system in the late sixteenth century.[49] Moreover, consultation of the statute book reveals a steady pressure against petty crime, with legislation against the vagrant again being of central importance, and the redefinition of a number of offences as being outside benefit of clergy: sodomy, witchcraft, picking pockets, horse-theft, and others.[50]

The changes delineated by Langbein, the laws against vagrants, and the increased harshness of the criminal code are symptomatic of a development of fundamental importance: the growing pretensions of the state. G. R. Elton's claim, made some twenty years ago, that the 1530s experienced revolutionary changes in the way in which England was governed, attracted much criticism and engendered a lively historical controversy.[51] Much of the controversy centred around the nature of change in the bureaucracy at Westminster, and the novelty or otherwise of some key concepts in political theory. These matters are of prime importance, but concentration upon them tended to obscure two basic points: that 'government', for many practical purposes, means making people do certain things and stopping them from doing others, and that in Tudor England these objectives were often achieved through coercion by the courts.[52] After the Reformation, the rulers of England were continually confronted by the grim spectre of religious, ideological, and social unrest, and they probably derived little comfort from the stress which protestant theology placed upon man's innate sinfulness and rebelliousness. Greater severity in the law of treason is the most obvious consequence of this, but it is impossible not to interpret the growing severity in criminal statutes as further evidence of a fundamental concern about social order. A striking example of governmental worries came in 1538, with the proposed revised standard charge to be delivered at 'inferior courts of inquisition' in the localities, in hopes that the 'ignorant and unlearned people' should be taught their duties to God, the King and the commonwealth. The charge was forty pages long, and listed 'every conceivable crime and misdemeanour'.[53] This intensification of concern over law and order makes the mid-sixteenth century an attractive point at which to begin a study of crime in early modern England.

Similarly, 1750 is an attractive point at which to terminate such a study. This attractiveness is largely due to our awareness of another major shift: 1750 is commonly held to be the point from which that compendium of changes which were to be labelled as the Industrial Revolution first began to pick up momentum. Doubtlessly, a number of continuities in crime, its punishment, and attitudes to these matters persisted well into the nineteenth century. Conversely, a study of crime in early modern England should logically be ended in a period when the rise of new socio-economic forces can be traced, and England was on the edge of making a decisive break with its pre-industrial past. Moreover, just as changing attitudes to crime can be traced in the mid sixteenth century, so can they in the years following 1750. This period saw the emergence of a growing body of criticism of the existing system of law and order, of which perhaps the earliest well known representative was Henry Fielding. Real law reform, and the emergence of a professional police force and a 'modern' system of prisons, were still the best part of a century away, but enough comment was already being aired in the decades immediately after 1750 to suggest that that year might serve as a useful point at which to end this book. Above all, the English translation of a work uniquely famous as the harbinger of new ideas on crime and punishment, Cesare Beccarria's *Dei Delitti e delle Pene*, was only some sixteen years away.

It would seem, therefore, that both the commencing and finishing dates of our study can be justified as representing some sort of change in attitudes to law and order. The problem remains, however, of determining how far the period 1550 to 1750 can be treated as a unit. This issue, in turn, raises the further question of the tension between continuity and change which, ultimately, underlies most historical writing. Obviously, many things changed between these two dates, although this is hardly the place at which to give a detailed account of the shifts in English society over these 200 years.[54] Arguably, the most attractive initial approach to the period is to see it as divided into two halves, with the division coming around 1650. In terms of political history, such a division would make considerable sense: the mid seventeenth century witnessed the massive political upheavals of the Civil Wars and the Interregnum. It can also be justified from the viewpoint of the social historian. It was at some indeterminable point just before the middle of the seventeenth century that there ended the great wave of demographic growth which had furnished the fundamental motor for historical change in England (and, indeed, most of Europe) since the late fifteenth century.[55] On a political level, England gives the impression of being a much more settled and stable country in the late rather than the early seventeenth century. Historians have, indeed, discerned a growth in political stability in the late seventeenth and early eighteenth centuries, and even such a crisis as the Glorious Revolution was passed without major social turmoil. It is also tempting to postulate a similar stability in the social realm. Demographic pressures were less, and, as we shall see, evidence about crime and punishment also suggests a society and economy that was somehow under less stress than it had been a century before.

Much changed politically in our period, the most familiar development being the victorious emergence of parliament from the constitutional struggles of the seventeenth century.[56] Socially, the nature and degree of change is less obvious and more contentious. England was more commercialized in 1750 than it had been two centuries before, but it was still a country in which the bulk of the population lived on, and derived their living from, the land. Much industry was still organized along traditional lines, factories were virtually unknown, and many commentators would have agreed that the most important variable in the annual performance of the economy was the state of the grain harvest. Behind these economic realities there lay an important social one: despite the rise of a monied interest, the landed classes were still the dominant group socially, politically, culturally, and, in many ways, economically. Although it would be otiose to claim that nothing changed between 1550 and 1750, it seems that the Englishman of the mid eighteenth century would have found much less to surprise him in the England of Edward VI then he would in that of George VI. Above all, as far as our immediate concerns are involved, few fundamental changes occurred in the criminal law. The subject is one which has so far been little studied, and one student has gone so far as to label the first half of our period as the dark age of legal history.[57] However, it is also undeniable that there were a number of minor tinkerings with the criminal law, that some important changes were beginning to emerge in the mid eighteenth century, and that the importance of the law as an ideological force in the constitutional struggles of the seventeenth century meant that, once those struggles were resolved, attitudes to the law were never quite the same again. Nonetheless both the statute book and what we can discover about the actual practices of the criminal courts combine to suggest a broad continuity in the basic assumptions of what the criminal law was about.

One last problem remains: that of how justified we are in describing crime in England as a whole. Early modern records do not permit the type of analysis of national trends which some historians have attempted for the nineteenth and early twentieth centuries. Both the current state of research and the sheer problem of record survival would make such an analysis impossible for our period. Few areas have been subject to really detailed studies, some courts (notably the central courts, especially the King's Bench and the Star Chamber) have only just begun to reveal their secrets to the researcher, while for some areas relevant sources simply do not survive throughout our period. In particular, to dwell further on this last point, assize records, recording felonies, are lacking for most of the country before the mid seventeenth century. A general work on crime in early modern England must, therefore, suffer from a number of gaps, both in subject matter and geographical spread. Conversely, as we have suggested, enough materials do survive to allow the delineation of both national trends and regional variations. Published monographs and essays, unpublished theses, records in print, and the massive body of hitherto unworked archive material all combine to make it possible to describe crime in most regions of England during at least selected points in our period, from the Scottish border to Sussex, from Cornwall to East Anglia. Much of this description will be tentative, and much of it will suggest directions for future research rather than provide definitive conclusions. This is a fair reflection of both the nature of the subject and the current level of work on it: it would be dishonest to attempt to be anything other than tentative on many points. Nevertheless, the exercise is a feasible one, and it is also more important than might appear at first sight: as we shall argue, studying crime leads us close to the core of some of the fundamental aspects of English society in the early modern period.

Chapter 2

COURTS, OFFICERS AND DOCUMENTS

Any student of crime must familiarize him or herself with the law-enforcement agencies of the society he or she studies. Crime has usually been detected, tried and punished within an institutional context: its very definition is often in large measure dependent upon rules laid down by the law-enforcement agencies of the society in which it is committed. Early modern England, as we shall see, was a country which enjoyed the presence of a large number of courts with a criminal jurisdiction, while there were also numerous officers charged with enforcing the law and maintaining the monarch's peace: indeed, even in 1550, England has the appearance of being a much-governed country.[1] This government had, by contemporary standards, a number of peculiarities, of which two are outstanding: the overwhelming importance of royal, as opposed to local or seigneurial, law; and the widespread dependence upon unpaid amateur local officials. The main purpose of this chapter therefore, will be to give some impression of the main elements of this system, in many ways unlike those obtaining in the other large European monarchies of the time. There is, however, a further reason for gaining a working knowledge of how the courts functioned and of how officials went about their business. Much of our argument in the three following chapters will be founded upon the study of archival materials generated by the courts: indeed, as we have suggested in the introduction, it is the availability of these archives, many of them still virtually unworked, which has made serious research on the history of crime possible. Accordingly, the final section of this chapter will consist of a brief discussion of the main types of document produced by the clerical staff of early modern English courts, and of their usefulness to the historian of crime.

In theory, the Court of King's Bench stood at the apex of the hierarchy of tribunals empowered to deal with crime.[2] It was the only one of the three superior common-law courts at Westminster to possess a criminal jurisdiction, and this jurisdiction was unlimited. It also had an important function as a court of review. It was empowered to remove into its purview cases from any inferior courts, and it could quash verdicts, or continue trial if this had not been completed. Particularly associated with the work of the King's Bench was the writ of *certiorari*, by which cases could be removed from inferior courts (most often the quarter sessions, occasionally the assizes or even the manorial leet). The use of the *certiorari*, originally intended as a means of circumventing the partiality of local juries and justices was, by our period, probably seen by litigants primarily as a delaying tactic. The King's Bench could also try cases presented by a grand jury of Middlesex, or arising from informations filed in the Crown Office.

Although details of the state trials held at King's Bench are accessible enough, the more mundane criminal business of the court awaits detailed investigation. Work that has been carried out, largely on cases in the Ancient Indictments series arising from the county of Essex,[3] suggests that most of the business reaching it on *certiorari* concerned misdemeanours, notably assault and riot, in which the yeomanry and gentry were concerned. The informations reaching it were concerned with a surprising range of economic and regulatory offences. The absence of trial for felony is striking. Even as a court of review, the King's Bench experienced a decline in serious business over the period we are considering, until by 1700 it was dealing mainly with disputes arising from summary convictions and settlement cases. Despite its theoretical powers to try even the most serious crime, therefore, the King's Bench was concerned mainly with misdemeanour and petty offences.

During the century between 1540 and 1640 the predominance of the King's Bench was challenged by that most celebrated of Tudor innovations, the Court of Star Chamber.[4] This tribunal was essentially the king's council sitting as a court, a more formal version of that jurisdictional authority which the council had traditionally exercised on the monarch's behalf. From the ancient right to receive petitions and redress grievances there gradually evolved, in the reign of Henry VIII, a true court with full public procedures. In theory, Star Chamber's main purpose was to punish breaches of the King's peace, notably riots, assaults, and acts of intimidation, while it also dealt extensively with cases of fraud, forgery, or perjury, offences which the other courts of common law could not deal with adequately. It was popular with litigants, and was thought of as providing speedy and flexible justice. It could, in fact, be argued that the court became too popular: recent research by T. G. Barnes has suggested that a large number of cases heard by Star Chamber were brought by plaintiffs who were already involved in parallel litigation, either in the other Westminster courts or in local tribunals, and who sought to embarrass their opponents by bringing malicious allegations of riot, assault, conspiracy or defamation.[5] The Star Chamber was also used by the central government as an instrument for implementing royal policy and, although it remained popular with litigants until the end, a number of state trials in the 1630s discredited it in the eyes of those hostile to Charles I's personal rule and to Arminianism. It was, therefore, one of the main targets of the Long Parliament, and was abolished in 1641. After that date its function, and, in all probability, much of what would have been its business, passed back to the King's Bench.

Throughout the period covered by this book, trial for felony was most commonly the business of the assizes.[6] The assizes had their origins in the reign of Henry II, and from shortly after that period until their eventual abolition in 1971 they constituted, some extraordinary exceptions apart, the country's principal criminal courts. By 1550, the country was divided for judicial purposes into six circuits, and two judges were sent out to ride these circuits twice annually, once in winter, once in summer. The assize judges were normally also judges in the superior courts of common law, although they derived their authority to conduct assize business from the commissions which they were given each time they rode a circuit. These commissions included the assize commission, the commission of oyer and terminer, and the commission of gaol delivery. It is these latter two commissions which are most important for our immediate purposes. It was the commission of oyer and terminer which empowered the judges to inquire into, and hear and determine, all offences in the counties within their circuit, while the comission of gaol delivery, as its name implies, empowered the judges to empty the gaols of the suspected felons held there, and try them.

The assizes were also concerned with other matters. Civil actions might be heard there, frequently on a writ of *nisi prius*. The assize judges also had an important function in passing the concerns of central government into the localities and collecting details of local grievances, notably through the medium of grand jury presentments. The assize also exercised close supervision of local government, and numerous regulatory offences were tried and local constables' presentments dealt with, along with the trial of more serious matters. In addition to this serious business, the arrival of the judges was an important event in the social life of the assize town, and of the county in which it was situated. The court itself, with its robed judges, the trumpeters and spearmen provided by the sheriff, the sermon which preceded it and the formality with which it was conducted, was intended to create an atmosphere of majesty, spectacle and ceremony: indeed, one observer declared in 1678 that the 'awful Solemnities' accompanying assizes might overawe defendants of 'low and common education'.[7] Conversely, by about this date the 'awful solemnities' were being supplemented by a number of more agreeable activities. Both the county elite and the commonalty seized on the assizes as an occasion to meet to discuss business, make marriage alliances, and exchange gossip. By the eighteenth century the coming of the judges from London was regularly greeted with assize balls and assize concerts.

Mention of these symptoms of the growing complexity of provincial cultural life should not deflect us from our main concern, the criminal business of the assizes. By the late sixteenth century, this court had established a virtual monopoly of trial for felony. In the earlier sixteenth century, a number of such cases might well have gone to quarter sessions, but in 1590 the reform of the commission of the peace by Sir Christopher Wray CJQB ensured that trial of serious felony became the prerogative of the assizes. Wray recommended that 'difficult cases' coming before the justices of the peace in their sessions should be referred to the assize judges, and it seems to have been generally accepted that any crime likely to result in capital punishment constituted a 'difficult case'. From the late sixteenth century most of the more serious felonies – homicide, grand larceny, burglary, arson, rape, and witchcraft – were tried at the assizes.

The growing monopoly of trial of more serious crime at the assizes had the concomitant effect of leaving the quarter sessions with the trial of petty offences, misdemeanours, and administrative and regulatory offences.[8] The criminal business of the quarter sessions became less important, and their function as the medium through which the administration of the county was carried out received greater emphasis. The sessions had their origins in the first half of the fourteenth century, but the most important step in their early development came when the 1351 Statute of Labourers provided that local justices should meet four times a year to enforce the new legislation. The times of meeting were fixed by a further Act of 1414, which confirmed earlier legislation in enacting that quarter sessions should be held at the Epiphany, in the week following Easter, at the Translation of St Thomas the Martyr, and in the week after Michaelmas. Legislation in 1360 had given justices the right to try felonies in their own counties, and in the late sixteenth century quarter sessions were still the scene of trials of felons. As we have seen, such trials became less common after 1590, and capital offences were usually left to the assizes. Death sentences might still occasionally be passed at the quarter sessions (the last hanging to be ordered by the North Riding sessions, for example, came in 1654[9]), but they were very unusual by the reign of Charles I. Even so, the quarter sessions activities are of great concern to the historian of crime: petty thieves and many of those accused of misdemeanour were tried there, while the numerous regulative offences indicted at the sessions help demonstrate the dimensions of control at which the authorities aimed.

The quarter sessions continued to constitute an essential part of both local government and crime control. By the late sixteenth century, however, it was becoming evident that the sheer volume of business being dealt with by local government demanded that justices' meetings should occur more frequently than once every three months. Local initiatives pointed the way, with justices in several counties arranging to meet between quarter sessions, or grafting their business onto other local government meetings. In such piecemeal initiatives lay the origins of the petty sessions, one of the distinctive elements in English local government by the late seventeenth century. A number of counties, notably Wiltshire and Norfolk, seem to have enjoyed something like regular petty sessions before 1600, while several others, among them Essex, Hampshire, Warwickshire and Worcestershire, set them up in response to a Privy Council order of 1605.[10] Something like a formal and national system of petty sessions finally emerged in the wake of the Book of Orders of 1631.[11] This instructed justices to meet in their neighbourhood every month to receive the presentments of constables, churchwardens and overseers of the poor, and generally to co-ordinate the work of local government. The system probably suffered during the Civil Wars, but with the return of order after about 1650 the petty sessions came into their own as frequent and intimate agencies of local government. Much of their work was administrative, concerning bastardy cases, poor law disputes, road repair, and the like, but they also dealt with some types of petty crime, notably drunkenness and minor forms of violence. By the Restoration the petty sessions, to quote a recent student of county government in Sussex, 'were recognized as convenient, necessary and effective'.[12]

In this the petty sessions had supplanted two other longer established types of court, those of the manor and the church. The manorial courts were of considerable antiquity, and their records have been much used by historians attempting to reconstruct medieval peasant society.[13] By the early seventeenth century, legal theorists had postulated the presence of two types of manorial court, the court baron and the court leet. The court baron was essentially the lord of the manor's court, and its main purpose was to record the transfer and inheritance of land within the manor. The court leet, which included the presentment of various petty offences in its business, is of more interest to the historian of crime. Together, the records of these manorial courts can be of unique value in illustrating the operations of the pre-industrial village community. For most of the inhabitants of late medieval, Tudor and early Stuart England, manorial institutions were the form of government which most continuously affected them, and it is important to grasp that this government, not least because nearly all landlords were absentees, was essentially self government: as the Elizabethan cartographer John Norden put it, 'is not every manor a little commonwealth, whereof the tenants are the members, the Lord the body, and the law the head?'[14]

Much of the running of these little commonwealths involved the curbing of certain forms of disruptive behaviour, and numerous minor delinquencies were presented before the leet jurors, themselves usually drawn from the more substantial tenants. As we shall see when we turn later to consider the court records of the Yorkshire manor of Acomb, many of these presentments involved the correction of nuisance offences and the settlement of interpersonal disputes: tenants might be presented for letting their livestock stray, failing to maintain their fences, or blocking the road with their dunghills. Other, more obviously criminal, matters might come before the jurors. Petty theft and pilfering, especially that involving wood-theft or arising from gleaning, might be presented. Cases of assault and bloodshed were regularly brought to the leet, as were many cases of verbal violence, notably scolding. To these matters arising from within the community might be added presentments prompted by central government directives: infringement of the settlement laws, for example, or of the laws against vagrancy. The manorial court, therefore, dealt essentially with the petty crime of the period, but a good set of manorial court leet records can provide us with a uniquely intimate impression of crime, conflict and control at a village level.[15] Manorial court records, more than those of any other tribunal, suggest that the nearer the court was to the wrongdoer, the greater the volume of evidence its archives are likely to provide. To take an extreme example, we know of twenty-three inhabitants of the Lancashire manor of Prescott who were indicted for assault at the county quarter sessions between 1615 and 1660. In the same period, 1,252 inhabitants of the manor were presented for assault before the leet. These figures endorse the view of a recent student of manorial courts that 'focusing upon only the higher courts misrepresents the nature and frequency of illegal activity'.[16]

The manorial courts have often been portrayed as the medieval 'peasants' court', where the will of the community (or powerful strata within it) might be expressed and community tensions aired and eased. By the late sixteenth century, the ecclesiastical courts were beginning to share some of these attributes.[17] Some earlier writers, seduced by the propaganda surrounding Hunne's case and the complaints of later Puritan writers, have asserted that the church courts were 'unpopular'. In fact, as we shall demonstrate at a later point, the church courts could not have operated without a wide degree of popular support and co-operation. If their correction business increased, as it appears to have done between about 1580 and the outbreak of the Civil Wars, it would seem likely that such support and co-operation was forthcoming. More work needs to be done on the church courts in the fifteenth and early sixteenth centuries but it seems that they survived the Reformation in fairly good shape, and emerged as a vital part of government in the reign of Elizabeth I. Their status after the Restoration awaits detailed research, but it is probable that their correction business after that date was increasingly limited to the enforcement of religious conformity.[18]

Before 1642, however, a much wider range of illicit behaviour was regularly presented before the church courts, of which that of the archdeacon was normally closest to grass-roots problems. The church courts were concerned not merely with the maintenance of doctrinal conformity but also with the upkeep of standards of christian behaviour. This responsibility became more urgent after the Reformation, when new stress was laid on the equation of the good citizen with the good christian: the population had to be not only adherents of the correct brand of christianity but also obedient, hardworking, sober and chaste. Sexual immorality was frequently presented before the church courts, whose archives, indeed, constitute a remarkable source for reconstructing contemporary attitudes on sexual and marital behaviour.[19] Drunkenness and other liquor offences, especially if committed upon the sabbath, likewise figured prominently in the business of the archdeaconry courts. Certain forms of slander and defamation, held by canon lawyers to be a breach of christian charity, were also presented there.[20] As with most other courts, very loosely defined types of disorderly behaviour, alarming or offensive to the respectable and powerful within the parish, might also come before the ecclesiastical tribunals. As with the manorial leet, the church courts were, in large measure, something which people used to settle their disputes or curb their disorderly neighbours. Again as with manorial courts, we lose much of the flavour of contemporary crime, delinquency, and law enforcement if we ignore the records of these lesser courts in favour of those more powerful tribunals empowered to try the serious offender.

The hierarchy of courts constituted, in theory, at least a powerful system of law enforcement. It had at their disposal an imposing array of sanctions against the lawbreaker. The assizes were empowered to hang felons, and might also impose lesser penalties: petty thieves were whipped, many thieves and manslayers escaped the noose through claiming benefit of clergy, while by the early eighteenth century many others avoided execution by being transported to the American colonies. Those convicted of misdemeanour at the assizes and quarter sessions were fined, while after about 1600 both these courts were regularly sending petty offenders to the house of correction. Those presented before the manorial courts were fined, while those found guilty by the ecclesiastical courts were made to do public penance, and excommunicated if they remained obdurate. However, institutions, whatever their theoretical powers, need competent officials to run them if they are to be effective, and we must now turn to discuss the law enforcement officers of the period.

Of all the officers of English local government, perhaps none has received so much favourable comment from the historian as the justice of the peace.[21] The immediate origins of this office, like those of the court of quarter sessions with which it was so intimately connected, lay in the fourteenth century. Originally conceived of as just one of a number of royal experiments for suppressing disorder, the office survived its rather shaky origins, and by the fifteenth century the justice of the peace was an essential part of local government. His importance, and his potential workload, were consolidated and extended by central government. Almost from the office's inception, statutes were passed adding to its duties and powers, perhaps 300 of them between the mid fourteenth and late sixteenth centuries. Throughout the period under discussion, the justice of the peace played a vital role in both law enforcement and county administration in general.

The solitary justice was empowered to conduct the preliminary examination of suspects and witnesses in cases of felony, take recognizances, commit suspected felons to prison, and bind over the unruly to be of good behaviour; he was to stop affrays, conserve rivers, and enquire into apprenticeship disputes and differences between master and servant; he could also take steps to suppress vagabonds, rogues, nightwalkers, nocturnal hunters in masks, and players of unlawful games; bind over soldiers who had sold their arms, equipment, or horses to appear at the sessions, or imprison them; he could deal in a similar fashion with those spreading false rumours; seize the goods of gypsies, search wax manufacturers for illicitly made candles, examine and bind over recusants, enquire into poaching cases, and have complaints about suits arising in the county courts referred to him; he could also, in times of dearth, supervise the sale of corn and the production of malt and, in the appropriate counties, control Thames watermen.

Two or more justices acting together had yet wider powers. They could look into cases of embracery and maintenance, riots, and poor scholars begging for fees; their local government functions included fixing poor rates and supervising the repair of the highways, and appointing overseers of cloth; they were empowered to take action against Jesuits and tax-evaders, take bail, grant alehouse licences, regulate the weights and measures used by tradesmen, and license pedlars or players; they were also to determine paternity in bastardy cases, order maintenance payments, and assess robbery rates.

These statutory duties were wide enough, but the justice also possessed extensive theoretical powers to hear and determine all forms of felony. In practice, however, as we have already seen, serious crime was being left increasingly to the assizes. The JP was still essential in the early stages of apprehending the serious criminal, by taking depositions, committing suspects to prison, and binding witnesses and prosecutors to appear at the relevant court. After about 1590, however, the justices in sessions became steadily less concerned with the trial of capital felony. By the late seventeenth century, the justices' main involvement in crime control was through the exercise of their extensive powers of summary conviction. Although felons had to be tried at the assizes, a wide range of petty offenders were simply tried before one or two justices, without any trial by jury.

The choice of the men to whom these duties were to be entrusted was obviously of great importance. Justices were appointed by the sovereign under the Great Seal, although in practice the Lord Chancellor or the Lord Keeper had responsibility for the composition of the commissions of the peace of the individual counties. As might be expected, those chosen were often the nominees of others in positions of authority: royal servants, courtiers, officials of central or local government, assize judges, even the monarch himself. The traditional qualification for membership of the bench, that the aspirant should be a £20 freeholder, was patently obsolete by the mid sixteenth century; long before that time, justices had been drawn from the upper echelons of rural society. In choosing justices, therefore, the central government had to square the age-old problem of finding local governors of sufficient wealth and local standing to command the respect due to the office, and yet ensuring that they were not so important as to become leaders of local faction. The Westminster authorities held the ultimate sanction against the negligent, persistently unjust, or politically unreliable justice: JPs were made or unmade at the central government's will. Once membership of the bench was seen as proof of arrival in the upper reaches of county society, and as a stepping-stone to further influence and prestige, the power to remove JPs from the commission of the peace provided a useful means of disciplining the gentry. Nevertheless, maintaining the necessary standards of dedication and co-operation among the justices was not always an easy business.

Describing the fortunes of the magistracy between 1550 and 1750 is difficult, not least because any general account must be modified by infinite local variations. Detailed county studies, for example Anthony Fletcher's account of local administration in Sussex, do suggest some general patterns. In the first half of our period the bench became more numerous, more wealthy, and better educated, but justices were not a homogenous body. They included Privy Councillors and courtier peers who might only have the most tenuous connections with the county, and what Fletcher describes as the 'magnate caucus' of important county families whose interest in the more mundane aspects of magisterial duties might be limited. To such men, a few honourable exceptions apart, the office of justice of the peace was a sign of status rather than an inducement to participate actively in local government. In Sussex, as elsewhere, the problem was to find 'able, loyal and energetic men' rather than 'turbulent, indolent and socialite magistrates'. Arguably, such paragons were more likely to be drawn from the members of solid and established gentry families who filled about half the bench in most counties, or from the representatives of those lesser gentry lines whose fortunes had only recently allowed them to enter the charmed circle of magistracy.

The workload of individual justices therefore varied greatly, and it is difficult to contrive a yardstick by which the diligence of JPs might be measured. Detailed examination of the relevant county archives, which could include counting the number of occasions on which individual justices attended quarter sessions or assizes, noted down witnesses' evidence in examinations or depositions, committed suspect persons to prison, or took recognizances, does, however, give some insight into who the active justices were. Other evidence can sometimes be used to demonstrate the nature and extent of the active justice's business. That paragon of magisterial virtues, William Lambarde, for example, left fascinating materials from which the workings of the bench in Elizabethan Kent can be reconstructed.[22] One suspects, nevertheless, that such justices were rare: for every Lambarde there must have been four or five less assiduous JPs, willing enough to perform their duties efficiently when called upon, but hardly over-anxious to seek out additional business.

If the responsibilities and powers of the justice of the peace between the fourteenth and late sixteenth centuries had increased, those of the sheriff had undergone a considerable decline.[23] The sheriff held an office of considerable antiquity, its origins shrouded in the mists of the pre-conquest era, which in the high middle ages had achieved almost viceregal status. In the twelfth century the sheriff had been responsible for the collection of royal revenue, military forces, police, gaols, courts, and the due execution of writs. His courts, the sheriff's tourn, and the county courts, had been vital parts of the machinery of justice. The sheriff had thus constituted a link between central and local government, but his office had barely reached its full splendour before a series of rival local government officials began to encroach upon it. Most importantly, the rise of the justice of the peace and the quarter sessions eroded the importance of the sheriff and his courts, the decisive step in this process being the statute 1 Edw. IV cap. 2 of 1463, which removed indictments from the sheriff's tourn to the quarter sessions. This diminution of jurisdictional powers was followed by a loss of the sheriff's military function, which was superseded by the mid-Tudor innovation of the Lord Lieutenant and the militia.

Despite the decline in its powers, the shrievalty was still of considerable significance. The sheriff remained responsible for collecting certain royal dues, running the county court (long since relegated to hearing civil actions where debt and damages did not exceed forty shillings), and supervising elections. More relevant to the historian of crime were the sheriff's continuing contributions to local policing, to the maintenance of local law and order, and to the exercise of the business of the common-law courts at Westminster in the locality. Writs from these courts commencing or continuing actions were sent to the sheriff, who served them and returned them through his under-officers. Similarly, he was responsible for serving and returning the writs of the assizes and quarter sessions, and played a vital role in the calling and smooth running of these two courts. The sheriff and his under-officers were responsible for publicizing the dates of meetings of these courts, for serving process upon persons required to attend them, for ensuring the presence of jurors, for holding prisoners in gaol before trial, for writing up the gaol calendars which recorded the presence of such prisoners, and for punishing those of them who were found guilty. The sheriff was also to organize the accommodation and entertainment of the judges of assize.

It seems probable that the social status of those filling the office fell steadily between 1550 and 1750. As ever, any suggestion of a general development must be modified by numerous local and individual exceptions, while, as is so often the case, more research has been done on this issue for the century before rather than that after the Restoration. Nevertheless, it seems that whereas sheriffs in 1550 were still drawn from the county elite, by 1750 they were usually gentry of middling fortune. Most recent authorities are agreed that it was the fees and expenses incumbent upon the office which made it so unpopular, and scattered evidence exists which would lend weight to such an interpretation. Typifying the retreat from the conspicuous consumption involved were the forty Derbyshire gentlemen who late in the seventeenth century made an agreement binding them to keep the costs of the sheriffwick as low as possible should they be appointed to it.[24] The sheriff was also responsible for money due to the crown left uncollected during his year of tenure, while the attractiveness of the office was decreased further by the obligation upon its encumbent to reside in his county during that year. The rumours circulating in 1622 that elevation to the office was being used as a form of 'gentle correction' for parliamentary critics of royal policy gives some impression of its potential appeal for the upper gentry.[25]

Despite the decline of the powers of the sheriff, and its lack of popularity among the county elite, the sheriff's under-officers continued to play an important, if at times disruptive, part in law enforcement. Most of the everyday duties of the shrievalty were in fact carried out by the undersheriff and a team of bailiffs, and it was these latter who in many respects represented the cutting edge of the legal system, serving writs and carrying out arrests. Such tasks, given contemporary attitudes to law officers, were hardly likely to attract weak or sensitive men, while inevitable problems were attendant upon the bailiff's dependence upon fees for his living. A clear distinction between the legitimate and the illegitimate fruits of office was rare in the upper reaches of national bureaucracy: it was even less common at the base

31

of the administrative machine, and complaints of bribery, corruption and extortion against bailiffs were all too widespread and all too plausible. The career of William Marshall, a Somerset bailiff in the years before the Civil Wars, provides a well-documented example of a common problem. In 1626 he was the subject of a complaint to the quarter sessions after he and his disorderly and unsworn assistants had broken into a woman's house and subjected her to obscene vilification; in 1631 he was taken to Star Chamber for bringing a false suit, and fined £20; in 1635 he was accused of multiple extortion in partnership with an attorney of the Common Pleas; and in the following year he was shot dead by a householder who he was attempting to arrest as part of a civil process and into whose residence he had broken without any legal justification. The coroner's jury investigating the fatality were willing to suffer a stiff fine rather than find against the killer.[26]

The upkeep of the county gaol and the safe keeping of those incarcerated within it was another of the cares of shrievalty. The records of every county are full of references to the decay of the structure of the gaol and of the unpleasant nature of life within it. Gaol was characteristically used as a place where suspects were held before trial rather than as a form of punishment in itself. Nevertheless, the impression lingers that even the briefest stay in a typical county prison cannot have been a very pleasant experience, while the state of the fabric of the prison might be so bad as to act as a positive inducement to escape. An extreme case is provided by a petition to the Warwickshire bench from the county gaoler in 1625. He complained that, owing to the lack of any alternative, he was forced to keep the prisoners in his own house. This was hardly a satisfactory situation, as the house in question was not really strong enough to hold prisoners; indeed, he reported, in the recent past all the inmates had managed to escape, and it had taken him considerable time and trouble to recapture them.[27]

Given the evident state of the structures used as prisons, the quality of life inside them may be imagined. Death through gaol fever, probably a form of dysentry, was common. Its virulence was dramatically demonstrated by a celebrated incident in 1577, when sick prisoners being tried at the Oxford assizes infected jurors and judges alike, with fatal results for several of them.[28] When other diseases, notably the plague, were rife, the prisoners, ill-fed and living in cramped and insanitary conditions, were obviously very vulnerable. They were dependent for food upon a county rate augmented by private charity. Those without friends were normally hungry at the best of times, while in times of death the poor felon went very hungry indeed. Conditions in gaol were also affected by the personality of the gaoler. This official, like the sheriff's bailiff, made his living from fees rather than a salary, and, as with the bailiff, was unlikely to be a sensitive or charitable man. As might be expected, numerous cases can be found of gaolers ill-treating prisoners, extracting extortionate fees from them, and indulging in such illegal activities as operating unlicensed alehouses in the gaol. It is hardly surprising that the gaoler, in common with the rest of the sheriff's officers, should enter a bond to protect the sheriff from the consequences of any negligence or illegal act on the part of his subordinates.

Whereas considerable evidence survives relevant to the functioning of the office of sheriff, the way in which the coroner carried out his duties is a shadowy subject which awaits detailed research.[29] The coroner, from the middle ages onwards, had enjoyed varied powers, but to the historian of crime the office's greatest significance lies in its responsibility for investigating suspicious deaths. The coroner had to convene a jury to assist him in such investigations, and also possessed such quasi-magisterial powers as the right to ensure the presence of witnesses and suspects at subsequent assizes or sessions by binding over, and the right to imprison persons suspected of homicide and to take depositions. He also had to be skilled enough to draft (or at least check the drafting of) the reports of inquests. Copies of these reports were sent to the King's Bench, and the large numbers of them, constituting one of the great unworked sources of English social history, survive in the archives of that court. Those dealing with homicide or suspected homicide were sent to the assizes, where trial took place. But, as we have suggested, so far little research has been done on the working of the office, or indeed on the social background of those filling it. Just after the beginning of our period Sir Thomas Smith asserted that the coroner was typically drawn from 'the meaner sort of gentleman, and for the most part a man seen in the lawes of the realme',[30] and this description probably holds broadly true for the remainder of the period. The fees that the office offered would have made it attractive to the lesser gentleman with a smattering of legal knowledge.

The 'meaner sort of gentleman', and the upper ranks of the yeomanry, might also participate in the system of law enforcement as hundred or high constables, vital links in the chain of authority. It was these officials, appointed for various sub-divisions within the county, who were responsible for passing the instructions of the quarter sessions down to the individual parishes. Their wider duties might be inferred from 'the othe of a high constable' which survives in the North Riding quarter sessions records from 1610. The high constable was to receive all informations and presentments made by the parish officers, and return and certify them to quarter sessions. He was to present all 'bloodsheddes, assaltes, affreyes and outcryes' occurring within his wapentake, and was to execute all writs, warrants and precepts sent to him. He was to endeavour diligently to apprehend all felons and vagabonds in his area of responsibility, and was also to enquire into the report to the sessions any faults among the under-officers. In general, the high constable was to 'well and truly behave' himself in all matters appertaining to his office.[31]

Beneath the high constable there came the most lowly officer in the whole system of law enforcement, the parish or petty constable. In the North Riding, the petty constable was required to swear an oath that set out his duties in plain terms:

> You shall . . . well and truly present all mannour of bloodsheddes, assaltes and affreys and outcryes there . . . done and commytted against the Kinges Ma[jes]ties peace: all manner of writtes, warrantes and preceptes to you lawfully directed you shall truly execute: the Kings Ma[jes]ties peace in your own person you shall conserve and keepe as much as in you lyeth: and in all thinges that apperteyne to your office you shall well and truly behave yourselfe.[32]

Ultimately, therefore, the maintenance of the king's peace and the functioning of the system of law enforcement depended upon the energies and efficiency of the unpaid parish constable, chosen to serve for a year from among his neighbours.

Understandably, many examples can be found of occasions when energy and efficiency was signally lacking among these local officers, and many historians, especially those unwilling to look any further than the more obvious literary sources, have tended to depict the parish constable in a very unfavourable light.[33] Recent research, however, has suggested that this portrayal is overdrawn, and rests upon very shaky evidence and a set of misconceptions about what policing in the early modern period was about. Before the early eighteenth century at least, most constables were drawn from the richer villagers, often were literate, and usually seem to have been reasonably efficient about their duties. Many of their alleged deficiencies were the outcome not of slackness, corruption or stupidity, but rather of their role as mediators between the state law and the desires of their communities. Keith Wrightson has described this problem in terms of 'two concepts of order', that of the village and that of the state, while Joan R. Kent has made some striking comparisons between the role of the seventeenth-century village constable and that of village headman in other agrarian societies.[34] What is undeniable, however, is that the state's concept of order was intruding steadily into the village. By the seventeenth century the parish constable's main function was to carry out the instructions of the county bench: his more traditional role of acting, in some respects, as a sort of representative for his neighbours, had been eroded.

The influence of the growth of the state manifested itself in another way: an increase in the efficiency of the bureaucratic staff of the various courts. England had enjoyed a relatively efficient bureaucracy in the middle ages, and the publications of the Selden Society constitute eloquent testimony of that bureaucracy's capacity for keeping legal records. Arguably, however, the early modern period saw an increase in this efficiency, or, perhaps more accurately, a diffusion of it away from the royal clerks at Westminster into the localities. As Professor Barnes informed us some years ago, it was the early Stuart period which saw the emergence of the clerk of the peace, the organizer of the clerical staff of the quarter sessions upon whose administrative ability so much depended.[35] The attention lavished upon the justices has tended to obscure the degree to which they depended upon the clerk and his helpers, not least because the Elizabethan and early Stuart periods saw an emphasis on the connection between more government and more paperwork. Similarly, work on the clerks of assizes and their staff has suggested a move towards a more bureaucratic ethos.[36] Work on other tribunals reinforces this suggestion: the amount of paperwork generated by the ecclesiastical courts between 1560 and 1642, for example, points to the existence of an efficient clerical staff.[37]

Much of the next three chapters will be based upon discussion of the materials produced by the efforts of the clerical staffs of various courts, and the final section of a chapter dealing with the structure of courts and office-holding is an apposite juncture at which to discuss these materials. As we have already commented, England has never been a police state, and has never experienced a fully inquisitorial system. For this reason the records upon which the historian of crime in England must work are less rich than the archives of a number of continental courts. To this intrinsic deficiency must be added the effects of the passing of time. Masses of relevant materials have been lost or destroyed, casualties of less record-conscious ages. Enough remains, however, to permit at least a partial reconstruction of the patterns of crime, and to understand something of the social processes which were involved in law enforcement.

Ironically, what is in many ways the most fascinating source is the one which has been most often destroyed, and in which both contemporary clerical staff and later legal historians took least interest: the deposition. The deposition, also known as the examination or the confession, was essentially the verbatim evidence noted by an examining magistrate or equivalent officer. Early examples of this type of document can be found in ecclesiastical court records, in borough records, or appended to coroners' inquests: its existence was formalized, however, by two statutes of Mary's reign, the first of them instructing justices to take relevant depositions before committing suspected felons and witnesses to bail, the second giving similar instructions to justices committing suspected felons to prison.[38] The deposition, therefore, can provide numerous insights into widely-held popular notions on crime, as well as providing information on the early stages of a prosecution. This class of document provides us with most of what we will ever know about the qualitative aspects of early modern English crime.

After taking depositions, the justice's next action in a case of suspected felony would be to bind the relevant parties over to attend the assizes or quarter sessions. By the early seventeenth century most suspected felons would be committed to the county gaol, but the more socially acceptable of them, in common with those accused of misdemeanours, would be bound over to the relevant court, together with complainants and witnesses, and required to give a financial guarantee of their attendance. The record of this practice, the recognizance, therefore provides some insights into pre-trial procedure, and might also be used to calculate how many cases known to the magistrate never came to trial. Further insights into other forms of criminal behaviour, notably violence, can be gained from recognizances recording binding over to keep the peace. Surety for the peace was granted against those who threatened the person or property of another. The potential victim would go to a justice, and declare on oath that he was in physical danger, or that his goods were threatened. If the complaint was credible, the person complained against would be bound over to keep the peace, sometimes on pain of forfeiture of a considerable sum of money. The system of binding over, therefore, constituted a cheap and in many ways effective method of curbing interpersonal violence: it has also bequeathed us a body of archival material upon which to found an impression of the extent of certain forms of tension in the past.[39]

As the next stage, the suspect would stand trial, either being delivered from the gaol, or attending the court rather than forfeit his recognizance.[40] The document formally recording this would be the indictment. In its standard form, the indictment should have recorded much of the information upon which the historian of crime might construct a statistical analysis: the name of the accused; his or her occupation or status; place of residence; the place where the crime was committed; the date upon which it was committed; the nature of the offence; the name of the victim; and, in many cases, the details of the punishment inflicted. Contemporary legal opinion suggested that the indictment should be an unusually accurate source. Between the fifteenth and the eighteenth century, writers and commentators on the law stated unequivocally that the indictment had to conform to certain essential standards of precision and accuracy. This insistence was buttressed by judicial decisions, especially from the King's Bench. It would seem, therefore, that an historical source could not have better credentials for accuracy than the assize or quarter sessions indictment.

Unfortunately, as rapidly becomes apparent to the alert student, the standards of accuracy prescribed in the law books and in judicial decisions were not invariably reflected in clerical practice in the provincial courts. J. S. Cockburn, the leading scholar of the early modern assizes, has used his knowledge of indictments between 1559 and 1625 to provide a cogent demonstration of the deficiencies of the source.[41] These need not be rehearsed in detail here, but even the more obvious of them demonstrate the limitations of the supposed accuracy of indictments. Firstly, details of occupation were frequently inaccurate, making analysis of those accused of felony by occupation or status a meaningless exercise. Secondly, the accused was usually simply described as being resident in the parish where the offences took place, which makes it impossible to determine how many crimes were committed by outsiders to the parish in question. Moreover, checking indictments against recognizances (a more reliable source) suggests that the dates given on them were inaccurate, which obviously impedes any discussion of the seasonality of crime. On this evidence, it is impossible not to agree with Professor Cockburn's conclusion that 'a moderately alert attorney could probably have made mincemeat of perhaps half the indictments considered at the assizes'.[42] Conversely, it should be remembered that the sample of documents studied by Cockburn was produced by courts suffering from the strain of ever-increasing business. It is probable that future research on indictments in other periods and for other areas will portray the indictment in a less gloomy light. In any case, we are indebted to Professor Cockburn for editing a multi-volume calendar of Home circuit indictments after arguing strenuously that this body of source material is, in many respects, useless.[43]

Trial procedure added further implications of the use of indictments. The first stage in this procedure was for the grand jury to decide if an accusation was sufficiently well-founded to warrant trial proper. When the jury's decision was affirmative, the indictment would be marked as a true bill. When its decision was negative, the indictment would be marked *ignoramus*, and often destroyed. In the case of a true bill, the accused would then go on to stand trial before a petty jury. In many cases, despite the eulogies lavished by all contemporary legal writers on the jury system, the jurors would simply bring in a verdict as directed by the judge.[44] In the late Elizabethan and Jacobean periods, the assize judges might be trying well over 100 felons at the rate of one every five or ten minutes over a period of two days. Such levels of business left little room for juries to agonize over their decisions. It also presented problems for accuracy of record keeping. One suspects that many of the deficiencies in indictments resulted from the sheer number of them that had to be processed in any one assize, while further problems of omission might occur at the trial stage, not least when clerks did not bother to record details of verdict or punishment on the indictment.

Happily, details of verdicts and punishments can often be reconstructed from other documents. Details of trial were often noted on gaol delivery calendars or on mainprise calendars which gave details of those bound over to answer at the court. Unfortunately, these calendars were often written on large pieces of parchment which made obvious outer wrappers for the other documents relating to the relevant session of the court. Accordingly, many of them are damaged or in poor condition. Often, however, the information on these rolls was noted in gaol books or crown books. These books, at their best containing a complete abstract of the business conducted at the assizes, can be excellent sources. In particular, they permit at least a partial reconstruction of levels of indicted crime in areas and periods for which indictments do not survive.

Whereas the indictment was the formal record of an accusation of felony or misdemeanour, less formal charges against less serious offenders were usually recorded in presentments. The dividing line between a presentment and an indictment was an obscure one in legal theory (the wording of indictments, for example, usually stated that the jury 'presented' the accused) and in practice. At the assizes or quarter sessions, presentments might include the comments of the grand jury on the county's grievances, or reports of petty delinquents by parish officers. At the manorial court, and on the correction side of the church courts, offenders were generally brought to trial on a presentment. At the manorial courts, details of these charges were engrossed, amid notes of other manorial business, on bulky parchment rolls, and discussion of bureaucratic efficiency should not ignore the high standards with which these most local of records were often kept. Such scribal perfection was rarely present among those responsible for noting details of presentments and subsequent trial in church court act books. Cases here were often recorded in heavily abbreviated Latin, sometimes amounting to little more than the clerk's private shorthand. Ecclesiastical depositions can present similar, if less serious, orthographical problems.

Depositions, recognizances, indictments, gaol books, and presentments all provide details of at least some aspects of crime in the past, and it is upon this formal documentation of the courts that the most useful work on the history of crime to have been completed in recent years has been based. These formal records can, of course, be supplemented by a number of less formal sources, many of them, like letters and diaries, far removed from the official law-enforcement system. Two further sources generated within that system do, however, require short mention. The first of these are the numerous petitions of complaint sent in to the clerk of the peace or the clerk of assize which enumerate the delinquent behaviour of individuals who had offended their local community. These have much in common with some of the less formal presentments and, like them, can provide useful qualitative information about petty crime and parochial reactions to it. Secondly, a number of justices' notebooks or collections of justices' papers survive, from which it is possible to reconstruct much of the routine activity of the justice which leaves so little trace in the formal record.[45] Only rarely do these books contain details of the justices' feelings about their activities, but from them it is frequently possible to infer something of their attitudes to their work, their colleagues, and those they sought to control.

No account of the machinery of law enforcement in early modern England can ever hope to be complete, and even a basic portrayal of the national system by which the law was administered has to make allowances for local variations, changes over time, and the accidents of record survival. Even so, a number of general conclusions can be drawn from the foregoing pages. Most importantly, anybody who has worked widely on the agencies of law enforcement and local administration must come away with the impression that England was a much-governed country. The assize system, a remarkably neat means of enforcing the royal law in the localities, is impressive enough. Even more remarkable is the way in which local jurisdictions seemed to have worked with commendable efficiency. Manorial court records, for some localities at least, give the impression of self-regulatory communities going about their business with deeply held concepts of lawfulness and order. The records of the quarter sessions and archdeaconry courts demonstrate a widespread willingness among local officers, drawn from the population at large, to participate in the running of the courts. Law enforcement in early modern England would have been impossible without a wide degree of public cooperation: as the work of the more active justices of the peace, as constables' presentments, as indeed the presence of most felons before the courts proves, this co-operation was often forthcoming.

The system of law enforcement in our period was not perfect, but it seems to have worked with more than tolerable efficiency. Two factors gave it a peculiar strength. Firstly, if we may state what will become a recurrent theme, the king's law was long established, and people were long used to settling disputes by recourse to that law. Secondly, the system was largely dependent upon unpaid amateur officials. This brought its problems, as complaints about venal 'basket' justices and ineffectual parish constables suggest: conversely, it also brought some peculiar advantages. Not least of these was that the hierarchy of office-holding corresponded to the social hierarchy: at a time when notions of the importance of degree, or stability, and of hierarchy itself were being constantly preached and at least partly accepted, such a correspondence made a good deal of sense. Moreover, the English system seems to have caused less oppression, and, indeed, less distortion of society, than the obvious contemporary alternative: one based on the purchase of office, with office-holders entirely dependent upon fees.

The English system may have generated less documentation than some of the continental ones, but it has bequeathed us enormous quantities of court records. That those which survive are perhaps a tithe of what was produced is a source of regret: as we shall see in the next chapter, it is difficult, if not impossible, to discuss 'crime patterns' in the modern sense in the two centuries before 1750. On the other hand, enough documentary material does survive to permit the construction of at least partial answers to a number of very relevant questions: the incidence of prosecuted crime; the incidence of different forms of punishment; shifts in the business of various courts; the identification of those social groups from which offenders were prosecuted; and the analysis of popular attitudes towards different types of crime and criminal. However incomplete the understanding which we shall gain on such matters, we can rest assured that consultation of court archives will usually bring us closer to an understanding of crime in the past than most other types of source material. The problems involved in using and interpreting these records are manifold: this should not, however, be used as an excuse for leaving them to collect yet more dust.

Chapter 3

MEASURING CRIME, MEASURING PUNISHMENT

One of the questions which the historians of crime is most often asked to answer is that of the nature of the rates and patterns of crime in the past. The question is a legitimate one, made all the more so by the evident willingness of historians of crime to adopt a statistical approach to their subject. The author of a major study of crime in colonial New York has declared crime in the past to be an 'eminently countable phenomenon',[1] and support has been lent to this proposition by such important pioneering works as those of Beattie and Samaha.[2] The logic behind such a methodology is a seductive one: as we have seen in the previous chapter, there existed in early modern England a large number of courts; despite the vicissitudes of time, a massive bulk of archival material survives from these courts; despite the difficulties of using this material, it might be expected that the industrious historian would be able to glean from it some criminal statistics, at least for isolated institutions or localities. Taken over a short period, such statistics might furnish details of a 'pattern of crime'. Over a longer timespan, they might produce evidence of fluctuations in levels of crime, which might in turn be compared against other socio-economic variables: demographic trends, harvest failures, inflation, trade depressions, the impact of war, and so on. Superficially, the study of crime statistics would seem to be the logical initial task of the historian of crime.

Materials for such an exercise are not lacking and, as we have seen, at least one student of the subject regards crime in the past as 'eminently countable'. Others are less sanguine. J. J. Tobias, dealing with the nineteenth century (a period in which, unlike that with which we are concerned, the government was actually collecting and publishing criminal statistics) comments that 'criminal statistics have little to tell us about crime and criminals'.[3] Certainly the opinions of nineteenth-century social commentators, upon whom Tobias draws, would seem to support this assertion. In particular, he mentions a lively debate from the 1890s, based on rival interpretations of the official crime figures, in the course of which

> the Chaplain of Wandsworth Prison argued that crime had increased, the Chairman of the Prison Commissioners argued that it had decreased, and the Chief Constable of Staffordshire argued that it was substantially unchanged in amount. The statistics provided ammunition impartially for all three, and the welter of figures leaves us none the wiser.[4]

In general, it is tempting to agree with an early nineteenth-century observer who thought the attempt to give precise statistical accounts of criminal activities was to indulge in 'accurate calculation upon subjects that do not admit of any calculation at all . . . how indeed can it be imagined that men who have the strongest of all motives for eluding observation, can be so open to it as to have their numbers as accurately defined as those of a regiment of foot'.[5] Given the force of such arguments and an awareness of the difficulties involved in obtaining any statistics before the nineteenth century, the temptation to regard the quantification of crime in the early modern period as a meaningless exercise is almost overwhelming.

The problems inherent in attempting to use criminal statistics are not peculiar to that period, and any quantification of crime is a risky enterprise.[6] This might seem at variance with simplistic, commonsense notions: crime exists 'out there', and criminal statistics are therefore an accurate measure of its extent and nature. Such notions, however, provoke a number of immediate objections. Firstly, all criminologists and historians of crime are sensitive to the existence of the 'dark figure', that body of criminal behaviour never prosecuted or even reported. Determining the dimensions of this behaviour, despite occasional guesses by contemporaries, is impossible. The problem of the dark figure would be lessened if we could be certain that the relationship between recorded and unrecorded crime was constant. If, for example, we could be sure that one-quarter of all crimes committed were invariably reported, it would be possible to accept fluctuations in prosecution statistics as indicative of fluctuations in the real level of criminal behaviour, even if not all crimes were prosecuted. Unfortunately, however, it would seem that the proportion of criminal behaviour which would be eventually prosecuted might vary, most usually because of changes in the public's willingness to prosecute. In a period of 'moral panic', for example, deviant behaviour which would be ignored in more normal periods might be prosecuted, and a higher proportion of deviant behaviour than usual would appear in the court record.[7]

Criminal statistics are also distorted by the actions of official crime control agencies. Crime statistics are especially likely to be affected by changes in institutional practices, or might vary in accordance with fluctuations in the efficiency of the officers of law enforcement or of the courts. Hence it might be argued that any employment of judicial statistics in quest of understanding crime, in the past or at present, is essentially misconceived. Quantification of judicial records tells us about changes in control, about changes in the system of the criminal law and its enforcement, but it can tell us little of value about changes in the levels of crime itself, or the real levels of illicit behaviour, an indeterminate sample of which is brought before the courts.

Clearly, any historian of crime ignoring these arguments would be extremely foolhardy. Equally, it is the conviction of the present author that, providing the difficulties inherent in the enterprise are born in mind, providing the statistics are accepted as being of limited usefulness, and providing that any conclusions drawn from them are presented with due caution, counting offences is a useful exercise. If nothing else, quantification provides a framework for future research, and a starting-point for future debate about the history of crime. Even if the argument that changes in prosecution statistics reveal nothing more than shifts in official attitudes or energies is accepted, it remains true that understanding the nature of these shifts is an essential component of understanding crime in the past. Additionally, the very nature of English sources dictates that the historian of crime in early modern England must spend at least part of his time counting. Deprived, as we have mentioned, of those rich qualitative sources which survive in some continental states, the English historian is forced to attempt to formulate his impressions of criminal behaviour in the past by patterning such information as is left to him.

Study of criminal statistics can also be justified on somewhat deeper grounds. In what is probably the most sensible discussion yet in print of the problems of quantifying pre-nineteenth-century criminal materials,[8] Douglas Hay has argued persuasively that, for property offences at least, statistics derived from assize and quarter sessions records do give an accurate impression of fluctuations in actual crime. Firstly, Hay lays considerable importance on the 'accidental' nature of court records: indictments were not drawn up to support arguments about levels of crime – indeed, one might easily imagine the perplexity with which the clerical staff of the assizes or quarter sessions would greet the news that the records they kept would be the subject of so much debate among scholars three or four centuries into the future. Viewed from this angle, indictments constitute one of those historical sources whose very usefulness lies in the fact that nobody writing them had the least notion that they would be used by future historians. Secondly, Hay makes much of the argument that most prosecutions for theft were privately initiated, and thus neatly turns the argument that criminal statistics merely reflect levels of control on its head. Theft prosecutions in the eighteenth century, to a large degree, were not affected by 'control' in the modern sense. Could it not therefore be argued that indictments for theft and other property offences in that period convey a less distorted impression of levels of crimes actually committed than do modern crime statistics?

Hay's arguments relate mainly to late-eighteenth-century materials, and it might seem over bold to suggest that they hold good for the whole of the period 1550 to 1750. Evidently, as Hay is perfectly aware, changes in criminal statistics at certain points within our period were caused by changes in the intensity of crime control activities. In Lancashire, to take an example cited by Hay, the arrival of a Puritan regime after the Civil Wars coincided with an increase of 156 per cent in indictments between 1626–40 and 1646–51.[9] Most of this increase, however, consisted of a heavier prosecution of regulatory offences: once more, we are reminded that 'crime' is a term which describes a very varied range of human conduct, and that there might be a variety of ways in which such conduct might enter the official record. Fluctuations in the prosecution of unlicensed alehouse-keepers, of bastard-bearers, of swearers of prophane oaths and the like were very likely to be reflections of 'control waves'. On the other hand, it is probable that the historian is on firmer ground when discussing changes in the level of property offences or homicide. At the very least, Hay's suggestion that the proposition that historical statistics of crime must be inferior reflections of reality to modern ones is 'far from self-evident' has an attractive ring to it.

Nevertheless, the difficulties peculiar to understanding the significance of criminal statistics in the early modern period must be faced.[10] As we have pointed out, understanding crime in any society is impeded by the existence of a 'dark figure' of unrecorded crime, and it was very much in the nature of things that the figure of unrecorded crime in early modern England would be very dark indeed. Contemporaries made estimates. Edward Hext, a Somerset JP, claimed in the 1590s that only one in five crimes committed in his native county were actually reported. Nearly two centuries later, Patrick Colquhoun, writing on London crime, thought that only one offence in ten reached the attention of the authorities.[11] Obviously enough, such estimates are little more than guesses, and too much should not be made of them: conversely, they serve to remind the would-be quantifier of crime in the past of the problems which must be confronted when attempting to establish connections between recorded and actual crime. These problems assume massive proportions when the full extent of the disincentives to prosecution and the alternatives to it current in the early modern period are realized.

The most obvious of these disincentives was the cost and trouble which prosecution might involve. Attending court might make serious inroads into the time of a complainant living, say, thirty or so miles from the town where the assizes or quarter sessions were held, while loss of earnings and the cost of recompensing witnesses for their time and trouble would be added to the usual expenses and frustrations of the period. Once at court, expenses would multiply rapidly, for the clerical staffs of the assizes, quarter sessions, central courts and ecclesiastical tribunals all depended upon fees for their living. Accordingly, a charge was made at each step in prosecution, and the total expenses incurred could be very heavy for a man of moderate means. Estimating the precise cost of a prosecution is difficult, as is estimating how fees would be split between accuser and accused, while, as we have suggested, defraying the costs of witnesses, let alone paying for legal advice, might add substantially to the fees charged by the clerical staff of the court. These fees do, nevertheless, provide some sort of base line, and it is therefore instructive to note that a clerk of assize in the mid seventeenth century might expect to make between 2/- and 16/8 from each indictment coming into the court,[12] a figure in all probability broadly similar to the profits to be expected by comparable officials in other tribunals in the system. Even allowing for the availability of cheaper justice for paupers, the costs of prosecution must have acted as a powerful deterrent. Edward Hext's observation of 1596 that the 'troble and chardge' involved in prosecuting a crime acted as a disincentive to the victim to take a case to law was probably broadly true throughout the period with which we are concerned.[13] Once more, we must remind ourselves of the essentially personal nature of law enforcement in the early modern era.

Costs, therefore, were one factor which might inhibit a desire to prosecute: another was the widespread contemporary practice of settling legal disputes out of court. Suits between parties were often settled by arbitration, and the courts of the common law, the civil law, and the ecclesiastical law all accepted, and in some respects encouraged, the practice. Even one of the superior courts at Westminster, the court of Chancery, accepted arbitration of cases as normal, and it has been suggested that this flexibility, this intermingling of official and informal justice, came close to satisfying popular expectations of how the law should operate.[14] This was probably as true of other courts handling suits between parties as it was of Chancery.[15] Indeed, it might be argued that the early modern taste for litigation, so often commented upon by historians, is partly explicable by attempts to solve otherwise intractable problems by starting a suit in the hopes of bringing on a properly regulated mediation, whose outcome would be confirmed by the acknowledgement of a court.

Arbitration is a process more readily applicable to civil actions than to criminal prosecutions. However, the distinction between the two methods of waging law was not so distinct in the early modern period as it is at present, and many criminal cases were settled out of court. Blackstone, for example, at the end of our period, describes the following practice in cases of battery and similar offences:

> It is not uncommon . . . for the court to permit the defendant to speak with the prosecutor, before any judgement is pronounced; and if the prosecutor declares himself satisfied, to inflict but a trivial punishment. This is done to reimburse the prosecutor his expenses, and to make him some private amends, without the trouble and circuitry of a civil action.[16]

Official countenancing of mediation can be traced at a much earlier period: indeed, on occasions it is possible to find the authorities encouraging the process. That reaching settlements of this type was unremarkable both to the populace at large and to the staff of the courts is demonstrated by a Staffordshire case of 1598. In that year a letter was sent to the clerk of the peace for Staffordshire, explaining the absence of Francis Henshawe from the last sessions, at which he had been bound to appear. Henshawe, it was claimed, had been absent as a consequence of his ignorance of the continued need for him to attend, 'the matter being compounded and agreed upon betwixte him and the other parties who were at difference w[i]th him'.[17]

Out-of-court settlements and the compounding of criminal cases raise some intriguing questions about contemporary expectations of the legal system. In particular, it would seem that individuals were sometimes more anxious to obtain satisfaction from the offender, pecuniary or otherwise, than to see the full rigour of the law brought to bear. In 1580, for example, Richard Dongon or Donghill the younger was brought before the borough authorities at Warwick for committing bloodshed on William Sharples. After Donghill had been in custody for two days, Sharples intervened and 'desired that he might be released in hope of a new lief'. Donghill was duly grateful; the record recounts how he 'being sent for fell downe uppon his knees, humbled himself, asked Sharples' forgiveness, besought the baileif to be good to him, promised to live from thensforth cyvilly and never to give cause of offence'. After these touching avowals the borough authorities released Donghill, although they were sufficiently cautious to plan to reinforce his promises of future good conduct by sending him to London '& their to plaice him so as he should never agayn trowble the towne'.[18] What emerges most clearly from this story is that for Sharples, the victim of an assault, a public apology and the promise of future good conduct was felt to be preferable to legal process against Donghill. The prosecutor's position in such matters was made very explicit by another man, victim of a theft a little later in the same year. He declared that after the solicitations of the accused 'and his freendes' he had decided that 'he woold not procede against him by lawe, but was content to forgive him so as he comytted no more the like'.[19] The existence of such attitudes must make us even more pessimistic about the possibilities of learning much about actual crime from criminal statistics.

These examples, apart from their role in enhancing a proper scepticism about crime statistics, are useful in displaying the flexibility of the law-enforcement system. In particular they suggest a willingness on the part of the authorities to countenance informal settlements in the laudable (if sometimes misplaced) hope of thereby ensuring future good relations between the two sides in a prosecution. More sinister, perhaps, were the numerous occasions on which felonies were simply compounded for money without any official blessing. As might be expected, surviving evidence suggests that this practice was most common when the offence in question was theft. Many instances, like that of the girl who, it was reported to the Gloucestershire assizes in 1698, had offered a man she had stolen from 'Seaven pounds in money in leiu [sic] of the money as was lost out of his house if he would not send her to gaol and prosecute her', must have gone unrecorded.[20] Even so, a trickle of cases suggest that thieves would think the return of stolen goods, or the offer of a sum of money in their place, a likely means of evading prosecution. One such was Robert Striven, reported to the Somerset quarter sessions in 1657 for theft. Striven had stolen a purse from his mistress, but on being challenged returned it and begged for forgiveness.[21] His pleas failed, but there seems to be little doubt that similar requests must often have been successful; one writer of 1701, at least, thought that the return of stolen goods often acted as a successful antidote to prosecution.[22] This opinion, and the scattered archival evidence which supports it, must render the 'dark figure' even darker.

Other crimes failed to enter the records in such a way as to make them candidates for criminal statistics simply because other forms of remedy were available, ranging from personal revenge to more or less official sanctions. At one end of this spectrum, it is likely that many crimes were punished on a local level, perhaps most commonly by the person offended against. Such punishment must frequently have taken the form of straightforward physical violence, although on occasion more subtle methods might be used. Richard Gough, in his account of his fellow parishioners at Myddle in Shropshire, describes the activities of the criminally-inclined Wenlockes. Reece Wenlocke, the head of the family, was a fairly typical rural petty criminal, whose 'greatest diskindness that he did to his neighbours' was breaking their hedges for firewood. Reports circulated that he had made a new oven, 'and, according to the manner of such things, it was at first to be burnt, to make it fit for use'. The villagers anticipated renewed depredations of their hedges, and the servant of one of them decided to take appropriate counter-action:

> as he walked by a hedge, which was near Reece's house, he saw there a great dry stick of wood, and took it home with him, and bored a hole in the end of it with an auger, and put a good quantity of gun powder in it, and a peg after

it, and put it again into the hedge. And it happened, that Reece Wenlocke, among other hedgewood, took this stick to burn in his oven; and when he cast it into the fire in the oven, it blew up the top of it, and set fire on the end of the house. [23]

It seems unlikely that prosecuting Wenlocke for theft would have provided the community with nearly as much satisfaction as did this spectacular informal sanction.

Other, more official, sanctions might be thought to be a more proper means of dealing with the petty offender than indictment. Binding over to keep the peace, or to be of good behaviour, was often used to counter indictable behaviour. The informal petitions to the bench, complaining against exceptionally delinquent behaviour by a member of a village, often illustrate this point. One of them, sent by Stafford-shire villagers in 1595, detailed the conduct of William Walker, whose misdeeds included assaulting a woman, killing the sheep and geese of his neighbours, and cutting down their hedges and gates. His victims sought to correct him not by indictment but by having him bound over to be of good behaviour. [24] Similarly, petty thieves, poachers, and perpetrators of other forms of disorder might be sent to the house of correction, even though their delinquent behaviour might well have been indictable. The house of correction, therefore, offered those seeking to curb the minor criminal an extremely effective weapon; it also constituted yet another factor widening the gap between actual and indicted crime.

As the previous few pages have suggested, those attempting to understand the 'nature and incidence' or 'patterns' of crime on the basis of early modern court records are choosing to involve themselves in an activity which is considerably more complex than it might appear at first sight. It must be remembered that any scholar analysing criminal statistics, be they of a past or a modern society, is dealing with recorded, known crime. The extent of the 'dark figure' must remain conjectural, and any change in recorded crime is therefore at least as likely to be evidence of changes in reporting as in crime actually committed. Despite these problems, historians persist, and will presumably continue to persist, in subjecting to statistical analysis the masses of court archives recording crime committed in the past. If they bear the limitations and inherent problems of such an approach in mind, there is little doubt that they will find much of interest and importance; at the very least, they will be forced to acquire an intimate knowledge of their sources. On the other hand, the quantification of court materials introduces a further confusion. If we accept the broad definition of crime given in the introductory chapter, it rapidly becomes apparent that different courts, by dealing with different types of offences, produced archives from which very different impressions about the nature or pattern of crime in the past might be formed. It could, in fact, be argued that it is meaningless to talk about crime patterns in the period 1550–1750 until all surviving court records for the period have been analysed, a task whose completion, to put it mildly, lies some way in the future. Examination of the statistics derived from a number of these courts will demonstrate some of the difficulties.

Concentrating on serious crime, which might be equated for our immediate purposes with felony, produces fairly straightforward results, which will be further discussed later in this chapter. Investigation of indictments at the assizes in Elizabethan Essex, for example, reveals what is emerging as the standard pattern of serious crime in early modern England: a generally low level of indictment, a predominance of property offences, against a smaller number of crimes against the person; and marked fluctuations in the level of property offences, compared with a comparative stability in murders and infanticides. Surviving indictments for Essex, 1559–1603, include 129 homicides and 28 infanticides, as opposed to 110 highway robberies, 320 burglaries, and 1,460 simple or compound larcenies. To this figure might be added 172 cases of witchcraft, an offence indicted with considerable frequency in Elizabethan Essex. Other forms of felony were brought to trial with surprising infrequency. These Essex indictments include only 28 cases of rape, 8 of buggery, and practically none of arson. On the basis of these figures, it has been postulated that Elizabethan Essex enjoyed a low crime rate, rising from 80 per 100,000 population in the 1560s to 200 per 100,000 by 1600.[25] At first sight, analysis of these indictments has performed a useful service; we are provided with a fairly definite notion of the nature of recorded crime in this period, and even with a 'crime rate' which can be compared with that obtaining in modern England, or any other society for which we have the necessary data.

Study of the archives of other courts, however, undermines any confidence we may have in such evidence. The fundamental problem is the impossibility of equating 'crime' with serious offences tried at the assizes. If we continue to focus our attention on Essex records, but move on half a century, we discover that prosecutions at the county's quarter sessions create a very different impression of the nature of crime and its incidence. In all, combining indictments and presentments, a total of 3,514 offences were prosecuted at this court between 1628 and 1632. These included some examples of the types of 'crime' tried at the assizes; 144 thefts, for example, and 48 assaults. Overwhelmingly, however, the offences dealt with by the Essex quarter sessions in this period either involved the failure of parishes or individuals to meet various forms of obligation, or were of a regulatory nature. Against the modest totals for theft and assault might be set 480 prosecutions for allowing roads or bridges to fall into decay, 229 for keeping a disorderly alehouse, and 684 for failing to attend church. These figures suggest a very different pattern of crime from that given by assize records, and also suggest an annual crime rate of about 700 offences per 100,000 population.[26]

The period 1628–32 was a difficult one, marked by severe economic disruption, and Essex was a much-governed county. Records from other areas however, confirm the view that after the early seventeenth century the quarter sessions were concerned mainly with the enforcement of various types of obligation and with regulative offences. Indictments at the Buckinghamshire quarter sessions between 1679 and 1711 totalled 1,394. Of these 93, or 6.5 per cent were for theft or breaking and entering, and 236, or 17 per cent, for assault. The remainder involved a number of minor offences, of which 20.5 per cent arose from the sale or consumption of alcohol, 11 per cent the repair or upkeep of roads and bridges, and 7.5 per cent the correction of negligent or corrupt officers or court officials.[27] Moving to a slightly later period and another county reveals a somewhat different but not totally surprising picture: of the 337 indictments tried at the East Riding sessions in the 1730s, 27.5 per cent were for theft, 12 per cent for assault, 38 per cent for highway repair, and 8 per cent for drink offences.[28] These figures suggest that the various preoccupations of different county benches might produce different patterns of crime; they also, however, demonstrate how different the whole phenomenon of 'crime' appears when approached from the perspective of the quarter sessions rather than that of the assizes.

Examination of offences presented at the various church courts of the period provides yet another impression of delinquent behaviour. Once more, the situation is obscured by regional variations, while the lack of much detailed work on the ecclesiastical courts after the Restoration makes it difficult at this stage to say very much about the types of offence brought before these courts in the second half of our period;[29] nevertheless, some pattern can be discerned. Seven hundred and fifty-six presentments against the inhabitants of the Essex village of Kelvedon Easterford were brought between 1600 and 1642 in the court of the Archdeacon of Colchester. The overwhelming majority of them fell into two categories: 234 involved various forms of sexual misbehaviour, adultery, fornication, bridal pregnancy, and so on: while 224 involved failure to attend church. The only other large group of presentments arose from disrupting the sabbath, either by misbehaving, usually by drinking in the alehouse (52 cases), allowing such misbehaviour (37 cases), or working (25 cases).[30] Isolated samples of presentments from Cheshire, Somerset, Suffolk and Yorkshire between 1590 and 1633 show broadly similar characteristics, with sexual immorality perhaps constituting a higher proportion of reported delinquency in the two northern counties.[31] Church court records, therefore, give a useful means of investigating certain forms

of petty criminality in the period. They also remind us of the dimensions of the behaviour which the contemporary authorities sought to
control.

Further information on the nature of petty crime and minor forms of
misbehaviour are to be found in the records of the manorial courts leet.
In villages where the manorial courts were still active they played a
vital function in regulating the lives of the local inhabitants and punishing petty crime. Analysis of the 198 presentments recorded on the
surviving rolls of the manor of Acomb, a township near York, between
1550 and 1600 gives a typical impression of the type of behaviour that
could be presented before a court leet. Many of the presentments, as
was appropriate in a court of this type, were concerned with purely
local issues, infractions of the customs and by-laws of the manor. Thus
about a tenth of presentments were concerned with infringements of
local laws, another tenth with the breaking of pinfolds or the rescue of
impounded livestock, some 14 per cent with failure to keep hedges or
fences in repair, and 8 per cent with allowing swine to stray. There
were also a large number of presentments of offences more familiar to
the modern observer's view of what might constitute 'crime'. Forty-
five presentments, about 15 per cent of the total, involved affrays and
bloodsheds, and a slightly greater number were concerned with thefts
of brushwood or firewood, or with hedgebreaking. There were also
occasional cases (about 10 of each) of keeping disorderly houses,
harbouring vagrants and other undesirables, scolding and slandering,
and poaching. The manorial court was still, therefore, playing an
active role both in regulating the community and in punishing certain
forms of offence, notably physical and verbal violence. It was able to
do so cheaply and locally, and was also a flexible enough institution to
bring pressure to bear on a wide range of ill-doers. The extent of this
range is demonstrated by the presentment of two women for eaves-
dropping and, in 1598, of the presentment of the inhabitants of Acomb
en masse for wearing felt hats on the sabbath contrary to Elizabethan
sumptuary legislation.[32] Manorial records, like those of the church
courts, remind the historian of the necessity of keeping as open a mind
as possible when attempting to define 'crime' in the early modern
period.

For a final demonstration of this point, let us turn from the local
manorial and archdeaconry courts to the archives of one of the Westminster courts, the Star Chamber. In contrast to the petty offences and
lowly offenders which were the staple concerns of local jurisdictions,
Star Chamber usually dealt with a better class of accused and (on
parchment at least) with a number of rather more serious crimes.
Interpreting Star Chamber records is, however, difficult; the distinction between civil actions and criminal proceedings was probably even
less clear here than elsewhere, while the most recent study of these
records has stressed that litigants in the Star Chamber were especially

given to tactical litigation.[33] Even so, some idea of the pattern of alleged offences brought to the notice of this court might be gained from analysis of the 8,500 cases tried there in the reign of James 1. These cases provide details of a broad spectrum of delinquent behaviour, most of it involving violence to either persons or property. The largest single category was formed by allegations of riot, rout, and unlawful assembly, which constituted just over 16 per cent of all cases. Assault constituted just over 11 per cent, while the destruction of property, forcible disseizin, forcible entry, and similar cases formed a slightly smaller proportion. Other common offences involved impeding or perverting the smooth running of the machinery of justice; contempt of court or abuse of process constituted just over 7 per cent of all suits, perjury slightly less, and malfeasance by officers 6 per cent. A further 12 per cent of cases involved conspiracy or combination, and 8 per cent forgery and fraud.[34] Once again, investigation of the archives of an individual court gives a very individualistic impression of the nature of 'crime'.

The logical conclusion to be drawn from all this is that discussion of patterns of crime on the basis of analysis of the records of one court is not a very profitable exercise. The only method by which the problem might be solved would be to study the records of *all* courts in a given area, an undertaking which, without the assistance of a squad of research assistants, would be far too large for the normal historian. For this reason, some of the most important findings about the nature and incidence of crime in the past have resulted, paradoxically enough, not from broadly-based studies but rather from the intensive study of individual village communities. A number of such studies have been completed or are in progress. They involve a thoroughgoing investigation of all documentary evidence relevant to the settlement in question, the objective being to provide as total an impression of life there as possible. Such studies are of immense consequence for the historian trying to understand crime in the past. Arguably, their greatest potential contribution to such an historian lies in what they reveal about matters outside the immediate scope of this chapter: on the other hand, such work as has been completed on projects of this type has already provided useful data about changing patterns of crime.

Perhaps the most relevant village study so far to appear is that completed by David Levine and Keith Wrightson on the parish of Terling in Essex. In their investigation of references in the assizes and quarter sessions records to crimes committed in the parish, they divided offences into three categories: 'interpersonal' disputes (theft, assault); 'obligation enforcement' (upkeep of roads, bridges, and so on); and 'regulative' offences (for example, control of alehouses, taking in inmates, building a cottage without four acres of land annexed to it). Over the period 1560–1699, they discovered 306 Terling cases which came to the two courts in question. Of these about a third were interpersonal, 9.5 per cent were concerned with obligation enforcement, and just over 56 per cent regulative. There were important chronological fluctuations within this overall pattern. Briefly, Levine and Wrightson found that there was a sharp increase in interpersonal offences at the turn of the sixteenth and seventeenth centuries, followed by a marked rise in the level of regulative prosecutions. This pattern corresponded roughly to that found when ecclesiastical court presentments involving Terling inhabitants were analysed. There was a steady rise in such presentments between 1570 and 1629, and presentments involving sexual misconduct, marital relations and other forms of interpersonal behaviour increased from a third of all presentments in the decade 1570–79 to two-thirds in that of 1620–29. The explanation offered for this rise in regulative prosecutions is an instructive one; it is argued that it was not the consequence of a 'real' increase in crime, but rather of an increased willingness on the part of some villagers to regulate the conduct of others through court prosecutions.[35] This study also provides a possible explanation for the fall in prosecuted crime in the second half of the seventeenth century; by this period, they argue, the petty offender would be regulated more efficiently through the operation of the poor law than by taking him to court.

Quantification of petty crime is, therefore, fraught with difficulties, many of them attendant upon the variety of courts which could deal with minor offences. Our major concern in this chapter, tracing patterns of serious crime (felony) is, however, superficially less complicated. For most of our period, felony was tried almost exclusively at the assizes, and hence having to cope with the records of a multiplicity of courts within any given area is not a problem. Unfortunately, the erratic survival of assize records presents its own problems. It is impossible to obtain anything like a national picture of crime much before the mid eighteenth century, as the relevant archival materials simply do not exist. Indictments for the Home circuit, comprising the counties of Essex, Hertfordshire, Kent, Surrey and Sussex, are extant from 1559, albeit in a very imperfect series, and most published work on fluctuations in serious crime has so far been concentrated on these records.[36] Northern circuit materials survive from about 1650, the indictments in this case being supplemented by a superb series of depositions, although as yet little detailed research has been carried out on these sources.[37] Imperfect assize rolls for the Oxford circuit survive from the Restoration, while on the Western circuit gaol books, giving at least skeletal information on prosecutions and punishments, are extant from the late seventeenth century. By the early eighteenth century the situation improves, and by the end of our period sufficient materials survive to permit the reconstruction of the incidence and nature of serious crime over much of the country.

The records of the assize circuits can, however, be supplemented by other materials. A number of regions enjoyed a palatinate jurisdiction, and exceptionally good record keeping has ensured the survival of criminal archives for a number of them. Lancashire, for example, seems to enjoy both a good run of indictments and a good series of depositions from about 1660.[38] The neighbouring county of Chester, although lacking a good series of depositions, does enjoy an unbroken series of gaol files from the reign of Edward III to 1831, recording the business of the Palatinate Court of Great Sessions, the local equivalent to the assizes. These records, which are supplemented by good local quarter sessions records, are largely untapped,[39] and it seems likely that future research on many aspects of crime in our period could be carried out on Cheshire materials. It is not part of my intention to pre-empt such research, but the Cheshire records do make an attractive basis for discussion of patterns of and fluctuations in crime, not least because they constitute an unbroken series of details of prosecution far removed from the much-studied south-east. The files await detailed investigation, but a good impression of the business of the Court of Great Sessions can be derived from the Crown Books, in which abstracts of what passed at each session were entered.[40] The clerical skill with which these abstracts were kept, and the degree of detail given, varied: it must be reiterated that much more work is needed on records of the court apart from the Crown Books. Even so, the date given in the Books are sufficient to permit the reconstruction of patterns of reported felony and its punishment in one English county between 1580, when the Books became well enough kept to allow detailed analysis, and 1712, when a hiatus occurs until the late 1750s. Cheshire archives, therefore, provide a good and virtually unbroken run of material against which evidence of a more limited chronological nature from other areas might be set.

Figures derived from these samples and the Cheshire materials are set out in Table 1. They indicate what seems to be a well established and national pattern which obtained throughout our period. Felony consisted overwhelmingly of property offences: larceny, burglary, housebreaking, highway robbery, robbery, and pickpocketing. These normally accounted for between two-thirds and three-quarters of prosecuted felony. The only other offences regularly to figure prominently were homicide and infanticide. Some localities experienced modifications in this pattern, as did Essex with witchcraft between 1560 and 1645, or most of the north of England with coining in the 1690s.[41] Such exceptions apart, prosecution other than for taking life or property was uncommon. Sexual offences, rape, sodomy, bestiality and bigamy, were very rare, less than 0.5 per cent of indictments in Cornwall 1700–49, to take an extreme example. Arson was rarely prosecuted. Even witchcraft, outside Essex and perhaps Kent, does

TABLE 1 Indictments for felony in nine counties, selected periods, 1550–1749

	Middlesex Sessions, 1550–1625		Sussex Assizes, 1559–1625		Hertfordshire Assizes, 1559–1625		Cheshire Court of Great Sessions, 1580–1709		Essex Assizes, 1620–80		Devon Assizes, 1700–9		Cornwall Assizes, 1700–49		Norfolk and Suffolk Assizes, 1734–7	
		(%)		(%)		(%)		(%)		(%)		(%)		(%)		(%)
Property offences	7.158	93	1.664	74	1.536	86	2.875	74	1.965	81	259	76	689	80	197	85
Homicide and Infanticide	400	5	219	10	83	5	623	16	279	11	52	15	113	13	19	9
Sexual offences	70	1	21	1	13	1	77	2	65	2	1	—	4	1	3	1
Witchcraft	21	—	16	1	41	2	34	1	101	4	1	—	—	—	—	—
Arson	1	—	*	*	*	*	17	—	9	—	10	3	11	1	5	2
Coining	5	—	*	*	*	*	96	2	10	—	7	2	10	1	1	—
Other	5	—	229	13†	138	8†	184	5	8	—	12	3	38	4	7	3

* Date not available. † Includes some misdemeanours
Sources as p. 220, n.8. All percentages rounded to nearest whole number. No percentage given if below 0.5%.

not seem to have figured prominently in prosecutions, and it seems that the incidence of prosecution of this offence does not in any way match its intrinsic interest. Even allowing for the deficiencies of record survival, the 33 prosecutions and 1 execution for witchcraft experienced by Sussex in the period when the witchcraft laws operated do suggest that the 'European witch craze' has been exaggerated.[42]

Future research will doubtless reveal some variations in this broad pattern. Work already completed does, however, suggest that it holds good in at least two areas which might have been expected to be atypical. London, for example, might have been expected to show different patterns from those provided by the mainly rural areas detailed in Table 1. Studying London crime is complicated by the threefold administrative division of metropolitan crime between the courts of Westminster, the City of London, and Middlesex, while serious crime in Southwark, the large and criminous suburb south of the river, fell under the jurisdiction of the Surrey assizes. Nevertheless, some impression of metropolitan crime early in our period is provided by a sample of 7,736 persons known to have been indicted for felony in Middlesex between 1550 and 1625.[43] This sample does show some differences from those derived from rural areas: in particular, crimes against property were apparently even more dominant numerically, 92.5 per cent of all of those accused of capital felony being charged with property offences. Those accused of murder and manslaughter, the only other capital felonies indicted in anything like large numbers, amounted to only just over 4 per cent. Once more, however, the paucity of prosecutions for other forms of felony is striking. Against 7,158 persons accused of property offences might be set the 70 tried for sexual offences and the 21 accused of witchcraft. The situation in the capital in the early eighteenth century was apparently very similar. Property offences predominated, accounting for 98 per cent of the accused at some Middlesex sessions towards the end of our period.[44] By that point fraud cases were beginning to occur regularly, a sign perhaps that crime in the capital was keeping pace with the growing complexity of commerical life. For the most part, however, the offences tried in London were still essentially those which formed the staple of business in country assizes: larceny, burglary, housebreaking, pickpocketing, and highway robbery.

If London might have been expected to have experienced distinctive patterns of crime, so, for rather different reasons, might the border country in the north. Obviously, the Anglo-Scottish border presented unique problems of law and order down to 1603, and continued to do so for some time afterwards. The area awaits further research, although a thesis recently completed by Dr Catherine M. F. Ferguson indicates that the border's law-enforcement problems were neither as serious nor as distinctive as ballads and legends from the heroic days of cattle-raiding and clan mayhem might suggest. Or Ferguson's main concern was with the comparative study of the English and Scottish administrative systems, but she has compiled some useful figures on crime in the border counties, based on Northern circuit assize records for the late seventeenth century. These demonstrate a higher level of assault indictments than that current at equivalent courts further south, indicative perhaps of lingering border violence. Nevertheless, analysis of indictments for felony provides a pattern which conforms very closely to what we have described as the national one. In Northumberland between 1660 and 1692, there were 687 indictments at the assizes for theft, 73 for murder, 9 for rape, and 17 for witchcraft, figures which are not unlike those obtained from the assize records of the Home circuit for the same period. In Cumberland, over the same period, there were 419 thefts and 31 murders (a ratio of nearly 16 to 1, roughly that obtaining in urbanized Middlesex), 15 cases of witchcraft and 2 rapes. By the late seventeenth century, therefore, patterns of indicted crime on the borders were roughly similar to those obtaining in the south, while fragmentary evidence from the early seventeenth century suggests that this was not a new situation.[45]

The nature of serious crime during our period does, therefore, seem to fall into a national pattern. Fluctuations in the incidence of that crime are somewhat harder to trace. Certainly, the evidence of the Cheshire Crown Books does indicate a dramatic change over the period 1580–1709 in the crime tried in that county. Figure 1 demonstrates the nature of this change. Indictments for felony rose steadily between 1580 and 1629, reaching their peak in the 1620s. The 1630s witnessed a slight decline, while the disruption caused by the Civil Wars caused a massive drop in the 1640s. It is striking, however, that the resumption of administrative normality after 1650, or even after 1660, did not witness any increase in crime levels. These were static for the remainder of the seventeenth century, the slight rise in the 1690s being caused entirely by a short-lived burst of prosecutions of coining offences. Little information has so far been collected on long-term fluctuations of this type, and record survival dictates that the areas for which such information will be forthcoming are limited. It would seem, however, that Cheshire's experience was an unusually marked example of a national trend. On the Home circuit, perhaps the only part of England apart from Cheshire for which relevant figures can be reconstructed over the whole timespan, a fundamentally similar pattern seems to have obtained. Indictments rose steadily from the middle years of Elizabeth's reign to reach a peak in Essex in the late 1590s, in Hertfordshire in the 1620s. Thereafter they fell, with Essex, Surrey, and Sussex all experiencing lower levels of indicted felony in the late seventeenth and early eighteenth century than they had between 1580 and the 1620s.[46] Evidence from Devon suggests that the same trend was experienced in the south-west. Surviving gaol delivery rolls show that on average 250 cases were tried annually at the Devon

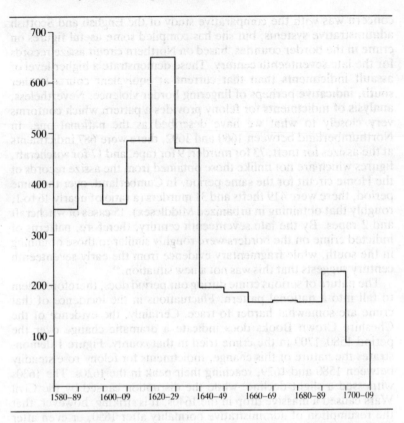

FIG. 1 Total indictments for felony, Court of Great Sessions, Palatinate of Chester, 1580–1709

Notes
1. Source for figures: P.R.O., CHES 21/1–5 (Court of Great Sessions, Palatinate of Chester, Crown Books).
2. Folios dealing with 1599 and 1600 are missing, so totals for 1590–1599 and 1600–1609 given in the figures are estimates extrapolated from the nine surviving years in each respective decade.

assizes between 1598 and 1640, while in the period 1700–09 this figure had fallen to approximately 38. London experienced much higher levels of indictment in the early eighteenth century than in the early seventeenth, but it seems that the levels of prosecution of serious crime in the remainder of the country fell drastically between the early seventeenth and the early eighteenth centuries.[47]

Perhaps the most surprising aspect of this trend was the fall in the level of indictment for property offences. Conventional wisdom on the history of crime has always assumed that property offences increased in number during the early modern period, keeping pace with that most familiar of phenomena, the rise of capitalism. The authors of a recent interpretative essay on crime and punishment between the medieval and the modern periods have restated the main elements of this process. As 'the increasing wealth of society during the later seventeenth and the eighteenth century' became more vulnerable, 'the commercial classes: merchants, shopkeepers and industrialists' formed a group 'which repeatedly called for more deterrents against crime'. The end product of all this was that 'theft steadily became by far the commonest crime before the courts – a situation significantly different from that of the preceding centuries'.[48] Thinking of this type was supported by some early work in the French provincial archives. A group of scholars claimed to have traced a distinctive transition in the early modern period, from a pattern dominated by crimes of violence in the sixteenth century to one dominated by property offences in the eighteenth. This model was based on a very small sample of cases, but it enjoyed considerable acceptance, not least because it fitted in with existing preconceptions about the supposed brutality of the later middle ages, and the supposed effects of the rise of capitalism upon patterns of crime.[49]

Unfortunately, evidence from English archives suggests that conventional wisdom on the development of crime patterns and notions of a *violence/vol* transition are sadly misconceived. Outside London, and perhaps a few other urban or industrial areas, crimes against property were indicted much less frequently in the early eighteenth century than in the Elizabethan and Jacobean periods. Figure 2, showing indictments for property offences in Cheshire between 1580 and 1709, demonstrates the premise for at least one English county. From 1590 to 1639 between 300 and 400 such offences were being indicted each decade at the Court of Great Sessions, a figure which rose to nearly 500 in the 1620s. By the first decade of the eighteenth century the number of indictments for crimes against property had dropped to about an eighth of that figure. In Essex, perhaps the only other county for which comparable information is at present available, much the same pattern seems to have obtained. The county experienced its highest levels of indicted property offences in the late 1590s, and thereafter, despite sharp increases in such offences in response to economic crisis in 1629–31, 1647–52, 1661 and the late 1690s, the secular trend was downwards. By the end of the first decade of the eighteenth century, the Essex assizes were also regularly trying a tenth of the property offences which would have come before that court in some of the bad years between 1597 and 1631.[50] Evidence for other counties is not yet forthcoming, but comparison of the figures given by Beattie for property offences in Surrey and Sussex between 1660 and 1750 with published calendars of assize records for the period 1559–1625 does not suggest a transition towards higher levels of property offence.[51]

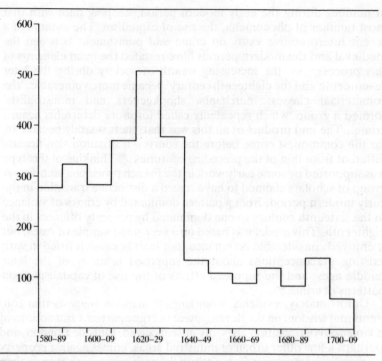

FIG. 2 Indictments for property offences, Court of Great Sessions, Palatinate of Chester, 1580–1709

Studying crimes of violence, especially homicide, gives the impression of a shift from a more to a less brutal society. Early attempts to examine changing levels of violence in England have claimed a progressive decrease in homicide between the middle ages and the mid twentieth century, and Beattie's work has certainly suggested that this trend can be traced for the years 1660–1800. Once more, Cheshire evidence can be adduced to illustrate the point for the earlier period. As Figure 3 shows, homicide was much more frequently indicted in the late sixteenth and early seventeenth centuries, although it is difficult to see why so many more cases should reach the court in the 1620s than in other decades. On balance, however, it would seem that there was a steady decline in the number of trials for homicide in our period. If the widely-held opinion that homicide trials bear a close relation to the number of violent deaths actually occurring is correct, this would suggest that some important changes took place in the social psychology of the English during our period.[52]

Study of homicide is, however, complicated by the emergence of infanticide as a new offence. Infanticide, or, more narrowly, the killing of new-born children by their mothers, was singled out for severe

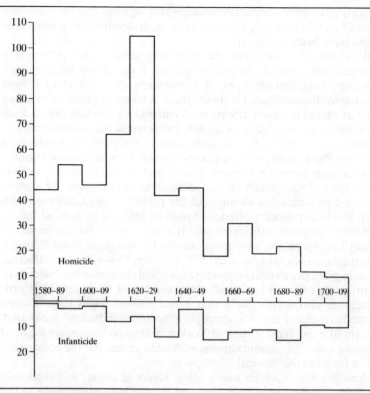

FIG. 3 Indictments and coroners' inquests for homicide and infanticide, Court of Great Sessions, Palatinate of Chester, 1580–1709

punishment by most European states in the sixteenth century, and in England a statute against the offence was passed in 1624. The objective of the English legislation was, to a large extent, the control of sexual morality as much as the defence of infant life. *Inter alia*, the 1624 statute made concealment of a stillbirth by an unmarried mother capital felony, obviously one aspect of wider attempts to control bastard-bearers. The 'infanticide wave', in England at least, may have resulted in more executions than the more familiar witch craze. The Cheshire records support this contention. The Crown Books show that 33 women were hanged for infanticides between 1580 and 1709, compared with 11 persons of both sexes for witchcraft. Cheshire also seems to have experienced a different pattern of prosecution for infanticide from that present in the south-east. There, it has been argued, more frequent prosecution of the offence preceded the Jacobean statute.[53] In Cheshire, this does not seem to have been the case, and infanticide was only indicted frequently after 1650. It is noteworthy, however, that by the late seventeenth century infanticide was being indicted roughly as often as simple homicide, which suggests that the transition away from violence may not have been as straightforward a process as might have been imagined.

It is possible, therefore, to trace long-term trends in property offences and homicide during our period. It should not be forgotten, however, that certain types of crime were also subject to violent short-term fluctuations. Of these, those relating to property offences have attracted the most attention. As might be expected, efforts have been made to relate crimes against property to economic variables, notably grain prices. It is an indication of the peculiar problems of studying the history of crime that even such a common sense connection as that between harvest failure and a rise in crimes against property has sometimes proved difficult to demonstrate. Nevertheless, it does seem that throughout the period we are concerned with here levels of property offences would be affected by harvest failure and other forms of economic crisis. It is also evident that the impact of a bad harvest might vary from county to county, or even between sub-regions within counties. As J. S. Cockburn has suggested, fluctuations in grain prices did not produce identical changes in the indictment of property offences in the adjacent counties of Essex and Hertfordshire.[54] It also seems likely that a bad harvest might have a more immediate effect on, for example, the proto-industrial areas of a county like the West Riding of Yorkshire than on the upland pastoral farming zone. Economic variables affected crime, but the connection was a far from mechanical or simplistic one.

Another factor which might affect levels of crime, and especially property offences, was war. Hay and Beattie have made much of the tendency for warfare in the eighteenth century to reduce crimes against property, principally because it removed from temptation those young males from the labouring poor who were most likely to become thieves.[55] Both their statistics and their marshalling of contemporary comment are convincing, not least when they show how demobilisation at the end of a conflict was accompanied both by a good deal of woeful prediction of social dislocation from contemporaries and by a rise in the crime rate. In early periods, the position is more obscure. It is noteworthy that what seem to have been the two most criminous decades in our period, the 1590s and the 1620s, were also periods of continual warfare. Certainly returning soldiers, as in the eighteenth century, created problems in Elizabethan and early Stuart England.[56] It is possible, however, that troops on the march to their embarkation ports also caused considerable trouble. The Essex lieutenancy letter book for the 1620s, for example, contains numerous complaints about the depredations of the soldiery and the need to combat stragglers and deserters: at one stage, indeed, armed watches were placed at all crossroads to supervise troop movements.[57] In the first half of our period, too, the outbreak of warfare normally entailed a stop in trade, with disastrous consequences for those areas with a large proto-industrial workforce dependent upon exports for their wages. Our delineation of a decline in crime would have brought little comfort to justices confronted by several thousand hungry and potentially riotous weavers.

As we have argued, measuring crime, although an essential and by no means pointless exercise, is fraught with difficulties. Superficially, measuring punishment should involve fewer problems. Given adequate documentation, there is no reason why the historian should not be able to reconstruct patterns of punishment. These, too, are of central importance: such questions as the total number and proportion of offenders undergoing different forms of punishment in different periods or in different areas are vital ones. In particular, given the nature of the law relating to felony in the period under consideration, fluctuations in capital punishment demand special attention. Most historians are familiar with the expansion in the number of capital felonies on the statute book after the Glorious Revolution, and it is tempting to assume that this legislative trend was paralleled by an increase in the number of persons hanged. Moreover, most of these new capital statutes concerned crimes against property and have, in fact, been interpreted as evidence of a hardening of attitudes as England became more commercialized and the rich became more hostile to the poor. This line of thinking, as we have seen, is contradicted by the decline in the level of indicted property offences: equally, evidence on changing patterns of execution for felony between the late sixteenth and the early eighteenth centuries seems to run against it.

Once more, we will take as our starting point the figures provided by the Chester Crown Books. Again, these provide a rough guide which must be checked against detailed work on the indictment files. Nevertheless, as figure 4 demonstrates, they do show a marked change in levels of execution between 1580 and 1709. Hangings were occurring at the rate of about 9 a year in the 1580s, increased in the difficult 1590s, then declined a little, only to increase to an annual average of nearly 17 in the 1620s, the decade which also experienced the highest levels of indicted crime. This level was more than halved in the 1630s, then the cessation of regular meetings of the courts in the war years produced a slump in executions. As with levels of recorded crime, however, levels of execution stayed very low and fairly stable in the second half of the seventeenth century. A hiatus in the records obscures the position in the early eighteenth, but a Crown Book recording business from the mid 1750s onwards demonstrates that low levels of indicted crime and of executions were still current at that point.[58] Evidence of long-term trends in hanging in Cheshire, therefore, suggests a dramatic break in the mid seventeenth century. A court which could execute 166 felons

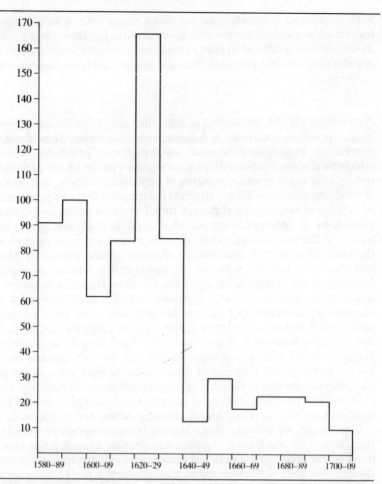

FIG. 4 Capital punishments inflicted for felony, Court of Great Sessions, Palatinate of Chester, 1580–1709.

in the 1620s and 10 in the first decade of the eighteenth century was obviously reflecting a fundamental transition.

Surviving records from other areas suggest that, as with patterns in indicted felony, Cheshire's experience was a very marked example of a national trend. In the south-east, we know that an average of 26 felons were executed each year by the Essex assizes between 1597 and 1603, a figure greater than the number executed on the whole of the Home circuit in an average year in the mid eighteenth century.[59] In Devon, surviving documentation allows us to estimate that approximately 250 felons were executed in the first decade of the seventeenth century, as opposed to 30 in the first decade of the eighteenth.[60] Even in London, with its massive and increasing population and its unique crime problem, the number of executions seems to have fallen over the same period. In 1887 a pioneer student of the Middlesex court records, using gaol delivery rolls from the middle years of James I's reign, postulated as a conservative estimate that nearly 150 felons were hanged annually in London in the Jacobean period. By the first half of the eighteenth century, the annual average of executions was a little over 20.[61] All surviving evidence suggests that levels of execution were much higher in the Elizabethan and Jacobean periods than they were in the first half of the eighteenth century.

Moreover, a lower percentage of those being tried for felony were being capitally convicted. In Elizabethan Essex, 26.4 per cent of the 2,432 felons whose fate is discussed by Professor Samaha were hanged. In Middlesex, 29 per cent of the 7,736 felons whose trial record survives between 1548 and 1625 were executed. In Cheshire, 22 per cent of those accused in the 1620s went to the gallows.[62] By the eighteenth century, the position had changed radically. To return to Cheshire, roughly 10 per cent of those tried for felony in the years 1700–09 were executed. In Devon, corresponding figures for the same period were 8 per cent. In London, over the years 1700–50, the proportion executed was around 10 per cent, while surviving evidence of the trial of 251 suspected felons in Norfolk and Suffolk between 1734–37 suggests that 12 per cent were executed.[63] It seems safe, therefore, to argue not only that the absolute totals of executions fell, but also that the proportion of those accused of felony who were eventually hanged had also dropped. To put it at its most basic level, a person accused of felony at the assizes in Elizabeth's reign stood a one in four chance of being executed: for his or her counterpart under Queen Anne, the chances were more like one in ten. This change, against the background of an increasingly severe legal code, is puzzling. It becomes less so when it is realized that, throughout our period, means were available by which persons accused of a capital offence might escape the noose. Analysis of any sample of assize court records illustrates the point: for example's sake, let us turn to a consideration of the disposition of cases tried in Norfolk and Suffolk in the years 1743–47. These provide a small but fairly typical sample of 251 accused, whose fate is set out in Table 2.

The first noteworthy feature of Table 2 is the relatively high proportion of the accused who were acquitted, just over 37 per cent. This seems to have been a fairly normal percentage of acquittals for the late seventeenth and early eighteenth centuries: at the Devon assizes, 1700–09, for example, acquittals ran at 45 per cent, while for Chester in the same decade the figure was over 30 per cent.[64] Even in earlier periods, in some areas at least, the acquittal rate was comparable. Although in Elizabethan Essex it only ran at 27.7 per cent, over 43 per cent of felons tried at the Devon assizes between 1598 and 1639 were

TABLE 2   Verdicts in felony cases, Norfolk and Suffolk assizes, 1734–37

	Hanged	Transported	Branded	Whipped	Remanded/Respited	Acquitted	Ignoramus	Other	Total
Homicide	3	—	2	—	—	16	1	—	22
Infanticide	—	—	—	—	—	3	—	—	3
Larceny	9	28	4	17	19	57	—	1	135
Robbery	—	—	—	2	—	—	—	—	2
Highway robbery	—	3	—	—	—	5	1	1	10
Housebreaking									
Burglary	16	17	—	1	11	12	2	—	59
Rape	—	—	—	—	—	1	—	—	1
Bigamy	—	—	1	—	—	—	—	1	2
Coining	—	—	—	—	—	—	—	1	1
Arson	—	—	—	—	1	2	1	—	4
Other	—	8	—	—	—	3	1	—	12
Total	31	53	7	18	38	94	8	3	251
%	12	21	3	7	15	37	3	1	—

Source: PRO, ASSI 33/1. Percentages are given to nearest whole number.

either acquitted or discharged.[65] This acquittal rate, far higher than that current in modern England, was probably the outcome of less efficient mechanisms for filtering out at an early stage cases that were unlikely to stand up in court. Conversely, it is interesting, given our earlier arguments about general unwillingness to take a case to court except as a last resort, that so many accusations should prove unsuccessful. The courts, it would seem, were favouring the accused on many occasions.

Fifty-three of our sample of East Anglian felons, or 21 per cent of the total, were transported to the American colonies. Transportation, the eighteenth-century equivalent of the medieval punishment of banishment, was obviously regarded as a handy means by which convicted felons who were thought to be not wicked enough to hang might be safely removed from the realm.[66] It was, in essence, one of a number of experiments tried by various European regimes which were coming to think that an automatic sentence of death was not invariably the appropriate way of dealing with all offenders: in France, for example, sentencing convicted criminals to serve in the royal galleys had much the same purpose as did transportation in England.[67] Sending convicts to the colonies was an idea which was tried well before the

Civil Wars, but it was not until the late seventeenth century that the practice became really common. After that date, the end of every assize saw another group of convicted felons contemplating a new life in the Americas.

Transportation had replaced claiming benefit of clergy and being branded as the means by which the serious offender might escape hanging. Benefit of clergy owed its origins to the conflicts between church and state of the high middle ages. One outcome of these conflicts was that clerics had the right to be tried for certain types of felony in the ecclesiastical, rather than the royal, courts. Proof of clerical status came to rest in the ability to read, a test which advancing lay literacy rendered increasingly meaningless. The situation was formalized in the reign of Henry VII, when it was declared by statute that those convicted of felony, notably theft and manslaughter, might escape hanging on a first conviction if they could read.[68] Recidivism was discouraged by branding a felon in the palm of his left hand, a supposedly indelible record of a previous conviction. Certain offences, notably murder with malice aforethought and rape, never lay within the scope of clergy, while later legislation rendered a number of crimes, among them burglary, sodomy, bestiality, witchcraft, and horse-theft, non-clergyable. Nevertheless, this loophole saved many felons from the gallows. Less than 3 per cent of the East Anglian sample – Table 2 were punished in this way but, as we have argued, at this late date clemency was being provided by ships to the colonies rather than antique legal anomalies: at earlier points in the period under discussion, a large proportion of those convicted for lesser felonies, theft and manslaughter, were saved by claiming their book and being branded as a clerk: perhaps 26 per cent of those accused at the Devon assizes in the first decade of the eighteenth century; just under 26 per cent of those accused in Elizabethan Essex; and nearly 20 per cent of those tried for felony in Middlesex between 1600 and 1625.[69] Benefit of clergy, therefore, provided the means by which many convicted felons escaped death: moreover, unless we are to revise most of our ideas on popular literacy in early modern England, it is obvious that the reading test was not being applied with any great rigour. Benefit of clergy was a nonsense, a proposition best supported by legislation of 1623 which extended the right to claim clergy to women in an age when the ordination of women as priests would have been unthinkable[70]: yet it was a nonsense which operated overwhelmingly to the benefit of the accused.

Another anomaly which might be manipulated to the advantage of the man or woman on trial was the traditional distinction between petty and grand larceny. Theft of goods worth more than a shilling constituted grand larceny, and might be punished by death: theft of goods worth less than that amount was petty larceny, most often punished by whipping. By the sixteenth century, inflation had removed such sense as there had ever been in such a division, and judges, jurors, and prosecutors alike seem to have been happy to have permitted the less dangerous thief to escape by altering the value of goods as given on the indictment, or by finding him or her guilty only to the value of a few pence. The majority of the seventeen thieves who were whipped for their offence in the East Anglian sample (Table 2) were originally charged with grand larceny. That a person originally charged with burglary was also whipped focuses attention on another way in which the courts were willing to bend the law to the accused's advantage: many accusations of burglary, felony without benefit of clergy, were adjusted to simple charges of grand (or even petty) larceny. This adjustment allowed many of those accused of burglary to escape the consequences of their actions.

Another escape route lay through the use of remands or pardons. Traditionally, as the preachers of assize sermons never tired of pointing out, mercy was an intrinsic part of justice, while the monarch's right to pardon was as glorious and necessary a power as his right to punish. By the mid eighteenth century this right was evidently being exercised to the full, with 15 per cent of those tried at the Norfolk and Suffolk assizes being pardoned, remanded or respited, most of them after sentence. It seems likely that a number of them were transported, although many must have gone scot free. Pardon might also be contingent upon other circumstances: pregnant women were reprieved on the grounds that an innocent embryo should not pay the penalty for its mother's transgressions; in theory, they were to be hanged after the birth of the child, although it seems likely that most women who escaped hanging through 'benefit of the womb' were later fully pardoned. Other suspects, either before or after trial, might be pardoned on condition that they entered military or naval service. Isolated examples exist from the Elizabethan and Jacobean periods: one man, for instance, was pardoned in Cheshire in 1620 on condition that he went to serve the protestant cause in Bohemia. It was, however, Marlborough's Wars which really encouraged the practice: quarter sessions records abound with references to the military, while the Devon assizes of 1704 released three men from the county workhouse 'on Condicon they goe Souldiers'.[71] Pardon might even be gained for less agreeable state service than enlistment in the army. At York, and possibly other assize towns, it was apparently customary in the mid seventeenth century to reprieve a convicted felon on condition that he acted as hangman.[72]

There were, then, a whole battery of alternatives to capital punishment in regular use during this period, and they combined to ensure that by 1750, the terminal date of our study, only about 10 per cent of those accused of felony at a normal assize would be executed. Circumstantial evidence from the mid eighteenth century, ably deployed by Professors Hay and Beattie, has afforded us some insights into the ways in which clemency might be sought and granted. Convicted felons would regularly engage the local gentry or other persons of authority to speak on their behalf, and attest to their previous good character or to the circumstances of their family background. Evidence from earlier periods is difficult to come by, although it is clear that something like the eighteenth-century situation portrayed by Hay obtained as far back as the fifteenth century.[73] Persons of influence were evidently willing to intercede on behalf of convicted felons, while judges were evidently willing to recommend pardon on the strength of such interventions: the formalized nature which the process might assume can be grasped from an example occurring at the Old Bailey in 1723, when the judge promptly recommended pardon when the prisoner at the bar announced that he had thirty or forty persons willing to speak on his behalf.[74] That clemency was so often extended, however, should not be allowed to obscure a concomitant question: what was so peculiar about those persons who *were* executed?

Absence of detailed depositions from most assize circuits makes it difficult to answer this question, although the immediate response must be that, by the eighteenth century at least, those who were hanged were either exceptionally unlucky or were felt to be exceptionally wicked. One obvious category of likely candidates for the gallows were those who could find no local notable to intercede for them. This was regarded by contemporary opinion as evidence of an extremely marginal, and hence suspicious, status, and eighteenth-century accounts of trials show how the inability to find anyone to speak on their behalf was a frequent preliminary to felons finding themselves on the gallows. In other cases, the court records do permit intelligent conjecture about the background to the decision to hang the accused: a person accused of an unusually heinous crime, or a multiple offender, was often felt to be especially deserving of death. Many of those hanged might have committed crimes for which legal escape routes were especially circumscribed: by the eighteenth century, for example, most of those hanged for theft had stolen horses, and horse-theft was felony without benefit of clergy; while a disproportionate number of those condemned for murder had killed by stabbing, an offence which had been made non-clergyable by a statute of 1604.[75] Behind all of this discussion of what might be termed, however anachronistically, sentencing policy, there lies one major theme: the flexibility of the criminal law, and the selectivity with which its ultimate sanction, death, was inflicted. Throughout the period, the criminal law was harsh, and becoming harsher: likewise, throughout the period its full harshness was being applied increasingly sparingly.

So far, the implications of this selectivity have only been discussed with reference to the fairly static situation in existence at the very end of the period covered by this book. The analysis which, in particular, Douglas Hay makes of this flexibility and selectivity, and the emphasis which he places upon the role of mercy in maintaining the credibility of the rule of law, are stimulating and, ultimately, persuasive.[76] Unfortunately, the analysis has a somewhat timeless quality: as figures for both prosecution of felony and capital punishment suggest, the criminal law in the period with which Hay concerns himself was not under any great pressure. In small counties, the assize judges might have to deal with only low levels of trial for felony by the mid eighteenth century. Even in Cheshire, not a small county by any standards, the Court of Great Sessions at its meeting of August 1760 found itself confronted by exactly one suspected felon, a man who was accused, and subsequently acquitted, of highway robbery.[77] The judges and clerical staff of that same court in the 1620s, when over 650 accusations of felony were tried and 166 felons sent to the gallows, would have found this situation incomprehensible, as would (for example) those responsible for running the Essex winter assize of 1598, when nearly 200 persons were accused of felony.[78] Fluctuations in capital punishment reinforce the conclusions that might be drawn from the study of fluctuations in recorded serious crime: that England experienced a growing crime problem from the early years of Elizabeth onwards; that this problem reached crisis proportions in many areas at some point between the late 1590s and 1630; and that the problem seemed to burn itself out in the mid seventeenth century, with levels of both indicted crime and capital punishment remaining stable and, by comparison with the previous half century, low, after that date. Study of levels of execution, like the study of prosecution of felony, refutes any simplistic model of the history of crime in England: ultimately, as we shall argue in a later chapter, it also refutes any simplistic model of the development of English society.

As the prefatory comments at the beginning of this chapter made clear, it is possible for one historian to regard crime as an 'eminently countable phenomenon' and for another to maintain that criminal statistics are of practically no value to those wishing to understand crime and criminals in the past. In the opinion of the present writer, it would not be unduly equivocal to suggest that the true merits of quantification lie somewhere between these two extreme positions. It must be reiterated that the would-be quantifier of court archives must beware of a number of pitfalls: there are the problems of attempting to wrest some impressions of fluctuations in recorded crime from imperfect series of documents; the problem of understanding the totality of 'criminal' prosecutions coming through a network of courts with overlapping jurisdictions; and, above all, the constant problem of the 'dark figure'. Awareness of these and a number of lesser problems urges caution upon the historian of crime, and emphasizes the dangers of naive quantification. Conversely, reconstructing patterns of prosecuted crime and punishment is a very useful exercise, provided that the limitations of that exercise are recognized. It is essential to gain a clear impression of the business of the courts. Analysis of the crime being handled over a limited period by a court or network of courts is the only way that an idea of patterns of prosecuted crime can be obtained. Comparison of such analyses from different areas and different periods allows the formulation of hypotheses about changes over time or varying types of crime in various economic contexts. The evidence from court archives can also be set against other forms of evidence: literary sources, for example, or the opinions of contemporaries. Crime may not be an eminently countable phenomenon: nevertheless, the reconstruction of patterns of recorded or prosecuted crime is an essential exercise.

Above all, we would emphasize again the importance of the patterns of indicted felony and capital punishment which we have delineated in this chapter. These contradict many of the expectations and much of the conventional wisdom about how long-term trends in such matters might have gone. Their significance is further reinforced because a wide range of geographical evidence suggests that here we are looking at a genuinely national trend. The massive decline in levels of indicted felony, whether attributable to a decline in crime actually committed, or to a decline in willingness to prosecute, is suggestive of some basic shifts in the nature of English society: it would be hard to deny, on either of these readings of the evidence, that England was a far more stable country in the early eighteenth century than it was in the late sixteenth. Trends in capital punishment support this view. It seems that over the whole of England, even in London, the absolute numbers of persons hanged declined between about 1600 and 1750, while the proportion of those accused of felony actually executed also fell appreciably. Fluctuations in petty crime tried at inferior jurisdictions are more complex, maybe too complex to permit the delineation of marked trends. Nevertheless, the pattern of long-term fluctuations in prosecutions for felony and in capital sentences does seem proven. The impression of crime in the past which the study of statistics provides might well be, to quote J. S. Cockburn, 'unclear and incomplete'[79]: it would seem, however, that there is enough clarity and completeness to permit us to claim that there were some fundamental changes in the prosecution and punishment of serious crime between 1550 and 1750.

Counting offences can also be justified on the grounds that it permits crime and punishment to be set against other more or less quantifiable phenomena. Thus even the most arid of English criminal documents, the indictment, can be put to good use, not least in permitting a discussion of crime in the past which rises above the merely anecdotal. Other sources might be better for providing the texture of crime and law enforcement in the past. Quantification of indictments, however much interpretations of the results of that quantification might vary, provides a context. Counting offences may be only the first step towards understanding crime in a given society, but it is an essential one. Nevertheless, as some of the earlier comments in this chapter have suggested, behind any formal prosecution there might lie a whole history of social processes, of interactions between the accuser and the accused. This conclusion suggests that the historian of crime might profit from examining a focal point far removed from the majestic and dignified assize court: the local community within which the victim and offender made their first contact, and from which the accusation which led to court proceedings originated.

Chapter 4

CONTROLLING THE PARISH

As we have seen in the previous chapter, quantitative study of court records, although an essential and in many respects intriguing exercise, provides an imperfect impression of the nature of crime in the past. We have also seen that this imperfection is especially marked in those studies which have concentrated on a statistical analysis of assize and quarter session indictments. It has, moreover, been argued that the major problem in attempting to develop criminal statistics for the period with which we are dealing is that the decision to prosecute was usually the outcome of an initiative made by an individual rather than a 'police' agency. Behind every indictment, presentment, and binding-over there lay an individual set of circumstances; to understand crime in early modern England, therefore, it is necessary to grasp something of the interpersonal relationships that preceded formal court action. Trying to do so inevitably leads us to an examination of the social milieu in which the victim and offender lived. Ultimately, we must endeavour to understand what was happening in the villages and small towns in which 90 per cent of the Englishmen and women of this period lived, and to try to connect the issues of crime and control with some of these wider problems of social history.

Generalizing about the nature of life in these villages and country towns is fraught with difficulties. Broadly speaking, it is possible to discern two main sets of problems. Firstly, there is the stumbling block of local and regional variations, and other variables more directly related to the study of crime: whether there was an active resident justice in the parish in question, whether there was a puritan clergyman, and so on. The second difficulty is that not much is really known about more than a handful of villages. Local, even parish, history is a long-established and respectable strand of historical scholarship: a number of historians, notably W. G. Hoskins,[1] have some years since demonstrated how the study of just one village can throw light on national developments. More recent work has, however, suggested that it is possible to understand the functioning of society in the past much more fully through the medium of village studies based upon an exhaustive use of archive materials. As the work of Alan Macfarlane and his research team has shown, given fairly lavish resources of time, money, and manpower, such studies will unlock tremendous potentialities for gaining a much deeper understanding of many aspects of our ancestors' lives.[2]

So far, intensive research on villages in the past has been limited to a few examples; given the complexity of the materials involved and the bulk of archive material which must be sifted in the course of such studies, it is doubtful if many more will be investigated. Such work as has been carried out has already confirmed earlier suspicions among historians that much of our received wisdom about the nature of life in the past is in urgent need of revision. In particular, the idea that our ancestors in the 'traditional' world lived in stable 'communities' has been questioned. Research on pre-industrial villages has revealed a massive turnover in population within relatively short timespans, and it is now evident that from the fifteenth century at the latest English rural society was marked by a very great degree of geographical mobility. Certainly, by 1550, many village communities in England were probably no more stable than the urban areas studied by modern sociologists. Such a conclusion must impose severe modifications upon our use of the term 'community': Macfarlane, indeed, begins his book on the methodology of reconstructing historical communities with a section devoted to exploding 'the myth of the community'.[3] Another student of village history, Keith Wrightson, has tried to deal with the problem by suggesting that there were three communities in the village: that of the established landholding families, the richer farmers; that of the servants in husbandry, about a tenth of the population, who would only be resident in any one township for a year; and that of the most transient element, the mobile poor, rootless and on the margins of society.[4] Even if we do not accept the specific reservations which these two writers have raised about using the term, it is clear that the social historian must be far more rigorous in his use of the word 'community'.

For our immediate purposes, the greatest difficulty lies in the gradual increase in social stratification which was such a feature of life in the English countryside in our period. By the late eighteenth century, English rural society was split into the tripartite division of landless labourer, wealthy tenant farmer, and *rentier* landlord. It was this distinctive hierarchy which was held by contemporaries to make English agriculture especially efficient, and which marked off the countryside of England from that of other nations, notably France. The origins of this social structure lay in the distant past, and were allegedly already discernible in the fourteenth century.[5] It seems incontrovertible, however, that it had developed most rapidly in the two centuries before 1750. Between the mid sixteenth and the mid seventeenth centuries a doubling of the population placed immense strains on English agriculture, the outcome of which, over much of lowland England at least, was the creation of a stratum of successful capitalist farmers and the emergence of a vast body of poverty-stricken labourers. In the following century, the slackening of population increase confirmed the outcome of these changes, so that by the mid eighteenth century village society was divided between the two groups to which we have alluded: a small body of relatively prosperous craftsmen, artisans, and capitalist farmers, and a much larger body of 'the poor'. This development did not, of course, come to maturity simultaneously in all areas: in Terling, in Essex, it was evident by 1600; in Myddle, Shropshire, it did not fully emerge until the 1720s.[6] But, broadly speaking, it seems that most of rural England in the years with which we are concerned witnessed an increased economic differentiation among its inhabitants.

This economic stratification was accompanied by a growing divergence between the *mores* and mentalities of the richer and poorer villagers. The late medieval peasantry, it has been argued, shared a common culture despite a degree of social stratification:[7] there existed within the village a 'moral community' which encompassed both the successful upper peasant and the near-landless labourer. From about 1550, long-term social, economic, and religious developments altered this. By the early seventeenth century, the yeomanry and other members of the rural 'middling sort' could be distinguished from the poor of the parish not only by their wealth, but also by differences in education, housing, clothing, stability of family life, and, perhaps most importantly, religious belief. In many parishes, especially those with a godly and active minister, attitudes towards sinfulness and disorder, increasingly identified with the poor, would be affected by puritan notions of what constituted acceptable conduct. By the late seventeenth century, therefore, many parishes were divided not only by differences in the wealth of their inhabitants, but also by differences in social and cultural values. This situation was by no means entirely novel: it was, however, increasingly marked. One outcome of the complex of demographic, economic, social, and cultural changes was that the village notables – the equivalents of the upper peasants in the fifteenth century and the wealthy tenant farmers of the late eighteenth – lost their sense of solidarity with their poorer neighbours; instead, their values and attitudes became much more closely identified with those of the gentry and, ultimately, of the nation's rulers.[8]

The gradual increase in social stratification and the steady divergence of the cultural values of the rich and the poor assume considerable importance when we turn to examine the problems of law enforcement during this period. Despite the attention given by historians to the justices of the peace, and the praise generally lavished upon the incumbents of that office, most of the daily round of county administration and law enforcement was carried out by inferior officers within the parish. The suppression of disorder and crime in this period was not merely the business of the justices: it also involved these parish officers, as well as those serving on assize, quarter sessions, coroner's or leet juries. Work on village records has suggested that these men were drawn overwhelmingly from the more prosperous layers of village society, from those better-off villagers who, we have argued, were increasingly identifying with the 'respectable' values of the state and godliness against the 'rough' values of the labouring poor. Early work by Hoskins suggested that it was the richer villagers who held office in Wigston Magna, Leicestershire, while detailed research on the Essex villages of Burnham-on-Crouch, Kelvedon, and Terling has demonstrated the same pattern. Work in progress by Joan R. Kent, based on a wide geographical sample, suggests that these isolated studies do, in fact, reflect a more general pattern. Parish officers were usually large or middling farmers, shopkeepers, or more substantial artisans.[9]

These men were responsible for the enforcement of the law at its most local level, and it is hardly surprising that they did not meet this responsibility as effectively as do the best modern police forces. Evidence can be found of parish officers who were partial, corrupt, inefficient, venal, and open to intimidation. The sessions order book for Warwickshire in the 1680s, for example, provides numerous examples of difficulties with local officers. We find constables bound over for allowing an escape; indicted for lodging vagrants and wandering persons; reprimanded for failing to execute warrants; and (a nice example of the problems involved in enforcing unpopular legislation) reported for failing or refusing to report religious conventicles.[10] There is also little doubt that parish officers might fail to report offenders through fear of retaliation. The incumbent of Beeford, Yorkshire, reported in 1743 that the parish's churchwardens had failed to present delinquents 'rather from fear than any other principle'. He added that 'the last that was presented immediately sought an opportunity of revenge upon the churchwarden', and concluded plaintively that 'was I to do it myself nothing would be safe about me'. More insidious constraints upon the efficiency of the churchwardens was reported from Sydenham in Oxfordshire in 1610. There the vicar ended a list of complaints against the disorderly Robert Sule by reporting that the churchwarden refused to co-operate in presenting him because he was the town miller and they were 'lothe to offend' such a man.[11]

Such examples, which could be multiplied to the point of tedium, have provided ammunition for those seeking to portray the inferior officers of law enforcement as typically inefficient, illiterate, and stupid. Many of the inferior officers' problems, however, arose from their ambiguous position in relation to both the machinery of law enforcement and their neighbours. As Keith Wrightson and Joan R.

Kent have argued, the parish officers were forced to mediate between two concepts of order; that of the state law, and that of the village, where 'order' often meant 'little more than a conformity to a fairly malleable local custom which was considerably more flexible than statute law'.[12] As we have pointed out, the 'stacks of statutes' which meant that the JP had his workload increased also implied an increase in the duties of the constable. Central government control over the localities was ultimately dependent upon the parish constable, who would often find the laws he was expected to enforce and the administrative instruction he had received from quarter sessions at odds with local ideas and the best interests of his fellow villagers. His difficulties would be aggravated by his more traditional role, as an officer with responsibilities to his parish as well as to the monarch. As Kent has recently suggested, 'like the village headman in other parts of Europe, or in nonwestern societies, he was the chief officer and representative of a local self-governing body . . . he not only enjoyed various responsibilities within its bounds, but he also acted as the village's executive agent in its dealings with outsiders'.[13] Chosen by the court leet, his responsibilities were still essentially local: constables often organized village festivities and rituals, and on at least one occasion, in a nice illustration of the connection between local custom and state morality, a parish constable can be found leading a *charivari* against a couple living together out of wedlock.[14]

Such considerations suggest that the usual image of the Tudor and Stuart constable is in need of reinterpretation. As I have suggested elsewhere,[15] much of the criticism that has been made of the constable and other parish officers has arisen from a failure to appreciate that contemporary assumptions about the role of such officers were very different from modern ideas on 'police'. Legislation and the instructions that came down via the hundred constable from quarter sessions might have been nudging the parish officer towards something like a police role, but much of his work still fell within the traditional area of keeping the king's peace. This consisted, to a large extent, of the essentially negative process of defusing problems before they got out of hand: nobody was going to promote a parish constable for the number of arrests he made and, in one sense, a lack of reports of indictable behaviour within his village could be interpreted as a sign of efficiency. Dependence on unpaid amateur officers had its drawbacks, but, given contemporary realities, we must agree with Kent's conclusion that 'it seems unlikely that other men would have achieved any greater success in linking the village and the state than did the relatively substantial villagers who usually filled the constableship'.[16]

Further peculiarities were inherent in the dependence upon individuals within the parish to act as prosecutors. Before formal prosecution, attempts might be made to get offenders to amend their ways through persuasion, warnings, or informal sanctions. The local petty offender might be allowed considerable latitude before being taken to court, and indictment at the assizes or quarter sessions must have seemed a very remote threat to such a delinquent. In most cases, prosecuting the local malefactor at these more powerful courts must have been regarded very much as a last resort, a consideration which lends yet more weight to our conviction that studying crime in our period takes us far beyond the records of the assizes and quarter sessions. It is, however, rather difficult to construct any very detailed picture of what might happen before a community, or individuals within a community, became sufficiently irritated with a delinquent's activities to consider indicting him. Nevertheless, it is possible to find clues in a number of more or less isolated cases.

Perhaps the most striking evidence comes from details of the background to witchcraft prosecutions. Depositions and pamphlet literature both show how an accusation of witchcraft was sometimes brought after many years of growing suspicions engendered by incidents which did not immediately provoke prosecution, but were recalled at a later date when another event led to indictment. In 1645, for example, witnesses in a mass persecution of witches in Suffolk were able to bring to mind suspicions of witchcraft that had been aroused seven years previously. In the following year, a witness giving evidence about an Essex witch described how she had hastened two men's deaths two or three years previously. When Elizabeth Crosley, a Yorkshire witch, was accused of bewitching Henry Cockcrofte's child, it was reported that she had inflicted similar harm on a child two years before. Pamphlets provide yet more detailed descriptions of how the witchcraft that led to indictment might be just the culminating incident in a long series of similar episodes. In 1578 Margery Stanton, another Essex witch, was indicted for bewitching a gelding. A pamphlet describing the trial gave an account of the harm she was thought to have done before this incident. She was supposed, through witchcraft, to have tormented a man, killed chickens, caused a woman to swell so that she looked pregnant and came near to bursting, made a cow give blood rather than milk, made a child ill, and tormented another. This example is by no means unusual.[17]

It therefore seems probable that an indictment for witchcraft was usually the outcome of a web of suspicion which was woven over a lengthy period of time, and which was based on a number of incidents which had not led to prosecution. Persons might be indicted for a specific act of *maleficium*, but they had usually been held to have been witches for some time. Hence Elizabeth Crosley, to whose case we have already alluded, was known by her alleged victim to have been in 'an evil report for witchinge'. Yet more conclusive were the opinions held about Ellen Smith, one of the Suffolk witches of 1645; it was deposed that 'the parents of this woman and this woman have been formerly counted and commonly reputed for a witch'.[18] Suspicions of witchcraft, therefore, were much more numerous than the total of indictments would suggest; indeed, one student of witchcraft in England has postulated that only one in three of those persons who thought themselves to have been bewitched actually initiated an indictment.[19] Thus a witchcraft prosecution was not the outcome of a single incident, but rather of a whole history of growing tensions in which a number of villagers might formulate suspicions against one of their number, normally a woman. This individual would acquire the 'fame' of being a witch, and eventually an indictment would be brought against her. Usually this would only happen after the woman had been defined as a witch, and frequently only after informal counteraction had been tried. This was often seen as a more useful initial line of defence than court action.[20]

There are obvious problems in treating witchcraft as a 'normal' crime, and it might be objected that this type of background is unique to it. There is, however, considerable evidence that a similar series of events might precede the indictment of other forms of offender. Something very like it seems frequently to have been operating in cases of theft, the felony most frequently tried at the assizes and quarter sessions throughout the period with which we are concerned here. Many of those indicted for stealing had a whole career of petty larceny and a growing reputation for thieving behind them; finally, their delinquencies grew so persistent that the parish became tired of them, or they irritated an individual into prosecution by stealing something of unusual value. One such was John Aston, a labourer living at Myddle in Shropshire in the second half of the seventeenth century. He was described as 'a sort of silly fellow, very idle and much given to stealing of poultry and small things', whose petty larcenies were tolerated for some time. Finally, however, he was tried at Shrewsbury assizes, where he was whipped after the trial jury saved him from a more serious fate by undervaluing at 11d. the poultry he had stolen. This experience apparently left him somewhat chastened, but we are informed by a contemporary that 'hee left not his old trade whoally'.[21]

Aston's story is an instructive one. It indicates that a parish might show considerable lenience towards the minor offender, especially if there were felt to be extenuating circumstances: if, for example (like Aston), the malefactor was thought of as a 'sort of silly fellow'. It is also noteworthy that his offence was reduced by the assize jury to petty larceny: one wonders if this was due to the initiative of the jurors, or to some intercession on his behalf from the parish. His return to Myddle after the trial, and his refusal to totally abandon his old ways, re-emphasizes the apparent ability of villages to tolerate a level of delinquency among their members. The presence of the persistent offender must have created considerable problems for the community, but in many cases his presence seems to have been accepted as part of the natural order of things.

The exact dimensions of this problem will not be fully apparent until more work has been done on village communities in this period. Such research as has been carried out has nevertheless shown that it is possible to construct criminal biographies of individuals who inhabited a parish for a lengthy period, and who were very persistent offenders. Investigation of crime in Kelvedon in Essex in the years 1600–40 has produced details of a number of such biographies. John Ayly, for example, keeper of the Unicorn inn, was guilty of most of the lesser forms of misbehaviour. Between 1613 and his death in 1636 he was in trouble for not coming to church; keeping disorder and selling drink on the sabbath; being drunk in sermon time; being a common swearer; living immorally with his maidservant; and committing adultery with a married woman. Another persistent offender from the same parish was Osias Johnson, whose activities were constantly reported to the courts between 1609 and 1621. His offences included assaulting the constables; fighting and quarrelling with one of his neighbours; fornication; refusing to pay church rates; remaining excommunicate; and obstructing the highway with a dunghill. Work on the parish of Earls Colne will probably bring similar case histories to light. An early survey of research in progress on its records has already provided details of the delinquencies of Henry Abbott, another habitual offender. In the late sixteenth and early seventeenth centuries Abbott was constantly presented before the local leet for a wide variety of misdemeanours, including bloodshed; refusing to watch and ward; using scandalous words against his neighbours; playing cards, dice, tables and other unlawful games; stirring up strife among his neighbours; cutting trees without permission; taking inmates; leaving ditches in disrepair; and contempt of court. To these offences before the leet were added frequent presentments before the archdeacon's court, for drunkenness, refusing to pay church rates, habitually failing to attend church, and leaving early when he did come.[22] As these case histories demonstrate, the local community had little success in curbing the determined local offender if he was sufficiently above the poverty line; Ayly was an innkeeper, and both Johnson and Abbott were fairly substantial men. They also show how much more will be learnt about delinquency in the past once detailed parish studies based on record linkage have been completed.

The ability of such offenders to continue their disruptive activities in the face of pressure from the parish should not obscure the importance of local opinion in bringing offenders to the notice of the authorities, and in influencing the nature of the treatment they received. Once again, we must remind ourselves that enforcing the law against the malefactor in this period was an essentially personal process, and that it seems to have been generally accepted that the severity of the law should be adjusted to meet peculiar circumstances. Detailed work on Essex and Sussex archives have demonstrated this point,[23] while scattered evidence from other areas demonstrates that it was perfectly usual for the presentment of offenders, or letters and petitions referring to them, to be accompanied by details of local opinion on the offenders or their misdeeds. Often, naturally enough, these opinions were very hostile: there was little point in sending a complaint to the clerk of the peace, for example, unless it were accompanied by some expression of disquiet at the conduct described. In 1635 John Musson of Rugby, for example, was imprisoned in Warwick County gaol for 'divers foul misdemeanours by him committed'. These were described at length in 'a certificate and petition under the hands of the best of the inhabitants of the said town testifying his lewd life and behaviour'.[24] Such petitions, normally urging speedy and severe action on the part of the authorities, were fairly common, and provide an important source for understanding the local offender in our period.

There were, however, a number of occasions on which the representatives of community opinion felt moved to write urging lenient treatment of offenders, or informing the court of extenuating circumstances. A man reported for fornication during the Archbishop of York's visitation in 1743 was dismissed 'on a certificate from the Churchwardens of his good life and conversation'. William Plombes of Great Lawton, Lancashire, presented for standing in the churchyard talking during service time, was dismissed after his vicar wrote a character reference on his behalf, attesting to his general good behaviour and regular church attendance. The presentment of Thomas West, of Thame in Oxfordshire, for fathering a bastard in 1718, provoked an imposing display of solidarity on his behalf from the respectable elements in the parish. The vicar, churchwardens, overseers of the poor and twenty-five other inhabitants signed a petition declaring that West was 'a very honest person & never suspected for an unchastity or Dishonesty', and that his accuser was a loose and dishonest girl who had become pregnant and who had accused West, a single man, in the hope that he would be forced to marry her. Similarly strong support came when an inn-keeper had his house suppressed by the Warwickshire quarter sessions in 1643. In this case a certificate was sent to the next sessions from the constables, churchwardens, and 'divers others of the better sort of the inhabitants' of his parish, testifying that he was a man of good behaviour and that his house was a fit place for victualling and selling alcohol. Even if an offence had definitely been committed, local opinion might be mobilized to help lessen the impact of punishment. In 1608 a bachelor, William Heifeelde, and a widow, Ellin Higges, of Sydenham in Oxfordshire, were presented before the church courts for fornication. The churchwardens and sidesmen of the parish wrote to the courts, asking the officials to show the couple 'what favoure possibly you maye', as they had since married, and were 'ij poore folkes, livinge ever since the former acte, honestly and orderly together'.[25]

Those in control of the parish might, therefore, allow considerable latitude to the known local offender, and might try to intercede on behalf of co-parishioners in trouble with the courts. Conversely, it seems probable that outsiders committing offences would be more liable to prosecution, and more likely to undergo stringent punishment if convicted. Certainly depositions relating to vagrant crimes gives the impression that the reaction against the itinerant thief would be swift, in contrast with the period of leniency which, we have suggested, might be allowed to the known resident pilferer. When, in 1596, a Kentish labourer found that his house had been burgled, he at once made a hue and cry which eventually caught up with the guilty parties, a returned soldier and two harvest workers. In 1600 Clement Crowhurst, a Gravesend mercer, was so incensed by a woman who had stolen some cloth from his shop that he pursued her to Rochester, where a search by the victim and the local constable revealed that the suspect had the stolen goods about her. The woman was from London, and claimed that she had come to Kent to visit an uncle at Canterbury.[26] This impressionistic evidence can be supported by more systematic findings. Investigation of a sample of persons accused of larceny and compound larceny in early seventeenth-century Wiltshire shows not only that local residents were least likely to be accused, but also that they were less frequently convicted. Of the permanent local residents who came to trial, 68 per cent were convicted; of the outsiders, 93 per cent. It is interesting to note that in this sample servants tried for larceny suffered a conviction rate which corresponded with their intermediate status of being somewhere between established residents and total outsiders; 88 per cent of them were convicted.[27] This point awaits further investigation: at present, nevertheless, it seems that outsiders to a parish who committed certain offences, notably theft and burglary, were more likely to be tried, and more likely to be convicted, than were local residents.

This evidence of a somewhat more lenient approach to the local offender, and of a correspondingly harsh one to the outsider, must not be allowed to create too rosy a picture of the village communities of the period. Some, indeed, have given a very different view. Lawrence Stone, for example, has recently portrayed life in the early modern village in terms which, in describing the dreadfulness of such an environment, verge on caricature. He assures us that it was a place 'filled with malice and hatred, its only unifying bond being the occasional episode of mass hysteria, which temporarily bound together the majority in order to harry and persecute the local witch'.[28] Such sentiments might serve as a useful corrective against those who have eulogized the 'community' of the 'traditional' world: but we must once more forgo any final conclusions until such time as those researching in depth on such communities are able to tell us more about interpersonal relationships and general attitudes.

More immediately relevant is the problem of the means by which control was exercised in these communities by those seeking to impose it. As we have seen, local thieves, and even witches, were allowed some leeway before their activities were indicted, while certain of those local offenders who were indicted were more likely than outsiders to escape conviction or serious punishment. Even so, the fact remains that there *were* delinquents within the parish, and that in many areas there were others within the community anxious to control their delinquencies. The 'well affected' had numerous sanctions, both institutional and informal, with which to combat the disorderly.

The longest established of these was the manorial court. This, along with other local franchises, had been the traditional means of controlling the community in the middle ages, and in some places at least had done so with surprising efficiency. By 1550, it is generally held, the manorial court was on the verge of its final decline: in some villages, nevertheless, it remained an essential agent in the struggle to maintain social discipline. Most leets were more or less defunct by 1650, but, as we have argued, in the first half of the period covered by this book the leet was still an institution of considerable importance for many communities. Some villages, indeed, were still run largely through the manorial courts. It was there that decisions were made, not only about agrarian organization, but also about wider issues of local government. They still appointed the local constable and other officers, and were often the place where local by-laws were passed and enforced. Such matters may sound trivial, parochial in the literal sense, but they were still of considerable importance to those living on the manor. More importantly for our immediate purposes, the manorial courts were still, in some places, very active in suppressing and punishing petty crime. For this reason, good leet records can provide us with very detailed insights into the nature of the small-scale crime of the period. They can also provide insights into the local power structure: an analysis of those serving as leet jurors, and those filling the manorial offices, frequently provides a roll-call of the village notables. Their control of manorial institutions, in those localities where such institutions were still flourishing, provided them with an important means of exercising control.

One such place, as we have seen in the previous chapter, was Acomb, near York, whose manorial courts were still very much alive in the late sixteenth and early seventeenth centuries.[29] Here the traditional self-regulatory aspects of manorial life were still apparent. The leet was still making by-laws, and adjusting them to fit new circumstances. However, this self-regulation did not imply democracy; the precise nature of the power structure within the village awaits further research, but examination of the names of leet jurors suggests that the manor was run by a loose oligarchy of the more substantial of its tenants. The business of the court was fairly varied. Most of it consisted of purely local, manorial problems. Persons were presented for such offences against neighbourly standards as letting infected horses graze on the common, breaking the pound, taking firewood from the common without permission, and not grinding at the lord's mill. These cases are fairly unremarkable, and had probably always formed the bulk of any manorial court's business. Another type of offence was that involving physical or verbal violence. Assaults and bloodshed were fairly frequent, and were usually punished by fines, sometimes to the value of 10/-. Scolding was also common enough, and was likewise punished by fining. Again, such presentments had been common in the middle ages, and although they can tell us much about interpersonal tensions in this period, they do not throw very much light on the problem of changes in the nature of control in the village.

What is perhaps more important was the tendency for this traditional business to be increasingly supplemented by the presentment of regulative offences. These had, of course, figured in the leet rolls of the middle ages: it seems, however, that they became more important at Acomb from the late sixteenth century onwards. It is difficult not to interpret this development as a local reaction to the national trend towards a greater regulation of various types of conduct to which we have alluded earlier in this chapter. Between 1614 and 1624 several inhabitants were presented for harbouring vagrants and told to get rid of them,[30] while in 1598 Robert Wright, apparently an habitual offender, was in trouble for lodging pedlars without the constable's consent.[31] The related problem of subtenants and inmates caused constant worry, and presentments against those 'entertaining' them were frequent. The object, of course, was to prevent such newcomers from obtaining the right to parish poor relief. In 1623, for example, John Wilkinson was presented for taking Thomas Waite into his house without entering bonds securing the township against claims for relief. Waite, it was reported, now lacked maintenance, and was a burden on the township. Other of the more marginal members of society were reported to the leet,[32] which also extended its activities to the control of sexual morality. Robert Wright was presented for harbouring a pregnant woman to 'the annoyance of his neighbours', while in 1600 three men were presented for each 'entertaining, receiving and keeping in his house a woman evilly disposed of her body'.[33] Given this involvement of the manorial courts in the regulation of conduct, it is not surprising that the 1631 Book of Orders, in its attempts to re-invigorate English local government, should give direction to those running leets to make special enquiry into certain types of local nuisance offender.[34]

The court leet, then, was still in many villages an important means by which the community, or those who controlled the community, could settle its differences, suppress certain types of crime, and maintain order. It had several advantages in this. It was essentially local, concerned with local issues and local people. It also provided cheap justice. By the second half of the sixteenth century, however, much of the suppression of petty crime which had once been the business of the leet was being dealt with by other institutions. Interestingly enough, the workings of at least one of these institutions, the archdeacon's court, demonstrate how far what was, in essence, an agency of the state church might find its operations being adjusted to local needs and popular attitudes.

The church courts, of which the archdeacon's court was the lowliest, have attracted unfavourable comment from historians. Certain aspects of their attempts at controlling sexual morality are repugnant to the modern observer; those steeped in the tradition that the development of the common law can be equated with progress have found aspects of the ecclesiastical law distasteful; while contemporary criticisms of the apparitor and other ecclesiastical court officers have been accepted far too uncritically. Despite such earlier views, more recent research on the archives of the church courts has led to a reappraisal of their significance.[35] The growth in their correction business after the mid sixteenth century was a natural consequence of the desire by the central government to enforce some of the wider aspects of the reformation. The central concern of the church courts, it might be argued, was to ensure that the laity came to church, and that they understood and accepted the religious teachings that they heard there. However, governments in this period were not merely concerned to ensure regular church attendance and religious conformity; they also aimed at enforcing godliness, morality, and discipline among their subjects. The attention lavished by the church courts upon sexual morality, drunkenness, indecent behaviour in church, and so on, was one aspect of the wider desire by the state to regulate the lives of those it ruled. The work of the English archdeaconry courts, therefore, was just one facet of broad trends which were common to countries where religion was reformed along catholic as well as protestant lines.

The wider discussion of these issues must be left for a later chapter: what must concern us at this point is the mechanics by which persons found themselves presented before the archdeacon. Recent research has completely rejected the older view that presentment at the church courts was normally at the instigation of the apparitor: on the contrary, it is now widely accepted that pressure for prosecution at the court of the archdeacon or at any other of the church courts was normally the result of pressure from below. Being presented before the archdeacon, like being indicted at the assizes or quarter sessions, was normally the result of the action of the person or persons offended against. In the former cases the offence was given to collective notions of proper behaviour, rather than to an individual. It remains problematic whether these collective notions were those of the 'community' or of its ruling stratum of relatively rich and perhaps relatively respectable yeoman and artisans. Certainly the desire to suppress 'ungodly' behaviour in general, and sexual immorality in particular, makes sense if we accept that there was a divergence in *mores* between the established village notables and the marginal poor. It was from the notables that the churchwardens were recruited; and, on the evidence of archdeaconry act books, most of those presented had had their alleged faults detected by the churchwardens. Again the impression is one of regulative laws being imposed upon the poorer members of village society by the richer.

This model should not be oversimplified. It is obvious from the records that a number of those appearing before the archdeacon had offended the moral values of a fairly wide range of their co-parishioners. It is this that has encouraged some historians to stress the intolerance and inflexibility of attitude of the early modern English villager. The successful operation of the archdeacon's court, more obviously than any other tribunal, rested upon a willingness by neighbours to mind each others' business. This they seem to have done in a very positive way; neighbours were only too willing to spy upon each other, and report what they had observed. It was through such actions that the 'common fame' that so often led to presentment arose, and examples of them are common in court records. Their flavour is conveyed perfectly by a Somerset case, in which a farmer reported how he came upon a young couple in 'a plot of grass under a hedge'. The couple began to have sexual intercourse, but

> when John and Hannah had almost ended what they were about this informant stept unto them and took John by the tail of his shirt and demanded of them why they were so wicked as to commit such a wicked act, to which John said that Hannah was his wife by promise and that he did intend to marry her the next morning at eight of the clock.[36]

This case of coitus being rudely interrupted is by no means unusual. It demonstrates the genuine dismay felt by many respectable parishioners at sexual misconduct, and their willingness to report such matters. The courts, we must reiterate, were not involved in simple repression, but were dependent upon active co-operation from the populace at large.

The archives of the archdeacon's court, therefore, provide useful insights into the lesser delinquents in the village and how the village, or at least its 'well affected' members, dealt with them. In the period between about 1560, when the need to enforce the Reformation and the growth of a desire to regulate the community provoked an increase in its business, and the early 1640s, when the outbreak of the Civil Wars caused it to fall into disuse, the archdeacon's court was vital in the suppression of petty delinquency. In this it was aided not only by its ability to elicit aid from within the parishes it sought to control, but also by the fact that it met frequently and locally. In term time the court met about once every three weeks, while its sittings were held on a small circuit within each deanery, so that parties appearing before it had usually only a few miles to travel. It seems, however, that this excellent means of imposing control never recovered from its period of abeyance. After 1660 the ecclesiastical courts were restored with the Stuart monarchy, but they probably never regained their pre-war vigour. The problem awaits detailed investigation: but, as we have seen, it appears safe to say that after the Restoration, the correction business of the archdeacon's court became smaller in volume and more restricted in scope. In contrast to the immensely varied presentments of the years 1560 to 1640, the archdeacon's court after 1660 seems to have concerned itself largely with the problems of church attendance and religious conformity.[37]

In the first half of our period, therefore, the local courts of the church and the manor provided not only a tool by which the richer villagers might control the poorer, but also constituted channels through which interpersonal disputes and neighbourly tensions might be articulated and resolved. The cases arising from these disputes and tensions can be regarded as less spectacular equivalents of those more familiar outcomes of neighbourly tensions, the witchcraft accusations tried at the assizes. These accusations, which also began to decline in number about halfway through the period covered by this book, were perhaps the most dramatic consequence of the state and church providing the legal framework and ideological cosmography within which village tensions could work themselves out. There were, however, a number of other types of case entering the courts which were equally expressive of disputes and tensions within the village. Perhaps the most notable of these arose from various types of verbal violence: ritual cursing, defamation, and scolding. These phenomena have not received the attention which they deserve. Detailed study of them can be justified on two grounds: firstly, they throw light on some very interesting but very obscure aspects of popular consciousness; secondly, they demonstrate the remarkable willingness of the English to settle their disputes by recourse to the courts.

Formal cursing is an activity which has connections with witchcraft, and it is no accident that the best recent discussion of it appears in Keith Thomas's magisterial work on magic and related beliefs.[38] Thomas argues that by the early seventeenth century 'the real source of the continuing belief in the efficacy of cursing lay, not in theology but in popular sentiment', the basis of this sentiment being that certain types of curse still retained their efficacy, especially when the curser's anger was justified.[39] Examples of formal cursing are rare in court records, but those which survive suggest that being cursed might be a traumatic experience. In a case brought to the Archbishop of York's consistory court in the early years of the seventeenth century, John Wood of Wetherby reported how his next-door neighbour, the widow Helen Hiley, had come to him 'and kneeled downe upon her knees and said a vengeance of god light upon the[e] Wood . . . and all thy children, and I shall trulie pray this praier for the[e] so long as I live'. A few years earlier, a Leeds man named John Metcalfe had told the same court how Anne Dixon had called him

> Whoremaster, whoremonger and harlott and did sit her downe upon her knees and cursed and banned him, and his wife, and badd a vengeance light upon the wife of the said John Metcalf and upon that whoremaster and whoremonger harlott her husbande . . . and prayed God that they might never thryve.[40]

Such ritual cursing, and the fact that reporting it to a court was felt to be an appropriate counter-measure, convey something of the peculiar flavour of interpersonal tensions in the early modern English village.

If such cases, despite their intrinsic interest, were rare, accusations of defamation were extremely common, and formed a major part of the business of all courts empowered to try them, from the Star Chamber down to the local ecclesiastical tribunals. Despite the mass of materials relating to it, however, the subject has attracted little attention from other than legal historians.[41] This is a pity, for even a preliminary investigation of the topic reveals that defamation could take very varied forms and might involve imputations of very different forms of illicit conduct. Sometimes, defamatory words could be very ornate and deliberate, as when Hugh Barker, from Chelmsford in Essex, was indicted in 1602 for composing a nineteen-verse ballad detailing the sexual misconduct of various of his fellow townsmen and women.[42] More commonly these suits for defamation arose from harsh and hasty words spoken in a quarrel: certainly, this is the impression that arises from detailed work which has been carried out on church court defamation in Wiltshire and Yorkshire.[43] As such cases suggest, study of defamation would tell us much about individual concepts of reputation and honour: conversely, the wilful spreader of defamation, rumour, and gossip might have a disruptive effect upon the community as a whole. When, for example, Thomas Hawkins declared that all the inhabitants of Goldenhill, Somerset, were infected with venereal disease, it was reported that 'differences and debates do arise between men and there wives in Goldenhill, and people do refrain from keeping company with those that are honest men there'.[44]

Perhaps the greatest threat to the tranquillity of the community as a whole, however, came from scolds. Scolding, like witchcraft, was one of the distinctive offences of the early modern period, although it has so far received little attention from modern historians. It was, moreover, usually dealt with by the local manorial or ecclesiastical courts, and hence has not been one of the major concerns of the legal historian. Nevertheless, the archives of the local courts demonstrate just how seriously the scolder might disrupt the township. Such individuals as Thomas Jackson of Eccleshall, in Staffordshire, of whom it was complained in 1599 that 'he useth to call all men yt he falleth out with and women also theeves, rogues, whores and queans and so greatly disquietes the townsmen' were obviously serious threats to the peace of the neighbourhood.[45] However, it should be noted that, such cases as Jackson's apart, the archetypal scold was female. Scolds presented before the archdeacon of Durham in 1600, for example, include Isabell Remmisson 'that she is a verrey idle scolde & a disquieter of hir neighbo[u]rs with malicious speeches'; Mary Taylor of Auckland, 'that she by her evill and rayling temper misusethe and formethe dissension amonge hir neighbours'; and two women of Denton presented because 'they are uncharitable scold[es] & disquiet their neighbo[ur]s'.[46] It would seem that scolding, so often written off by historians merely as a joke, contains some important clues not only to contemporary views on harmony and order, but also on attitudes to differences in behaviour between the sexes.

After the Restoration, despite some isolated local exceptions, it would seem that both the manorial leets and the archdeaconry courts were less active in suppressing petty crime and moral delinquencies. The manorial courts, essentially the tribunal of the local community, and the lesser ecclesiastical courts, whose workings still in many ways reflected popular attitudes, were being replaced by the justices' monthly meetings, known at a later point as petty sessions. It is, unfortunately, easier to postulate that this development occurred than it is to prove it. Little archival evidence of the functioning of petty sessions and justices' meetings survives before the late eighteenth century. There are some signs that these meetings were of real importance, although these are largely of a piecemeal or a literary nature. The petty sessions obviously had most of the attractions of the arch-deacon's court; they were capable of dispensing cheap, local, and speedy justice. It was obviously easier to get a petty offender fined or bound over by the justices at their meeting than it was to indict him at the assizes and quarter sessions, and probably just as effective.

The pressure that resulted in the keepers of disorderly alehouses, parents of bastards, pilferers, and other disorderly livers being presented before or reported to the petty sessions were probably essentially similar to those which so often lay behind other forms of prosecution: a growing dismay with the conduct of the delinquent, and an eventual decision to take some form of action. Petty sessions were an obvious place to take such action, and by the late seventeenth century the meeting of the sessions constituted an important event in the immediate locality; some idea of the attendance at a petty sessions might be derived from a report of a floor collapsing under the 200 people attending a petty sessions at an inn in Essex in 1692.[47] A further impression of the conditions under which the petty sessions were held can be gained from a writer who in 1700 described caustically how the justices' business was conducted 'amidst the smoaking of Pipes, the cluttering of Pots, and the noise and ordure of a narrow Room infected with Drinking and a Throng'. Arguing that petty sessions should be held in 'some Town-house or Market-House' rather than an inn, he continued

> the Magistrate should sit aloft, and conspicuous upon the Bench (as it's becoming a Place of Judicature), and not be oblig'd (as may be seen sometimes) to hold a Glass in one hand, whilst he signs a Warrant with the other; tho' much more Eminent was he, who to shew the stediness of his Hand, writ and sign'd a Warrant upon the heaving Belly of a boggy Hostess'.[48]

The country petty sessions might not have been the most decorous or orderly of tribunals; by the early eighteenth century it nevertheless played a vital role in the suppression of small-scale crime and delinquency in rural and small-town England.

Discussion of the use of the inferior courts in dealing with the local petty offender should not, of course, obscure the existence of a variety of other sanctions, both formal and informal, which could be used against the disorderly. Official sanctions included binding over to keep the peace, or to be of good behaviour (cheap and immediate means of controlling the violent or the troublesome), and committal to the house of correction. Metropolitan house of correction calendars show how many offenders who might otherwise have been prosecuted were simply incarcerated for a few months' hard labour,[49] while other criminals who might have been indicted or presented at an earlier date were, by the mid eighteenth century, simply being dealt with on summary conviction by a single justice. Informal sanctions were more numerous, if more difficult to document. Employers of labour had wide powers of discipline, and might punish disorder, pilfering, or sexual misconduct among their employees by physical chastisement or simply by dismissing them. The gentry might exercise similar controls over their tenants, while the parish priest would attempt to ensure the discipline of his flock by mediating disputes among them and by exhorting the ungodly to better standards of conduct. The villagers themselves were perfectly capable of expressing their disapproval of delinquent or deviant behaviour through the communal satire of the *charivari* or through straightforward ostracism. Prosecution at a court was, therefore, only one of a whole battery of sanctions which might be brought against the criminal and the disorderly.[50]

By the late seventeenth century the 'well affected' of the parish had another method of control to supplement court action and informal exhortation. This was the poor law. It has been argued that in the closing decades of the seventeenth and throughout the eighteenth century the administration of the poor law gave the members of the parish vestry a very effective means of disciplining the labouring poor.[51] The general economic changes in Tudor and Stuart England had produced a large body of poor which contemporaries saw as the stratum of society from which most criminals would be drawn. As we shall see in the next chapter, this attitude was from their point of view basically correct: one of the major themes in the history of crime in early modern England is the way in which behaviour classed as criminal came to be regarded as characteristically the prerogative of the poor. However, the development of an efficient poor relief system, despite the inroads it made into the pockets of the village notables, provided a ready means of disciplining this potentially disorderly element in society. This discipline must have been doubly attractive in that it avoided the costs and trouble involved in formal prosecution.

By the late seventeenth century, therefore, a number of developments had ensured, in many parishes, the ascendancy of a local elite of comparatively rich yeomen, tradesmen and artisans. This group, we have argued, grew in importance throughout the period 1550–1750, and by the latter date was marked off from the poor of the parish both by its relative affluence and by its adherence to a somewhat different set of cultural values. It must, of course, be remembered that this overall picture is subject to infinite local variations: in the north and west of the country, in particular, such changes probably came later and were less absolute than in the lowland zone. Moreover, the different strata of a community were still able to show a solidarity of attitude over some matters; the game laws, for example, may well have been equally abhorrent to the tenant farmer and the village labourer. Even so, an increase in social stratification in rural society is one of the most striking features of the social history of England in this period, and is of manifest importance to the historian of crime; it was on the minor property owners that the system of law and order ultimately depended. The work of the JP was doubtless of great significance, especially given the growth in the powers of the petty sessions and the augmentation of the justices' powers of summary conviction. On the other hand, the system would have been inoperable without the co-operation of inferior officers, whether as parish constables, churchwardens, or overseers of the poor. It was they who were responsible for the fundamental tasks of reporting crime and disorder, and executing the justices' instructions for suppressing them.

Our realization of the importance of the parish officers and, ultimately, of the significance of the nature of the social structure within the village, must remind us yet again that the suppression of crime in early modern England was an essentially personal business. In an earlier chapter we have pointed out that the decision to prosecute usually lay with an individual, and for this reason it is very difficult to see criminal statistics in this period as more than the roughest guide to the real level of crime. Study of the criminal in his local environment re-emphasizes this point: as we have seen, villages were able to cope with habitual offenders in their midst over fairly long periods without indicting them at the assizes or quarter sessions. For most known local offenders informal admonition, control through the poor law, and presentment at the local leet or the archdeacon's court seem to have been considered the most effective method of control. When a local delinquent did fall foul of the assizes or quarter sessions, parochial opinion was often willing to exert itself sufficiently to send petitions or letters to the courts stressing the special circumstances of particular offenders. That these petitions might be either in defence of the criminal or against him hardly matters; in either case, they demonstrate that the application of the criminal law in this period was essentially adjusted to particular cases. This theme will be developed in the concluding chapter of this book, where it will be argued that this selectivity in the treatment of the offender, within the context of a severe legal code, is one of the distinctive features of law enforcement in early modern England.

Study of the petty criminal and his or her relationships with the more orderly members of the village also raises the question of what contemporaries wanted from the system of law enforcement. Obviously, they preferred a system which was cheap, speedy in its operation, and local (the first quality, most would have agreed, was dependent on the other two). Arguably, the court leet, the archdeacon's court, and the petty sessions met these requirements. It is, moreover, probable that these institutions provided punishments which were felt by the community to be appropriate to the local offender's misdeeds. The decision to present an offender at the leet or the archdeacon's court does suggest that the presenter thought the punishments inflicted by those institutions were adequate ones. The adulterer, for example, sentenced by the church courts to do penance before the congregation in a white sheet, must have been a reassuring spectacle for the godly and the chaste, and perhaps a deterrent for those contemplating sexual immorality. The regular presentment of adulterers before the archdeaconry court is, therefore, perfectly understandable. When, however, the Rump Parliament introduced the death penalty for the female adulterer in 1650, the law proved virtually unenforceable.[52] The 'well affected' of the village might wish to see the adultress punished, but they apparently had little desire to see her hanged. The severity of punishment which an offender might expect to receive before a court had to correspond roughly to what the community, or those running the community, felt to be appropriate to the crime in question.

However, before such matters as community attitudes to crime, or even the exact extent or nature of crime in this period can be understood, we will need to know far more about the structure and workings of village and small-town society. Future research will surely demonstrate variations between the different types of community: between the supposedly well-disciplined nucleated settlements of the corn-growing areas; the allegedly more egalitarian and undisciplined settlements of the forest and upland areas; and the socially divided proto-industrial village. They will also provide clues to help explain the sometimes dramatic differences in recorded crime between close or even neighbouring parishes. Doubtless, in each case where a parish is studied in depth the broad lines of the argument put forward in this chapter will be subjected to innumerable exceptions and modifications. Conversely, it is unlikely that they will negate the two most persistent themes in my argument, the importance of small property owners in, and the intensely personal nature of, the enforcement of the law in the early modern period.

It is also unlikely that future research will negate the impression, formed from this initial study of a wide geographical range of court records, of a general transition away from a local court system geared essentially to facilitating the settlement of interpersonal disputes to one which emphasized the control of the richer over the poorer villagers and which, ultimately, demonstrated the penetration of the state into the parish. In the previous chapter, we postulated the existence of massive changes in the levels of prosecution of felony over the period with which we are concerned, and in the levels of capital punishment of felony. Fluctuations in the prosecution and punishment of petty crime are more difficult to trace, but it is possible that an equally important, and perhaps not unrelated, shift took place there too. In 1550, the petty offender was most likely to be dealt with in a local manorial court. Often, of course, presentment of offenders there was the outcome of pressure from richer villagers, for in many areas the situation traced by Wrightson and Levine in Terling had obtained long before the sixteenth century. Many presentments, however, give the impression of an attempt to resolve a dispute or conflict between two persons of roughly equal status. More research is needed, but at the time of writing it seems likely that the 'village tension' offences – scolding, witchcraft, defamation – were considerably less likely to be brought to court by the mid eighteenth century. By that date the petty offender was dealt with in the justice's parlour rather than before the leet jury, and curbing his activities was therefore more obviously the business of the state rather than that of the community, however defined. This process should not be oversimplified, and its local variations need further study. Nevertheless, it is difficult to deny that, when studying petty crime after a transitional phase perhaps best represented by the archdeaconry court, we see the replacement of the local justice of the manor by a justice which, however flexible in relation to specific local circumstances, was essentially that of the gentry and, at one or two removes, of the state.[53]

Chapter 5

THE CRIMINAL ORDERS OF EARLY MODERN ENGLAND

One of the major contributions of Victorian social debate to modern British attitudes was the acceptance of the concept of a 'criminal class'. By 1850, contemporary observers were convinced that such a social stratum existed.[1] They saw it as the product of rapid industrialization and urbanization which, it was felt, had concentrated the lower orders in desperately poor and intrinsically dangerous masses. In the lowest quarters of every major city, it was thought, there existed a geographical area whose inhabitants lived mainly on the proceeds of crime, who enjoyed a lifestyle different from those of both the bourgeoisie and the respectable poor, who spoke a distinctive argot, and who were organized into a unique social hierarchy. This idea of the criminal as a lumpenproletarian, living a separate existence in the city slum, is still with us. Until the rise of a radical approach to criminology in the mid twentieth century, practitioners of the subject still based their approach to the criminal on this stereotype. Poor toilet training, irregular church attendance, and an unwillingness (when of an appropriate age) to participate in youth club activities were among a number of similar factors which were felt to predispose individual young people towards a criminal career: it is no accident that these characteristics were readily attributable to the non-respectable working class. This traditional stereotype of the criminal is still strong among newspaper editors, the writers of television crime series, and the public at large. Its significance as a force for defining deviant behaviour in modern society is, perhaps fortunately, outside the scope of this book: recently, of course, criminologists with a more radical approach to their discipline have had much to say in criticism of it.[2]

To the Victorians, the newly formed 'criminal classes' were essentially the product of economic and social change. Such a view leads us back to the general problem of the connection of crime, and thus criminals, to the general lines of socio-economic development. As we have already argued, the idea that such a connection existed is an attractive and logical one. Conversely, as the discussion of fluctuations in the prosecution of serious crime and its punishment suggested in chapter 3, surviving evidence makes the nature of the connection more obscure than might have been expected. As we shall see at a later point, it is possible to trace shifts in the official or semi-official perceptions of the criminal in this period, although again the problem needs rather more subtle handling than the straightforward 'rise of the capitalist state' approach might suggest. In this chapter, however, we shall address ourselves to the central problem: who, in the England of our study, were the criminals? In what way were they drawn from new social groups, produced by social and economic change? And how far were they organized, or professionalized, into some form of 'criminal class'?

One change which does seem to have occurred in the social profile of the English criminal was the decline of upper-class involvement in criminal acts. In the middle ages, the upper reaches of English landed society had felt no qualms about breaking the law. This trait should not, of course, be overstated: our view of the problem has been distorted by the historical folklore of the big bad feudal baron, and by an historiographical tradition which purveys a somewhat curious view of the Tudors' relationship with the English nobility. As one recent historian of the nobility in the late middle ages has put it, 'medieval nobles, like modern teenagers, receive disproportionate publicity for their delinquencies'.[3] Nevertheless, in both instances evidence of a solid core of misbehaviour exists. Setting modern teenagers aside, we can find numerous examples of indulgence in criminal acts by medieval nobles. Violence was common, usually in pursuit of local prestige or power: local office holding, parliamentary elections, the short-circuiting of law suits, disputes over boundaries or real estate, all might be the occasion for fighting or disorder. Such incidents might be episodes in feuds which could result in severe local problems. From about 1441, for example, the west of England was seriously disturbed by a dispute between the Earl of Devon and the Lord William Bonville, the initial conflict being over the stewardship of the Duchy of Cornwall. The climax of this feud came in 1455 when, among other delinquencies, the earl murdered a lawyer who was a member of Bonville's council, and looted Exeter Cathedral.[4]

Such acts (if on a somewhat less dramatic scale) were common enough and, as we shall see, persisted well into the period with which we are concerned. More remarkable, however, is the involvement of members of the gentry in regular, organized criminal activities. One historian, taking a lead from E. H. Sutherland's more modern concept of 'white collar crime', has gone so far as to claim that 'fur collar crime' was a distinctive form of deviance in the late middle ages.[5] One gentry family whose criminal career has been extremely well documented was the Folvilles of Ashby-Folville, Leicestershire. Six brothers from the family (a seventh, paradoxically, was a royal keeper of the peace), perpetrated a series of murders, robberies, rapes and extortions between 1326 and 1341. The worst of them was Eustace de Folville, whose crimes included five murders and a score of other felonies. Their greatest coup was to capture a judge, justice Richard Willoughby, while he was on his circuit, and extract a ransom of 1,300 marks from him. There was a strong element of organization in their activities (Eustace was, in fact, referred to as the *'capitalis de societate'* on one indictment), and they obviously formed a nucleus around which other rogues in the area gathered. Moreover, they seem to have enjoyed considerable support in their locality: on occasion, the survival of the band was assured, or its survival made easier, by the assistance of local individuals ranging in social status from poor peasants to the gentry.[6]

By 1550 the gentry were less likely to be involved in organized crime of this type; they were, however, still capable of acts of savage violence. The greatest scholar of the late Tudor and early Stuart aristocracy has commented that 'in the sixteenth and seventeenth centuries tempers were short and weapons to hand'. The behaviour of the propertied classes, like that of the poor, was characterized by the 'ferocity, childishness, and lack of self-control of the Homeric age'.[7] As the examples he adduces to support this contention demonstrate, the aristocracy and gentry of mid Tudor England were as likely as their fifteenth-century forebears to indulge in individual acts of physical or verbal violence, or to encourage gangs of retainers or hired thugs to assault enemies as a means of paying off private grudges or pursuing local power politics. Gradually, however, things changed, and habits or restraint spread among the landed orders. Partly, this may have been an outcome of Tudor policy towards noble troublemakers: it seems more likely, however, that the shift in conduct is mainly attributable to an even less tangible phenomenon, a change in fashionable opinion as to what constituted proper aristocratic conduct. The taste for Castiglione and his English imitators demonstrates an increasingly civilized and sophisticated view of the proper behaviour of the gentleman. These renaissance values were, curiously enough, reinforced by puritanism, which had its vogue in at least some gentry circles in the decades before the Civil Wars. A number of cultural influences, therefore, made the upper echelons of society somewhat less prone to indulge in acts of violence. The case of Lord Ferrers, tried and executed in 1760 for murdering his steward, became a *cause célèbre*, and passed into folklore as an example of the equality with which the law of England was applied.[8] One suspects that it would have attracted rather less attention had it been tried two centuries earlier.

One aspect of changing fashions among the aristocracy was the arrival of the duel as a recognized social institution.[9] The first fencing school in England was opened at Blackfriars in 1576 by an Italian named Rocco Bonetti, and the art of fencing rapidly acquired upper-class patrons. Bonetti advertised his high-class clientele by hanging the coats of arms of his students around his walls, while Vincentio Saviola, another Italian fencing-master, was the protégé of the Earl of Essex. Although duelling in England never became as extensive a problem as it did in France, it enjoyed a vogue among at least some English gentry: indeed, so adept did they become at the use of the rapier that one of them, named Cheese, even managed to kill Jeronimo Saviola, Vincentio's brother and himself a fencing-master. The custom, it seems flourished in the post-Restoration period. Those wishing to learn how to conduct a quarrel could do no better than model themselves on the political elite. George Villiers, for example, the second duke of Buckingham, was involved in a number of duels and challenges. In 1666 Buckingham's disparagement of the Irish nation during a debate in the House of Lords provoked the wrath of Lord Ossory, who challenged him. On this occasion Buckingham avoided fighting by complaining about Ossory to the House and having him incarcerated in the Tower. Four years later, however, he was involved in a duel with the Earl of Shrewsbury. The fight was provoked by Buckingham's adultery with the Duchess of Shrewsbury, and ended with him inflicting serious wounds on the earl, from which he died about two months later. In 1672 Buckingham, who was pardoned after this killing, was again challenged, this time by Sir William Coventry. As this evidence, involving one of the leading peers of the realm, suggests, violence was still something in which the upper reaches of society were wont to indulge until well into the seventeenth century.

Mention of the misdeeds of the second duke of Buckingham serves as a useful reminder of the extent of aristocratic delinquency in the Restoration. The reign of Charles II witnessed an upsurge in upper-class debauchery, for which most of the participants passed largely unpunished. Charles Sackville, the Earl of Dorset, his brother, and three gentry cronies were accused in 1662 of robbing and murdering a tanner named Hoppy during a drunken evening, although the case was dropped when they pleaded that they thought he was a highwayman. John Wilmot, the second Earl of Rochester, was another courtier of vicious life whose career included involvement in a fight in 1676 between a group of gentry roisterers and the watch at Epsom, in the course of which one of the gentlemen was killed. Another familiar figure at Charles II's court, Sir Charles Sedley, perpetrated a vicious assault on an actor named Edward Kynaston when the latter, who bore a close physical resemblance to Sedley, was impertinent enough to appear in public dressed like the knight. Sedley also distinguished himself by being fined £500 after running an orgy at the Cock tavern in Bow Street. On this occasion, the judge added to the financial punishment by upbraiding the malefactor in tones redolent of pre-1660 morality. He declared that it was for Sedley 'and such wicked wretches as he was that God's anger and judgements hung over us, calling him sirrah many times'.[10]

Needless to say, the lesser gentry aped the manners of the *nobilitas major*. Reports of crime in late seventeenth-century London contain numerous references to gentlemen (many of them, one suspects, essentially of the *soi disant* variety) who were ready to indulge in acts of violence, often in defence of what they conceived of as their honour. A pamphlet in 1684, describing the death of a poor waterman who was murdered after bumping accidentally into a gentleman in a dark alley, commented how the 'Bullys and Hectors' about London would kill in response to the slightest affront. It deplored the common attitude which felt 'nothing but the blood of a man were a satisfaction it may be for an innocent takeing the wall of, or a neglectful stumble upon one of these night-walking gentlemen'.[11] Other cases give an impression of the shortness of temper among the gentry. Sir William Estcourt, one of a panel of Wiltshire jurors brought up from their native county to hear a case between two of their compatriots in London, was killed by one of his fellows when a fight broke out after an argument over horse-racing in a London Tavern.[12] Another gentleman was killed in a duel which followed an argument over payment of a bill in a tavern,[13] while other descriptions of murders in the capital suggest that such a background was not uncommon for gentry violence there.[14] Tempers were doubtless often heated by drink, but the underlying cause of incidents of this type was a lack of psychological restraint over violent conduct. One gentleman murderer, enjoined not to fight, replied to those seeking to restrain him 'he would not be pist upon for a coward, but fight he would'.[15] As long as such attitudes persisted, observers would continue to complain of 'the wild hectorian gentlemen, wherewith this age and city too much abounds'.[16]

Gentry violence was by no means restricted to those members of the class visiting the metropolis. Records of rural areas reveal a similar willingness on the part of the country gentry to indulge in violence. The Northern circuit assize records, to quote their Victorian editor, 'give rather an unfavourable picture of the Yorkshire gentry'.[17] In a number of cases violence erupted in the form of a duel, with an argument in an alehouse often forming the background to the incident. One such killing, involving an unusually high-class murderer, occurred in 1681 when the Earl of Eglington killed a Mr Maddox. The two had been playing dice in an alehouse at Doncaster, and the killing followed a dispute over the money gambled, exacerbated by Maddox's uncharitable observations upon the Scottish peerage.[18] Other cases, although of a different nature, point to a general intemperance in the behaviour of the high gentry. In 1664 Lionel Copley Esq., a gentleman of a county family of considerable influence in the Sheffield area, was indicted for beating a man, putting a bridle into his mouth, mounting on his back and riding him for half an hour. Renaissance concepts of aristocratic behaviour were evidently late in spreading as far as South Yorkshire.[19]

The involvement of the gentry in acts of violence, and in such standard areas of debauch as drunkenness and womanizing, suggests that the propertied classes' retreat into respectability was more complex and more lengthy a matter than has sometimes been made out. Nevertheless, gentry violence does seem to have become less widespread as the period we are considering unfolded, less likely to involve groups of thugs hired or encouraged by gentlemen, and, thanks to the institution of the duel, more likely to be restricted to members of the class. Such a generalization needs to be tested against detailed local studies, and it will doubtless be modified by regional differences and a host of individual exceptions. Even so, one is left with a sense that violence by a gentleman was felt to be less acceptable, and was less common, in 1750 than in 1550. Certainly, gentry involvement in other forms of crime was more limited. The gentry frequently indulged in poaching, and some were involved to at least some degree in smuggling gangs and wrecking; but the robber barons of the late middle ages, the upper-class heads of organized crime, were a thing of the past. Individual gentry may have been involved in random and unpremeditated acts of violence; others may have poached; but gangs like those run by the fourteenth-century Folvilles no longer existed. By 1750 the aristocracy found it easier to augment their income on the stock exchange or by improving their estates rather than by ransoming royal judges.

The robber baron, a distinctive type of medieval criminal, was thus largely obsolete by the late sixteenth century. Already, however, contemporary observers in England, as in much of Western Europe, were commenting in fearful tones on the arrival of a new type of criminal stereotype, the vagrant. The increase in vagrancy in the late sixteenth century was the outcome of those socio-economic changes to which we have already referred, of which population increase was the most important, if perhaps the least identifiable by the inhabitants of what was essentially a pre-statistical society. There were more people around, and a high proportion of them were poor. In what passed for good times in the sixteenth century, there would never be enough work to go round.[20] The rythms of the pre-industrial economy might provide full employment for a month or so at harvest time, but in the slack periods of the agricultural year there would simply not be sufficient work to do. In bad times, those who enjoyed at best a marginal economic existence would be thrown into acute poverty. Bad harvests would send the price of bread, the staple food, up beyond the level at which the poor could afford to buy it. A stop in trade, something to which the export-based English textile industry was especially vulnerable, would threaten the position of those dependent on by-employments. The problem of vagrancy, therefore, can be seen against two interlocking phenomena: the gradual population increase, which perhaps doubled the number of inhabitants in England between 1500 and 1630, and which created severe long-term pressure on resources by producing a large body of poor; and the tendency for this period of steady pressure on resources to be punctuated by periods of short, sharp disaster when the harvest failed or when trade ceased.

Literate contemporary observers, although acutely aware that all was not well in the body politic, were unable to take so detached a view as might the modern historian. As we shall see, the vagrant emerged as *the* criminal stereotype in the late sixteenth century. His importance in the eyes of those bent on keeping English society orderly was demonstrated by a mass of legislation and a substantial body of popular literature, the former aimed at curbing his escapades, the second at horrifying the public with sensational accounts of them. R. H. Tawney's aphorism that 'the sixteenth century lives in terror of the tramp'[21] is seemingly born out by a mass of contemporary opinion.[22] The nature of this stereotype, and its implications, will be discussed further in a later chapter: for the present, our purpose is to analyse the reality of vagrant crime, and to assess the extent of the threat it posed to contemporary society.

The first impression to strike anyone turning from the statutes and the rogue literature to court archives is that the vagrant emerges as a much tamer phenomenon from the second than from the first. The large bands of vagrants, generally speaking, are absent; there is little evidence of a 'fraternity of vagabonds'; and the justices examining vagabonds seem not to have been in any way concerned about such matters. Most of those apprehended do not seem to have been the professional rogues legislated against in parliament, but were usually unremarkable representatives of the lower, and hence more vulnerable, strata of society. Individuals drawn from one parish's poor might easily turn up as vagrants in another area, and behind many decisions to take to the road there lay stories of personal disaster and failure in the face of those random setbacks or adverse economic conditions to which the poor of the period were so prone. Other vagrants might be young servants dismissed from their service for one reason or other, or servant girls thrown out of service for pregnancy, perhaps the result of a liaison with their employer.

The study of vagrancy is further complicated by the high level of geographical mobility containing in early modern England. Those who had decided or had been forced to leave their parish after some disaster, or servants turned out of service, would mingle on the road with migrant workers, harvest workers, and youngsters in search of service or apprenticeships. To such people, begging, stealing or working might well have been equally attractive methods of getting by, each of them to be employed when appropriate. This stratum of mobile poor must have irritated many contemporaries, but it is difficult to see it as a universally subversive threat.

As we have suggested, the literary image of the Elizabethan vagrant evaporates as soon as court records are examined. Vagabonds examined by the town authorities at Warwick, for example, were almost always far less threatening than their counterparts in the popular literature of the period. Most of them claimed to be wandering in search of employment. A girl from Cheltenham claimed that she was going in search of service in the north country; a man from Henley-on-Thames declared that 'he hath no trade to live by but onely a labourer, an is come into the country to seek woork, but can fynd none'; another man explained that 'he had bene that time in divers places to seek work of his occupacion being a silk wever an now was determyned to goo towards London'. Others had hard luck stories to tell. William Wilson told how he had once kept an inn at Southwark, but 'being fallen in debt was fayne to come from there', while John Weaver of Stratford-upon-Avon claimed that 'he hath bene an occupeier of small wares, and was robbed of them & so forced to go abrode'. For such people, begging must have been the obvious alternative when there was no work to be had. Richard Boney told how 'he hath bene in woork with dyvers men . . . and confesseth that many times he got his living by begging', and his companion, Thomas Corbet alias Lock, explained that he 'most commonly got his living by the Charytie of good folks'.[23] With Boney and Corbet we encounter individuals on the very margins of society.

Other vagrants were less pathetic, if somewhat puzzling, figures. Many claimed to be on the road in order to visit friends or relatives, whether in hopes of being assisted to find work or purely for social reasons. In 1580, the Warwick authorities questioned Arthur Sackfield a 'skoler in Mawdlen college in Oxford' who was travelling 'to seek his freends for exhibiccien'.[24] Numerous people seemed to have been travelling around England for more or less licit reasons: indeed, it is possible to find what might be described as primitive tourists. Henry Bristow, apprehended in Southampton in 1641, had in his possession a map of England, and explained that 'he bought it at the Exchange in London being desirous to travel to see the country'. John Bodle, examined by the authorities of the same town in December 1639, informed them that he was 'by profession a bricklayer, and that hee doth not use to worke at his profession in the winter time, but doth use to go abroad to see fashions'.[25]

Vagrants, therefore, included the pathetic and the bizarre: they also included the criminal. Most of the crimes they committed, however, were opportunistic and small-scale thefts. Typical vagrant criminals were the two northerners taken at Warwick in 1580 who confessed to having stolen ducks, geese and pigs on their travels, which they either consumed at the houses where they stayed or bartered for their lodging.[26] There is also evidence that, although the level of sexual promiscuity so eagerly recounted by Harman and other writers probably did not obtain, the vagrant's attitude to formal marriage was often as casual as the authorities feared.[27] There was, of course, a hard core of 'criminal' vagrants whose activities are recorded in the archives. Many pickpockets, a relatively skilled group of criminals, seem to have been vagrants, like the Lincoln woman apprehended by the Warwick authorities in 1584.[28] There are also isolated reports of organization, as, for example, when the Warwickshire sessions ordered local constables to search a barn which was thought to be a haunt of vagrants in 1625.[29] When we read of vagrants admitting to purchasing counterfeit passes from characters called 'Dick Skoler' and 'Giles of London', or when we encounter a female vagrant named 'Dorothee Grene alias Coosyning doll'[30] we do get the sense of a reality lurking behind the pamphlet writers' description of the vagrant problem. Conversely, there was little evidence of the hierarchy of vagabonds, of the canting tongue, and above all of the high level of organization to which they refer.

Although the vagrants may not have enjoyed the degree of professionalized roguery and organization which the writers of rogue pamphlets attributed to them, there is ample evidence that they enjoyed informal associations and knew where to find support in the countryside through which they passed. Those examined in cases of theft frequently gave accounts of how they had fallen into loose associations on the road. Mary Gessy, a spinster vagrant questioned by the Staffordshire justices in 1596 in connection with a theft, explained how she had met casually with those upon whom stolen goods had been found.[31] Mark Lewes, a Southwark man accused of theft in Kent in the same year, gave a more elaborate account of his associates. He told how he had left his home to go into Kent to seek harvest work, and how he had met John Stafford, a soldier, while on the road. Lewes had known Stafford while himself serving as a soldier in Brittany, and recounted how his former companion committed a theft, and promised to meet him later at Woolwich. While *en route* for that place, Lewes fell in with 'one being a stranger to him', who was planning to travel to London by way of Eltham. On Lewes's insistence that he intended to go to Woolwich, the stranger replied 'I do not greatly care yf I do goe allso that way', and agreeing together in this fashion the two made off and were eventually apprehended.[32] Some of these stories may well have been covers for criminal associations: together, however, they do suggest that the large ambulatory population of England in this period were willing to accompany each other on the road, and to enjoy some feelings of mutual identity, if not of solidarity.

It would seem, therefore, that the vagrant was a lesser problem in reality than he or she was in the popular literature of the period. Doubtless a hard core of 'sturdy beggars' did exist, but it did not hold a monopoly of law-breaking. Rather, crime seems to have been committed by the poor as a whole. The poor, of course, should not be regarded as an undifferentiated mass: they could perhaps be represented as a continuum, with prefigurations of the 'respectable' poor of the Victorian era at one end, and the real-life equivalents of the rogues and vagabonds of the pamphlets at the other. In particular, as I have argued elsewhere,[33] it is difficult to draw any real distinction between the vagrant and the unstable poor of the parish, the migrant workers, servants or poor labourers who had no real stake in the community, and who were terribly vulnerable to the economic crises of the period. Once misfortune sent such people on a downward path, the circumstances of the time made it very difficult for them to maintain respectability; for many of them, as we have seen, begging, stealing and working must have been regarded as equally useful aids to survival, each of them suited to certain occasions. Such people did not constitute the organized menace to social norms portrayed by the pamphlet writers, but rather formed a constant irritant. Something of the mentality of these marginal people is conveyed in the Kentish JP Thomas Harman's report of an interview with a 'walking mort' in the 1560s. The justice upbraided the girl for her 'filthy living and wretched conversation', and advised her to seek employment. 'God help!' she replied, 'How should I live? None will take me into service. But I labour in harvest time honestly.'[34] The need for such people to survive in the months outside harvest time contributed greatly to England's theft rate.

The problems of controlling the poor were exacerbated by the custom of sending young people out to seek service, or of putting them into apprenticeships. Many left their employers before their time had expired, and many others seem only to have worked for a short term, so that at any one time the vagrants and migratory workers on the road might be joined by a number of people on the move between services. Moreover, by the late eighteenth century, it had become axiomatic that servants were constantly on the lookout for opportunities to rob or cheat their masters.[35] Court records suggest that these fears were all too frequently justified. Often, it appears, pilfering would be tolerated over a lengthy period before a report was made to the authorities. Richard Burges of Wolverton, Somerset, for example, reported that his servant, at the instigation of other residents of the parish, had been stealing food and apples from him for two years.[36] Servants might also attempt more sophisticated frauds. In the early seventeenth century a Warwickshire baker told how his servant, apparently at the instigation of his father, had defrauded him of £3/10/-. The youth had pocketed the money with which customers had paid their bills, and then told the baker that they had 'received the bread upon the score and not paid the same'. This had serious consequences, for not only was the baker defrauded of his money, but 'variance' was caused between him and his customers when he attempted to collect what he thought was the money due to him.[37] Quarter sessions records abound with these tales of pilfering and fraud by servants and apprentices, and they also recount occasional instances of violence or sexual delinquency on their part.

Problems could, moreover, be caused by residents of the parish, both rich and poor. A number of the forms which these problems might take have been examined in the previous chapter: it must, however, be reiterated that as well as the vagrant, so familiar to the general historian, there existed a number of resident disorderly, dealing with whom might cause considerable trouble. Petitions from the 'well affected' of the community against such individuals often give the impression of lives devoted to drunkenness, sexual immorality, pilfering and minor acts of violence. Four examples chosen at random from the Staffordshire sessions records illustrate the point. In 1595 the bench heard of William Walker who had assaulted a women, killed the sheep and geese of his neighbours, and cut down their hedges and gates. In 1601 William Hardey was reported because he stole small amounts of corn, grazed his cattle on other men's pasture, and 'liveth altogether idelie, a common brawler amongst his neighbours'. John Whistons, who had resisted mustering, threatened and beaten the constable, and stolen both corn and timber from his neighbours, was described as 'one that labreth not to get his livinge by truth so that his neighbours known not howe he liveth except it be uppon the spoile of the countrey'. William Alcocke, it was reported, was constantly involved in suits against his neighbours over the fencing of land, refused to pay taxes or rates, was an habitual thief, and threatened his neighbours with violence. Indeed, the petition against him complained, 'he thinketh hymselfe a man lawlesse and therefore lyvethe without the compasse of all good order . . . he goeth gallantilie and hath to supplye his wants that which men of far greater lyveing hath not, and howe he cometh upon yet no man knoweth.'[38]

Such individuals, the complaints of the 'well affected' inform us, usually patronized those unlicensed and disorderly alehouses which were the bane both of legislators and of the local authorities. John Fielding, writing at the end of our period, thought that

> at the ale-house the idle meet to game and quarrel; here the gamblers form their strategems; here the pick-pockets hide themselves till dusk, and gangs of thieves form their plots and routs; here conspirators contrive their hellish devices; and here the combinations of journeymen are made to execute their silly schemes.[39]

Combinations of journeymen were probably uncommon before the middle of the eighteenth century, but records from earlier periods reveal that the alehouse might easily contain criminals of one sort of another. County authorities were fond of making orders against ale-houses, which were normally portrayed as the nests of all forms of sin, while complaints from within the parish demonstrate how local opinion might be offended by the unlicensed and disorderly alehouse. Typical was a petition which reached the Somerset bench in 1627 from the vicar, churchwardens, overseers of the poor, constable and other inhabitants of Somerton, against a disorderly house kept by Thomas Merrett. They declared that

> there are to our knowledge sundry foul and filthy abuses committed daily in his house, and the said house is esteemed among us (and that upon some proofs and other strong presumptions) to be little better than a thievish and whorish bawdy house, to the great scandal and annoyance of our town.[40]

There can have been few parishes from which a similar complaint may not have been made at some point within our period.

With alehouses of this type we are confronted with the problem of establishing the degree to which rural crime was organized during this period. Fielding's description was of London alehouses, but there seems to be no reason why the disorderly alehouse tucked into a 'blind' corner of the parish should not also serve as a centre for organized criminal activity: such places would obviously have their attractions for 'thievish and whorish' individuals in the village, while some of the accounts of the deeds of highwaymen in the eighteenth century refer to the use made of a network of 'flash houses' in the countryside. Could it be argued that these were symptomatic of a more widespread organized crime in rural areas?

Certainly, some types of rural crime were very organized. Poaching, which by the end of the period was in large measure a commercial activity dependent on trade outlets, was obviously in this category, and will be described at length in the next chapter. Similarly, smuggling was dependent upon an organized distribution network: eighteenth-century observers estimated that 3,000,000 lb of tea were smuggled into the country annually, which suggests that a fairly sophisticated criminality existed in some coastal regions. So far, however, little serious research on smuggling has been done, least of all for the sixteenth and seventeenth centuries. A recent study of smuggling in Sussex, centred on the 1740s, has shown that the trade was indeed well organized.[41] At the base of this organization lay the fact that the smuggling gangs enjoyed a wide measure of popular support in the area. Many local people did not think that smuggling was wrong: indeed, one smuggler, hanged in 1749, told a clergyman present at the execution that 'as to the charge of smuggling, he owned he had been concerned in that trade for a great many years, and did not think there was any harm in it'.[42] Such attitudes formed the context within which the Kent and Sussex smugglers, notably the infamous Hawkhurst gang, operated. They carried out a virtual guerrilla war against the officers of the government, and enjoyed a wide measure of popular support even after they had murdered a revenue officer and an informer under particularly brutal circumstances. Comparative work on smugglers in other areas and other periods is needed. Nevertheless, smuggling does have many of the outward signs of organized crime by the mid eighteenth century: a large number of participants; some degree of division of labour; an intelligence and informative system; and a sophisticated network for distributing the goods in question.

Other criminal activities manifested some of these characteristics. Although the only full-scale study of coining is focused a little later than the period with which we are concerned here,[43] it does portray what is in many ways organized crime. The subject awaits further study for earlier periods, but it is probable that in some regions at least coining was widespread and, on an informal basis at least, organized by the end of the seventeenth century. A Yorkshire diarist recorded how a debtor tried to restore his fortunes by turning king's evidence against a group of coiners in 1682. The local justices went to the building used by the coiners, 'a retired house in the country', and apprehended thirteen coin clippers 'at work in their drawers and shirts', along with £30–£40 of clipped silver and the criminals' tools. Investigations continued, and among those brought in were Foster and Woodworth, 'the two great masters in this faculty for making stamps in steel and iron or making moulds of all sorts of coin, clipping coining and melting down all sorts of metals'. These also turned king's evidence, and implicated about 140 further people living in Lancashire and Yorkshire.[44] The problem continued to be endemic in the north, and Palatinate of Lancaster records and Northern circuit assize depositions suggest that further research would reveal a network of coiners in the 1690s spreading from Derbyshire to Northumberland.[45]

Another group of criminals who depended on something like an organized network of contacts and who may have showed something like a 'professional' attitude to their delinquences were horse-thieves. People involved in the horse trade in early modern England seem to have displayed the standards of honesty and fair-dealing popularly attributed to used-car dealers in modern Britain. Many suspected horse-thieves were dealers in horses, or claimed to have got rid of the stolen animals without too many questions being asked. Hence Richard Evans, questioned about a horse-theft at Warwick in 1583, gave an account of trading all over the midlands, while John Stables, apprehended in Lancashire a century later, confessed to stealing a gelding, but then told how he simply rode it to Manchester and exchanged it for another.[46] The appearance or colouring of horses might be changed, the early modern equivalent of false number plates and a respray. A Bristol woman, apprehended in Gloucestershire in 1696, told how she had been encouraged to steal by William Lynch, who promised that 'if shee would keep his councill' he would teach her how to obliterate and change marks on horses.[47] Horse dealers were obviously viewed with suspicion. Two were taken by the Staffordshire bench early in the seventeenth century, and it was later learnt that they were of 'an ill name' for horse-theft in Derbyshire. The horses they had with them were examined, and found to be 'riffraffe horses not fitt for horsecoursers to traffic withall' which had probably been stolen 'out of some commons or forests far off'. One of the men was thought to be living unusually well in prison, and it is instructive that this was attributed to 'his fellowe horstealers which peradventure will not see him wante, for feare of disclosinge the brotherhood & fraternity that is amongst them'.[48] Such comments, and the evidence of depositions, suggest that horse-theft was an important aspect of organized crime.

The historian might well expect to find the highwayman at the most advanced level of organized crime in the country. The traditional image of the highwayman with its emphasis upon skilled and daring men carrying out well-planned criminal operations, together with the continuous governmental pronouncements about the existence of organized gangs of highwayman, would seem to support such a hypothesis. But even here we find that the level of organization was not high, specialisms were not exclusive, and criminal associations were often formed on an extremely casual basis. The point is well illustrated by the career of that most famous highwaymen of all, Dick Turpin.

Turpin was born in Essex, served out his apprenticeship as a butcher, married, and resettled in his native county. Unfortunately, he soon fell on hard times, and found himself 'reduced to the necessity of maintaining himself by indirect practices'. These consisted of a progress through the theft of sheep and cattle to association with smuggling gangs along the Essex coast, and thence to membership of a gang which carried out a number of burglaries and robberies in the area. Essex became too hot for Turpin, and he was forced to roam further abroad. While so doing he fell in with another highwayman, named King, with whom he carried out a number of successful crimes: that this liaison began when Turpin attempted to hold King up is indicative of the essentially loose organization which prevailed even among highwaymen. Eventually circumstances forced the team to split. Turpin decided to try his luck further north, and turned to stealing horses and trading them in Lincolnshire and the East Riding of Yorkshire. He fell foul of the authorities because of a minor breach of the peace, and while he was being held for investigation on that account suspicions of horse-theft were formed against him. He was held for trial, during which period evidence was adduced that he was the Essex robber Turpin. This clinched his fate, and he was eventually hanged at York in April 1739. His career is an instructive one. It illustrates the extreme geographical mobility of the professional criminal in this period, although his eventual fate also illustrates the mobility of information about criminals, even in a period when no central system of collecting such information existed. It also, moreover, illustrates the limitations of contemporary criminal professionalism and organization. Most of the criminal associations which Turpin was involved in were essentially short-term, while his career shows none of that specialization that is held to be one of the hallmarks of organized crime: after all, this most celebrated of English highwaymen went to the gallows on two charges of horse-theft.[49]

That Turpin's career, if not his notoriety, was not atypical is confirmed by the fullest study yet to appear of rural criminal organization, that provided by Alan Macfarlane's recent account of the activities of the gang headed by the Smorthwaite brothers.[50] The Smorthwaites and their confederates operated in Westmorland and the neighbouring counties in the 1680s, and constituted the nearest approximation to an organized group that Macfarlane was able to discover in his extensive work on the Northern circuit assize records of the period. Their misdeeds included a series of burglaries and highway robberies, while they were also involved with coiners and coin-clippers. Their offences, however, are once more suggestive of a criminality that was at best semi-organized. The crimes were normally planned, but membership of the gang, and the recruitment of accomplices, was usually on a very haphazard basis. There was, moreover, little attempt at specialization. As well as the offences already mentioned, the members of the gang also carried out pickpocketing and various thefts, normally of animals, often on an essentially opportunistic basis. It is difficult to accept such offenders as representatives of organized crime in the modern sense, or of anything which might be described as a 'criminal sub-culture'. It is undeniable, however, that there existed a network of people known to operate, on occasion at least, outside the law, and to whom support and assistance might be given, more or less casually, by like-minded persons.

It is striking that our discussion of such organized crime as existed has concentrated mainly on the male offender. Female crime, except for witchcraft, perhaps, is a subject which has so far attracted surprisingly little attention,[51] one facet of the regrettably undeveloped nature of the study of women's history in the early modern period. This is a pity, not least because (as with other aspects of women's history) scholarly studies are needed to redress some of the more extravagant absurdities perpetrated in the name of women's studies.[52] Early research has, however, indicated that, as in modern society, the more familiar offences were committed overwhelmingly by males. In Elizabethan Hertfordshire, for example, men formed 85 per cent of those accused of theft at the quarter sessions, and 86 per cent of those similarly accused at the assizes. Only 5 per cent of those accused of

fraud and other commercial offences were female. Females also constituted a minority of those accused of assault or murder, while their
victims tended to be drawn largely (in the case of homicide overwhelmingly) from within the domestic circle. Further analysis of theft
indictments demonstrates that women tended to be involved in the less
daring larcenies, usually stole goods of small value, often stole in
company, and generally showed less bravado and initiative in their
crimes, often merely acting as accomplices and decoys. Contemporary
expectations of female criminal behaviour throughout the early
modern period are neatly summed up by the reactions of a man who at
Romford in 1735 had the unusual experience of falling victim to a
female highway robber, 'a woman well mounted on a side saddle . . .
who presented a pistol and demanded his money'. His reaction was
evidently one of surprise: he recounted how 'he being amaz'd at her
behaviour told her, he did not understand what she wanted'.[53]

Such evidence demonstrates how study of crime can illustrate other
areas of human behaviour, for it shows how sex roles in early modern
England probably differed little from modern ones. As one student of
the subject has suggested, 'men and women in Elizabethan England
displayed clearly distinct modes of criminal behaviour, and . . . these
distinctions were similar to those observable between the sexes
today'.[54] Eighteenth-century evidence, while broadly supportive of
these observations, suggests a further level of complexity. Comparison
of the sex of those accused of crime in the rural and urban parts of
Surrey between 1660 and 1800, for example, shows that a higher
proportion of those accused of both property offences and crimes of
violence were female in the urban areas. It has been suggested that this
is explicable by the freer if more precarious life of women in cities,
compared to the countryside, which was more patriarchal, and which
enjoyed better cushioning against adversity, and more protection
against extreme disaster.[55] More evidence is required, and more needs
to be known about both changes over time and regional variations
before such hypotheses can be verified fully. It is nevertheless clear
that larceny, burglary, murder and assault in early modern England
were overwhelmingly male activities.

Some types of crime, on the other hand, were peculiarly female.
Only 23 of the 192 persons accused of witchcraft at the Essex assizes in
the period we are studying were male, and it is instructive that the most
potent 'criminal stereotype' of the period, that of the witch, should be
female.[56] Similarly scolding, an offence which has so far received
insufficient attention from historians, was a predominantly female
activity. Perhaps the most specifically female crime in our period,
however, was infanticide.[57] Men might be occasionally involved as
accomplices or accessories, but the overwhelming majority of those
accused and convicted of this offence were women. Indeed, many
aspects of infanticide were linked to the social position of women, and

of unmarried women from the lower orders in particular. The typical infanticidal mother was an unmarried servant girl, and her motives were usually a desire to avoid the shame and consequent loss of position which unmarried motherhood would bring. For such women, discovery of pregnancy or the arrival of a bastard would result in dismissal from service, probably without a character reference, and a life-long stigma which would probably ensure that future employment in any but the most demeaning of jobs would be unobtainable. The pressure upon them to do away with the child immediately after birth would be great, and they probably accounted for well over half of those accused of infanticide. The rise of infanticide in the second half of the sixteenth century, and its eighteenth-century decline which led to the repeal of the Jacobean statute in 1803, makes it, as we have commented, one of the distinctive offences of the period. The fact that it was an almost exclusively female crime underlines its importance both to the historian of crime and to those attempting to understand the position of women in early modern England.

Another distinctively female offence was prostitution. Again, little scholarly attention has been focused on this phenomenon in our period, and, as we shall see, most of what has been written, and most of the more accessible evidence, concerns London. Little is known about prostitution in provincial towns (indeed, English urban historians have been strangely reticent about the whole subject of crime), while only limited work has been carried out in rural prostitution. This latter suggests that prostitution, in the sense of a direct transaction involving the exchange of sexual intercourse for cash or other forms of payment, was very rare on any more than the most casual basis in the countryside. The fullest treatment of the subject, dealing with Somerset in the mid seventeenth century,[58] reveals a fair level of prostitution, but little of an organized nature. The typical rural prostitute was either a vagrant, wandering from parish to parish augmenting her income by soliciting *en route*, or the village whore operating from a particular inn or bawdy house. Such women might approach the status of the modern professional prostitute, and some of the inns or other houses they operated in must have been very similar to fully fledged brothels: the disorderly alehouse in Elizabethan Essex which was equipped with a drinking vessel in the shape of male genitals is certainly suggestive of this.[59] It seems likely, however, that most rural and small town prostitutes were part-timers, willing to supplement their income when occasion arose. Ann Morgan of Wells, for example, was obviously a regular prostitute. Her house was known to the watch, she had a sliding scale of fees, and was wont to call on the assistance of several of her female neighbours when she had more 'lewd company' than she could cope with alone. Even Morgan, however, was apparently given to certain forms of licit economic activity: on one occasion, it was reported, she attempted to negotiate a higher fee (18 pence) with a client on the grounds that he had 'hindered' her 'the knitting of half a hose'.[60]

In the countryside, therefore, apart from some smuggling and coining gangs, crime rarely reached more than a very casual level of organization, and professional criminals were few and far between. Most accounts would suggest that, throughout this period, a radically different situation obtained in London. So far, little work has been done on crime in urban centres outside the capital, and it is therefore difficult to say if other cities experienced forms of criminality which were different from those existing in their rural hinterlands. London, however, with a population rising from perhaps 400,000 in the mid seventeenth century to nearly a million by the late eighteenth[61] was generally held to offer unique opportunities for vice and crime. By the end of the early modern period, this opinion was a commonplace. The sheer mass of the population, it was felt, made control more difficult than in the country areas. The concentration of wealth gave the thief and burglar infinitely more targets, while the growth of London as a leisure centre made business for the owners of gambling houses and brothels. Above all, the size of the metropolis made for anonymity and concealment. To Henry Fielding, writing in 1751, it seemed that the cities of London and Wetminster and their suburbs, because of 'the great irregularity of their buildings, the immense number of lanes, alleys, courts and byplaces' could 'scarce have been better contrived' for 'the very purpose of concealment'.[62] In the early eighteenth century, a new problem joined the familiar ones: gin. Despite a suspicion that for many of the respectable the availability of cheap spirits provided a handy stock explanation for the destitution and depravity of the London poor, it is impossible to deny the adverse effects of that 'grand preservator of sloth, Jeneva, that infallible antidote against care and frugal reflexion'.[63]

It was the early eighteenth century, indeed, which really introduced the criminal entrepreneur into English history in the person of Jonathan Wild. As ever with such figures, it is difficult to separate legend from truth: nevertheless, Wild's reputation is most impressive. His early career reads like the prototype for contemporary criminal biographies. Born of honest parents in Wolverhampton in 1682, Wild served out his apprenticeship and began to trade as a buckle-maker. Circumstances prompted him to leave his wife and son, and go to seek his fortune in London. Initially, the search proved fruitless, and Wild found himself imprisoned for debt. During his incarceration he apparently made contact with members of the criminal underworld, and after his release set up as a brothel-keeper with an ex-prostitute that he had met in gaol. He found his true *métier*, however, when he set up as a receiver of stolen goods. From that point, according to both

111

legend and what can be pieced together of the historical record, his fortunes increased rapidly.

Wild persuaded thieves to bring stolen property to him, and, after the goods had been sold by Wild or his agents, the proceeds, minus a commission, were returned to them. After a short period the receiver made an important discovery: the original owners of stolen property were often willing to pay more for its recovery than a fence would be prepared to offer. The thieves with whom Wild was in contact were therefore encouraged only to rob persons they could identify, so that the victims could be contacted about the return of their stolen goods with a minimum of effort. Simultaneously, Wild began the practice which earned him considerable opprobrium, and became a thief-taker. Thieves operating outside his control or in opposition to him were informed against, and his competitors were thus removed via the gallows or the transport ship. According to some accounts his criminal activities became very sophisticated. Individual gangs of thieves were allocated to each of the roads coming in to the capital, while areas within the capital which were likely to afford rich pickings were likewise allocated to specific teams of malefactors. Warehouses were rented within which stolen goods were kept, watches and jewellery were altered by craftsmen hired for the purpose, and a sloop was purchased for the purpose of transporting to the continent spoils that could not be safely disposed of at home. Meanwhile Wild assumed an air of respectability, and even petitioned the Corporation of London in January 1724 in hopes of being recognized as a Freeman of the City as an acknowledgement of his services as a thief-taker. Needless to say, the law eventually caught up with him. Early in 1725 the captain of his sloop, one Johnson, was captured. Wild engineered a riot in the course of which Johnson made his escape, but Wild was captured and more serious charges were prepared against him while he languished in gaol. He was eventually hanged for receiving stolen goods, and his head and trunk were displayed as late as 1860, a grisly reminder of a remarkable career.[64]

Wild's career coincided with that of one of the first English criminals to acquire legendary status, Jack Sheppard. Once more it is difficult to disentangle myth from history when recounting Sheppard's story, but his exploits, whether true or not, would have been impossible in a milieu where a fairly sophisticated level of crime did not exist. Unlike so many of those who ended their days at Tyburn, Sheppard was a native Londoner, born at Stepney in 1702. His father, a Spitalfields carpenter, died when Sheppard was a year old, and the youngster experienced various early vicissitudes before being apprenticed to a carpenter. From that point, his career, like Wild's, assumed the character of a dreadful warning to potentially idle apprentices. He became slothful in his work, and fell into bad company at the Black Lion in Drury Lane, his most notable companion being a prostitute named Bess Lyon, alias 'Edgeworth Bess'. She and her associates lured Sheppard into thieving, and he was eventually captured. His incarceration in the St Giles's Roundhouse marked the first step on his road to fame, for Sheppard was best remembered in the popular mind for his daring escapes from prison. A little after breaking out of the Roundhouse, Sheppard was imprisoned again, this time in the New Prison. It was from this institution that he made his most remarkable escape, which involved breaking from his irons, cutting through a double grille of oaken and iron bars, descending 25 feet with the aid of a sheet and a blanket, and scaling a wall 22 feet high with a companion on his back. He resumed his life of theft and burglary, but crossed Wild at some point, and was turned in by the thief-taker. He promptly escaped, this time from Newgate, and resumed his old ways, being recaptured again by a posse of armed men headed by one of the turnkeys of the prison. Undeterred by being placed in what might be described as the maximum security area of Newgate, Sheppard broke out yet again. He was, however, recaptured a little later, having become incapably inebriated after drinking brandy with his mother. This time the authorities made no mistake, and Sheppard was executed at Tyburn, before (according to some accounts) a crowd numbering 200,000.[65]

The careers of Wild and Sheppard, despite being exaggerated by legend and tradition, do suggest that London, by the 1720s, was experiencing something like highly organized crime, much of it committed by professional criminals. Earlier evidence suggests that roughly the same situation obtained in the Elizabethan and Jacobean periods. Certainly, the popular literature of the period took it as axiomatic that London contained, along with so many other marks of sophistication, an organized body of thieves, prostitutes, cheats, coseners, and 'cony-catchers'.[66] Similarly, the legislation of the period often assumed that organized crime existed and was increasing: the Elizabethan statute against pickpockets, for example, was insistent that there was a number of trained pickpockets and cut-purses in the capital, carrying out crimes so daring as to include picking pockets at court.[67] Literary evidence and governmental fears are not the most infallible guides to reality: nevertheless, more reliable evidence survives which suggests that organized crime, in many ways a prefiguration of that which existed in Wild's day, was already well established in the capital by the late sixteenth century.

One of the most likely symptoms of the presence of organized crime, as the career of Wild suggests, is the existence of organized thieving and of the organized disposal of stolen goods. Eighteenth-century observers were aware of this. Henry Zouch expressed the opinion that 'in the metropolis particularly, robbery is actually become a science'; Henry Fielding claimed that London contained a body of rogues who had 'reduced theft and robbery into a regular system'.[68] Behind this 'system' of theft and robbery there lay the receivers of stolen goods. Fielding thought that 'one of the great encouragements to theft of all kinds is the ease and safety with which stolen goods may be disposed of', and a commentator in the 1720s remarked that 'the mischief that one man can do as a thief, is a very trifle to what he may be the occasion of, as an agent or concealer of felons'.[69] The earlier period may have left us no figure comparable to Wild, but the crime literature of the day often assumes the existence of receivers of stolen goods, while the printed calendars of Middlesex sessions records for the Jacobean period contain numerous references to prosecution for receiving such goods.[70] Occasional evidence also points to the existence of organized and professional thieves. One such piece of evidence dates from 1585. In that year, following what appears to have been an unusually active drive against crime by the London authorities, a remarkable report was sent to Lord Burghley. This not only listed a number of notorious thieves and forty-five 'habouringe howses' for criminals, but also described a school for pickpockets suggestive of the presence of an Elizabethan Fagin. 'One Wotton, a gentilman borne', the report ran, had 'procured all the cutpurses about this cittie to repair to his said howse. There was a schole howse sett upp to learne younge boyes to cutt purses.' Among the teaching aids at this unusual academy was a purse containing counters and money which was hung with bells. The youngsters were taught to take money out of the purse without sounding the bells, 'and he that could take a peece of sylver out of the purse without the noyse of any of the bells, he was adjudged a *judiciall Nypper*'. Such accounts do lend substance to literary evidence of the existence of an 'Elizabethan underworld'.[71]

Further substance is lent by the existence of another pointer to the presence of organized crime in general: organized prostitution. As we have seen, there is little evidence of more than casual prostitution in rural areas. In London, however, the brothel and the professional prostitute were long established. Most contemporary writers regarded it as axiomatic that organized vice was one of the major law-and-order problems in the capital. John Disney was just one of a host of commentators who complained of 'the impudent sollicitations of lewd women in our streets, the nests of bawdry that are known and settled in particular houses'.[72] By the 1690s, indeed, it was possible to read a monthly publication, John Dunton's *The Nightwalker*, which described prostitution in the capital in a style of social reportage which anticipated Mayhew. To Dunton, London was 'a second Sodom', and he considered that English morality and English liberty were endangered by 'that same unclean spirit, which prompted the false prophet Balaam to advise Balak to corrupt the manners of the Israelites, by sending his loose Midianitish women amongst them'. His publications provide a lively portrayal of prostitution in the capital, and, if accurate, do suggest a high degree of organization. Dunton described one madam who ran an establishment with girls at varied prices, and who also had a couple of unpleasant sidelines. On occasion, she would make her girls start a fight in the street, and then have pickpockets work the crowd that gathered to watch. She also 'drove a trade . . . of curing her guests if they were clapped', and any customers that feared infection could, on payment of a fee, have the prostitute of their choice searched for the signs of venereal disease before them. Some of his reported conversations with prostitutes have an almost timeless ring: one girl reported how she had drifted into prostitution at the age of sixteen, while being servant to a tradesman, since 'neither his wages nor way of living suited with my haughty mind, for I did very much admire finery in others, and was impatient to be as fine as they'.[73]

Perhaps the most remarkable account of prostitution in the capital, however, is contained in a pamphlet of 1608 commemorating the execution of Margaret Ferneseed, who was burnt for murdering her husband. Although she claimed to be innocent of the killing to the last, she confessed to having been a whore since puberty and to having run a brothel. Her recruiting methods were well planned. She kept close contact with carriers, so that she could 'make spoile of yong maidens who were sent out of the countrie by their friends, here with hope to advance themselves'. These girls were debauched, and put on the streets, each of them being compelled to give 'ten shillings a week out of their gettings' to Ferneseed. She also made use of discontented wives. She would note 'any breach or discontent' between likely women and their husbands, and would then persuade them that 'they were not beloved of their husbands', or that 'their husbands maintained them not sufficiently to expresse their beauty, and according to their owne deserts'. Once these women had prostituted themselves, Ferneseed ensured their continued service by a simple form of blackmail, threatening to expose them to their husbands if they refused to continue to accommodate her customers.[74] Other pamphlets of the period confirm the impression of organized prostitution based on established brothels, and of the dangers and inconveniences attendant on organized vice. In 1620, for example, Henry Goodcole, the first of the ordinaries of Newgate to publish accounts of the misdeeds of the prisoners passing through that institution, described the careers of a prostitute named Elizabeth Evans and her associate, Thomas Shearwood. This couple worked one of the most familiar crimes associated with prostitution. Evans would pick up drunks, and the couple would later murder and rob them. Shearwood in his confession gave information concerning 'many base persons of his condition, and the dispersed places of secret harbouring such unprofitable obnoxious members unto a state and commonwealth'. Goodcole rounded the lesson off by giving a list of places where those unfamiliar with the ways of the town were warned not to go.[75] Such evidence suggests that

London was a dangerous city, full of hardened criminals.

However, as with rural vagrancy, court records give a somewhat different impression of London criminals from that found in didactory pamphlets dealing with spectacular cases. Document survival obscures the problem for the first half of our period, although A. L. Beier's work in progress on the London Bridewell will doubtless add much to our knowledge of vagrancy and petty crime in the capital before the late seventeenth century. From about that time, however, extant records from the City of London, the City of Westminster, and urban Middlesex all combine to allow us to supplement our knowledge of the serious criminals condemned at Tyburn with insights into their less threatening counterparts. Many of them were petty delinquents not much different from those recorded in the archives of courts in rural areas or small towns. In the same decade as Wild was running his criminal empire, the Lord Mayor's court of the City of London was dealing with all sorts of minor delinquents: Richard Spileman, complained against by John French 'for being a loose disorderly person haveing no vizible way of liveing and comeing into his house and cheating him of victuals and drink'; a woman brought in 'for selling stinking mackerell'; a customer in an alehouse complained against by the landlord 'for endeavouring to defraud him of his reckoning after calling for liquor'; and an apprentice reported by his master 'for assaulting, beating and bruising him over his stomach'.[76]

Accusations of larceny suggest that even in an age when robbery was held to be becoming a 'science', the typical London thief was essentially opportunistic and interested in small-scale thieving. In the 1680s we find persons accused of 'pilfering of severall sugar loafs', or of 'pilfering a p[ar] cell of cotton wool out of cotton baggs'. In 1729 we find such examples as the 'loose disorderly app[rentice] suspected of pilfering three handkerchiefs', or the woman accused of 'pilfering a quartern loaf'.[77] Prostitutes, too, seem to have most typically operated on an amateurish and opportunistic basis. Doubtless, well-equipped brothels, catering for a variety of tastes, did exist: court records, however, suggest the existence of an underclass of unimpressive and possibly part-time prostitutes: Celia Lilly, apprehended in 1729 'for being a night walker & taken in the streets at an unseasonable time of night & picking up men'; Amy Prust, reported 'for walking the streets & picking up men at an unseasonable time of night'; and the two women apprehended 'for being disorderly persons & common night walkers & talking obscene discourse at unseasonable time of night'. It is difficult to see such figures as representatives of sophisticated and organized vice, and it is possibly significant that they were often discharged 'on promise of future amendment'.[78]

Those who did not receive such lenient treatment were most often sent to one of the numerous houses of correction in the metropolitan area. These institutions were obviously regarded as the proper means of combating a wide range of minor offences, and their archives constitute one of the great unworked sources for the criminal and social history of the capital. Many petty criminals were sentenced, as the City of London authorities put it in the 1680s, 'to bee set to hard labour & to receive the correction of the house',[79] and even the most cursory inspection of the relevant archival materials supports the contention that houses of correction in the capital, like those in the country, were actively used against such offenders. In January 1690, for example, the house of correction for the City of Westminster held 107 persons, of whom 36 were prostitutes, 15 pilferers, and 40 simply classified as idle and disorderly. In January 1710, the same institution held 82 people, among them 14 prostitutes, 8 vagrants, 34 petty thieves, and 20 idle disorderly persons.[80]

Such evidence of the extent and nature of petty crime in London suggests some important conclusions. It seems arguable that too much attention has been focused on criminal entrepreneurs, on the possibilities for the existence of organized crime in London, and on the serious and often daring criminals hanged at Tyburn. It is, of course, perfectly understandable that attention should be lavished on such subjects: they attract our interest, and, whatever arguments are put forward about the importance of petty crime, serious crime is a subject which demands serious attention. Nevertheless, it must be reiterated that the court records and house of correction calendars present a different image of the criminal from that given in such sources as *The Complete Newgate Calendar*. The runaway apprentices, small-time whores, pilferers and sneak-thieves, drunkards and cheats who appear in such sources come across as essentially pathetic figures, and as criminals who did not differ significantly from their rural counterparts. Such a conclusion makes any simplistic idea of London as a crucible of advanced, professional, organized criminality a little less easy to maintain. London was still essentially a pre-industrial town, and hence it is hardly surprising that its crime should correspond in many ways to that obtaining in the countryside. For every Johnathan Wild or Jack Sheppard there might well have been a thousand opportunistic pickpockets or shoplifters, concerned with immediate survival rather than running a criminal enterprise. Some of them might graduate to full-blown professional criminality: it is inherently probable that the majority did not. Even in the capital, the typical law-breaker, whether thief or prostitute, was essentially opportunistic in his or her approach and modest in his or her criminal ambitions.

In this chapter we have attempted to delineate the salient features of what was a very complex phenomenon. Here, as elsewhere in this book, we have tried to study a subject on a national level over two centuries, and it is only proper that we should be very tentative in any

117

conclusions we reach. As we have argued, there are many subjects within the orbit of those tackled in this chapter which need further research: gentry crime; female crime; organized crime in provincial towns. Not until more detailed work has been carried out on such topics as these will we be able to discuss the early modern criminal in more than very cautious terms. Nevertheless, it is possible to discern a few developments, of which the most important, perhaps, was the growing tendency for the authorities to define criminal and disorderly behaviour as the prerogative of the poor. Court records at the beginning of our period, for example those of the Court of Great Sessions at Chester in the reigns of Edward VI and Mary, or the Marian quarter sessions rolls for Essex, show that a fairly high proportion of those accused were described as gentlemen or yeoman, and that they were often involved in such old-style offences as forcible disseisin or riot.[81] By the mid eighteenth century, as materials from such disparate counties as Wiltshire, Surrey, and the East Riding of Yorkshire suggest, the main task of the forces of law and order was to combat the disorders of the poor.[82] Doubtless, despite the presence of the occasional gentry-led gang, the poor had provided most criminals in the late middle ages: certainly, work completed on fourteenth-century crime would support this view.[83] Even so, the interpretation which emphasizes the 'criminalization' of the poor in the sixteenth and seventeenth centuries has much to command it: there were simply more of them, and providing for them and controlling them became a major preoccupation of both central and local government.

Our discussion has suggested, however, that despite governmental fears and the warnings of sensational literature, there was little by way of organized or professional crime in our period. There was probably a comparatively high level of organized crime in London, although it is difficult to appraise it accurately through the distorting mirrors of popular literature and the penumbra of myth surrounding such figures as Johnathan Wild or Jack Sheppard. The presence of organized crime in the metropolitan area should not obscure the fact that the pathetic, small-time whore and the opportunistic pilferer were more typical, if more elusive, figures than the high-class madame or the criminal entrepreneur. In the countryside and small towns, the situation was only slightly less complex. There were, of course, types of crime which, by the eighteenth century at least, were highly organized: smuggling, poaching and coining, for example, although, as we shall discuss in the next chapter, there is a strong possibility that these activities flourished because of a widespread public feeling that they did not constitute 'real' crime. With offences which did not elicit such sympathy from the local populace, such criminal organization as existed was essentially casual. There was a permanent network of people on the wrong side of the law, but, as we have seen, even such notorious figures as Turpin would form their criminal associations in an essentially *ad hoc* manner.

Highwaymen, horse-thieves, and the hardened 'professional' vagrant rogue were often known to each other over surprisingly wide geographical distances, and seem to have been able to pick up local contacts fairly rapidly when they moved into a new area. Moreover, in certain areas at certain times organized gangs of highwaymen and horse-thieves might exist. But, as the career of the Smorthwaite gang suggests, organized crime outside London was rarely very sophisticated or permanent. Even in the extreme north, as the history of the Smorthwaites again demonstrates, there was, by the late seventeenth century, little sign of the banditry or vendettas celebrated in border ballads. Cattle-reivers and feuds across the borderlands might still have been a problem in the reign of Elizabeth,[84] but by the late seventeenth century criminal behaviour in the extreme north seems to have been well on the way to corresponding with that in the south. It is perhaps instructive that by 1700 the execution rate at the assizes in the northern counties of Westmorland, Northumberland and Cumberland was the same as that obtaining elsewhere, about 10 per cent of those accused of felony, indicating that no special law-and-order problem was felt to exist there.[85]

We must therefore conclude that there was little professional crime in our period and, equally, few traces of a 'criminal class' or a 'criminal subculture', at least outside the capital. Could it therefore be argued that committing crime was a normal part of the life experience of labourers and the poorer artisans? Edward Thompson has suggested that 'crime – in the sense of being on the wrong side of the law – was, for the vast numbers of undifferentiated working people, normal', and has also commented that those hanged at Tyburn as portrayed by the Ordinary of Newgate, were not members of a 'subculture' but rather representatives of 'the commonplace mundane culture of plebeian England . . . unremarkable people, distinguished from their fellows by little else except that fact that by bad luck or worse judgement they got caught up in the toils of the law'.[86] Moreover, if the labouring or artisanal poor constituted a 'dangerous class', even the briefest acquaintance with court archives suggests that they were more dangerous to each other than to anybody else. The poor stole from each other; they killed each other; and they raped each other. Such cases as that of the two East Riding farm labourers who in 1763 raped a girl after she refused half a crown to lie with them are difficult to fit in to any notion of a 'criminal sub-culture'.[87] Early modern observers, used to explaining crime in terms of mankind's innate depravity and sinfulness, would have had less trouble in fitting the incident into their own conceptual framework.

At the back of most current thinking on crime and criminals, in present-day England as in earlier periods, lurks the idea of the criminal as a menace to society. Preambles to statutes and the rogue pamphlets of the period accepted it as axiomatic that, 'out there' there existed groups of organized criminals who, if left unchecked by wholesome laws and an alert public opinion, would overturn all social values. Obviously, this could happen: Wild's career impeded the normal operation of justice in the capital, while the more recent careers of Al Capone and the Kray twins demonstrate how much progress has been made in such matters since the early eighteenth century. For the most part, whatever the damage to their individual victims, it would seem more sensible to regard the criminal as an irritant to honest people rather than a menace. Criminal entrepreneurs and organized gangs doubtless existed in our period. Their activities are sometimes well-documented, and some of the participants emerge as interesting figures. They were not, however, typical of the early modern criminal. More representative, to take a very pertinent example, were the two servant girls taken for theft at Doncaster in 1629, Elizabeth Robinson and Elizabeth Sharpe. In their depositions, Sharpe claimed that she had been led on by Robinson, who encouraged her to steal a few pence, and told her 'to saye if it weare knowne, that the said eight or nyne single pence were putt in this examinant's shooe by the ffairies'.[88] It is difficult to see such people as a threat to society.

Chapter 6

SOCIAL CRIME AND LEGITIMIZING NOTIONS

As was argued in the introduction to this book, one of the problems in studying crime in the past is the temptation to do so from the perspective of the bodies and social groups responsible for framing and implementing the criminal law. Three main reasons might be adduced for this: firstly, the predominance of the legal-historical approach, which has laid undue emphasis on the decisions of the legislature and the judiciary; secondly, the tendency to regard social history as somehow below the 'dignity of the historian'; and thirdly, the established view which sees English history in terms of a progressive evolution. The Whig interpretation, albeit in a diluted form, has died hard, and still informs many of the basic assumptions of history as it is taught to schoolchildren and undergraduates. Seen from such perspectives, crime, like so many aspects of the life of the poor, only becomes of interest when it constitutes a 'problem' for the country's rulers. Recently, however, some historians have attempted a rather different analysis of crime in the past, and have claimed that at least some forms of offence are best interpreted as rational and coherent actions arising from or justified by a set of attitudes different from those of officialdom. Whereas emphasis has previously been placed on legislation, or the machinery used to enforce it, recent research and recent re-thinking of the relevant issues has revealed the potentialities of what might be described as a 'history from below' approach to crime in the past. Once more, we are reminded of how court records provide unique insights into the mentalities, attitudes and aspirations of the lower orders of early modern England.

This approach to the subject is, sadly, as fraught with problems as any other. In one sense, it might be argued, any criminal committing a criminal act demonstrates that his attitudes to law and order are different from those of the legislature and the forces of law enforcement. Moreover, analysis of crime in any reasonably developed society might lead the Marxist or radical scholar to conclude that all crime might be interpreted either as the product of a system based on

121

inequalities of wealth and power, or as a revolt against that system. Hence the thief steals to alter the distribution of property in his society, the murderer kills because the society in which he lives has blunted his sensibilities over such matters, and the rapist rapes because he has been brought up in a world which emphasizes male dominance and insists on its periodical assertion. Such ideas are stimulating, but the current level of research on the history of crime suggests that it would be dangerous to attempt to apply them too crudely to past criminality. They are, perhaps, best left to modern criminologists who have both a sufficiently developed conceptual framework and enough empirical evidence to sustain a debate on such matters. In any case, our immediate concern is with other problems.

The crucial difference between the offences with which we shall deal in this chapter and the generality of crime depends on the extent to which the perpetrator of the offence felt that what he was doing was not wrong, and the extent to which his views were a reflection of widely-held values. Again, we must acknowledge the possibility that most criminals could find justifications for what they do. Property offenders, for example, might justify or excuse their actions by reference to the general corruption of the world of business and commerce, and pamphlet evidence suggests that they were already doing so in Elizabethan London.[1] There is, after all, a tradition that Al Capone once said 'I'm just a businessman.' Despite such spurious claims, the historian of crime must confront the problem that several forms of conduct classified as criminal by the courts and the statute book were regarded as legal, or at least justifiable on quasi-legal grounds, by large sections of the population at large: on occasion, indeed, popular attitudes might even have encouraged such conduct. The objectives and morality of legislation were not invariably shared by those subjected to it, and many practices which the statute book declared illegal were considered legitimate in at least some circles.

Awareness of the existence of popular notions of legality and legitimacy, at odds with those of officialdom, has given rise to the concept of 'social crime'. Crime, according to the classic formulation of this concept, can be regarded as 'social' when it represents 'a conscious, almost a political, challenge to the prevailing social and political order and its values'. It occurs when there exist conflicting sets of official and unofficial interpretations of the legal system, when acts of law-breaking contain clear elements of social protest, or when such acts are firmly connected to the development of social and political unrest.[2] The idea of social crime is an exciting one, not least because it can be used as the starting-point for the construction of a different perspective on the history of crime. In positing a distinction between the 'good' social criminal and the 'bad' normal criminal it seems to allow for a more subtle analysis of the actions of at least some offenders and to provide a conceptual tool for understanding the reactions of the populace to at least some forms of law-breaking. It has also led some historians to regard certain types of illegal activity as being morally different from others. Hence we find a group of writers, themselves interested primarily in social crime, warning against too easy a division between ' "good" criminals, who are premature revolutionaries or reformers, forerunners of popular movements – all kinds of rioters, smugglers, poachers, primitive rebels in industry', as distinct from 'those who commit crime without qualification: thieves, robbers, highwaymen, forgers, arsonists and murderers'.[3]

Even so, this is the distinction which must be made if the concept of social crime is to be sustained. The problems are numerous, not least because, as one commentator has remarked, even if the social and normal criminal can be distinguished, there is every possibility that they inhabited a common culture, 'that of the exploited labouring poor'.[4]Nevertheless, occasional comments from those living within that culture do suggest the existence of interpretations of the law different from official ones. In 1735, for example, a Gloucestershire turnpike rioter awaiting execution declared that 'he had never committed any theft nor murder nor done any crime in his life . . . and did not think that crime [i.e. turnpike cutting] had been of so heanious a nature as to bring him to that unhappy end'.[5] Less dramatically, it is possible to find occasional comments from the lower orders about other offences, notably poaching,[6] which suggest that they held different opinions about at least some areas of the law from those current among their rulers. The problem remains of ascertaining how typical such views were, to what extent they reflected the long-term thinking of individuals, and how widely held they were among the populace at large: in short, how far they were indicative of a 'culture' in which are embedded coherent views on the legality or illegality of certain forms of conduct.

Much of the argument about the existence of such views, and hence about the validity of the concept of social crime, revolves around attitudes to property. Poaching is perhaps the most familiar aspect of this problem, but there were others of equal contemporary importance which reflected popular attitudes. Gleaning, for example, played a vital part in the economy of the poor, and the poor's assertion of what they considered their customary right to glean sometimes led to disputes as the onward march of agrarian capitalism led landowners and farmers to oppose these rights. Scattered evidence from Hertfordshire and Essex in the early Stuart period, showing the poor justifying gleaning by appeal to custom,[7] could probably be matched by evidence from other regions. Divergent views on the nature of, and on rights of access to property, can be found elsewhere. Numerous disputes arose over rights to gather firewood, a commodity secondary only to food in its importance to the rural poor. In some areas it is possible to trace a long history of tension over wood-rights. In the forest of Grovely in

Wiltshire, to take one well-documented case, charters of 1597 and 1603 confirmed the rights of the inhabitants of Wishford Magna and Barford St. Martin to gather 'all kinds of dead snapping wood, boughs and sticks', according to an 'old custom' that 'time out of mind hath been'. The later history of the area was to provide numerous examples of the customary rights reaffirmed to these charters coming into conflict with the pretensions of the local landlords, the Earls of Pembroke.[8] In many areas gathering firewood, like gleaning, was a custom which was redefined as crime.

While such redefinition of property rights was engendering friction in the agrarian world, essentially similar processes were causing essentially similar problems to industrial production, both rural and urban. In many trades, workers benefited from traditional perquisites which were basically analogous to the rural worker's traditional rights to glean or gather firewood. Certainly, entrepreneurs in those industries dependent upon the putting-out system had long been concerned with the embezzlement of materials by workers to whom they had been entrusted for processing, and as early as 1609 a statute had been passed against abuses of this kind in the wool trade.[9] The virtual impossibility of supervising workers before the advent of the factory meant that the taking of 'perks' was endemic in many trades, and some workmen, notably miners and shipyard workers, became notorious for the amount of material they took from their workplaces. The eighteenth century witnessed increased tension over such matters in a number of industries, and concomitant legislation, notably an Act of 1749.[10] It is difficult to see how great a change such legislation made in reality, not least because a number of the practices criminalized by the new statutes might simply have been previously dealt with by summary conviction before a magistrate. The whole subject is one which obviously awaits detailed study, but it is difficult not to interpret the eighteenth-century legislation as symptomatic of a wide concern to erode traditional perquisites. By the end of that century, embezzlement from the workplace was thought of as a major evil: the police reformer and stipendary magistrate Patrick Colquhoun, indeed, went so far as to suggest that perquisites should be abolished from royal dock yards and similar governmental institutions, and the workforce compensated for this loss of privilege by increased wages.[11]

There would seem, therefore, to be scattered but telling evidence that something like social crime did exist, not least in terms of differing attitudes between the populace and their rulers and employers over the illegality of some practices. Unfortunately, evidence on such matters is scattered, and work on a number of aspects of the problem is at a very early stage. Two types of offence, both of them very germane to the topic under consideration have, however, received considerable attention: poaching and rioting. The first of these was early singled out as a form of social crime, since it was 'often justified on the grounds that no private property in wild animals can legitimately exist'.[12] The second is becoming recognized as one of the distinctive forms of action by the lower orders in pre-industrial society. Arguably, therefore, if evidence of social crime, and on popular ideas of legitimacy, is to be found anywhere, it will be through examining these two offences.

The English game laws were, by the end of the period we are concerned with, a tangled mass of confused and often contradictory legislation.[13] They consisted of a series of statutes, the earliest of which dated from the fourteenth century. Even when superseded, these statutes were rarely repealed, while their wording and exact meaning were often obscure. Early eighteenth-century observers were fully aware of this legislative labyrinth. That fictitious repository of squirely virtues, Sir Roger de Coverley, provided evidence of his 'great abilities' as a justice of the peace when he 'gain'd universal applause by explaining a passage in the game Act'.[14] On a more austere level, we find Blackstone himself very critical of the game laws. Poaching, he wrote, was covered by

> a variety of acts of parliament, which are so numerous and so confused, and the crime itself of so questionable a nature, that I shall not detain the reader with many observations thereupon . . . the statutes for preserving the game are many and various, and not a little obscure and intricate; it being remarked that in one statute only, 5 Ann c. 14, there is false grammar in no fewer than six places, besides other mistakes.[15]

The present writer shares Blackstone's unwillingness to burden his readers with a detailed list of the laws in protection of game. Perhaps the best introduciton to the problem might be provided by an examination of the Game Act of 1671,[16] which summarized the existing situation and set out the framework within which the game laws operated until 1831.

By the provisions of this Act the taking of game was prohibited to persons who did not fall into one of four categories: firstly, those who held freeholds worth at least £100 a year; secondly, those who had leaseholds 'of ninety-nine years or for any longer term', worth at least £150 a year; thirdly, those who were 'son and heir apparent of an Esquire, or other person of higher degree'; and, fourthly, the owners of franchises, as far as their liberties extended. Thus the act, in effect, restricted the right to hunt game to persons holding landed wealth; in its way, it was as much a symbol of the ascendancy of the aristocracy and gentry as was the Glorious Revolution of 1688. Moreover, the 1671 Act did not limit the qualified person's right to take game merely to that found on his own land: if he hunted elsewhere he might be sued for trespass, but this was hardly an effective deterrent. The qualified person could, therefore, for most practical purposes hunt where he wished, while the unqualified could not even take game on his own land. The end product of this legislation was that the game of England was regarded, in a sense, as the common property of the gentry of England, and the gentry became almost fanatical in their desire to preserve their privilege to hunt it from other social groups. As Blackstone remarked sourly, poaching was 'an offence which the sportsmen of England seem to think of the highest importance; and a matter, perhaps the only one, of general and national concern'.[17]

Whatever the complications of the game laws, and however obscure certain of their clauses, their overall intent had been clear from their inception. The original Game Act of 1389 set the tone for the future by declaring that 'no manner of artificer, labourer, nor any other layman, which hath not lands or tenements to the value of x 1s [40s] by year' should be allowed to either keep hunting dogs nor own any other animals or equipment that would allow them 'to take or destroy deer, hares, nor conies, nor other gentleman's game'.[18] Later legislation continued in this vein: the right to hunt game belonged essentially to the men of landed property, not to artificers and labourers. In time, indeed, it became a commonplace that the game laws, however tangled and however unjust, at least constituted a handy means of deterring idleness and other evil courses among the lower orders. Bacon argued that the game laws were there 'to prevent persons of inferior rank, from squandering that time, which their station in life requireth to be more profitably employed'.[19] Similarly Blackstone, when considering poaching, wrote that 'the only rational footing, upon which we can consider it a crime, is that in low and indigent persons it promotes idleness, and takes them away from their proper employments and callings; which is an offence against the public police and economy'.[20] The leisured class must have its sport: to allow the labouring poor similar leisure was a manifest absurdity.

Unfortunately, the poor did not share their betters' views on the landed orders' exclusive right to hunt game. The small landholder and tenant farmer ignored the prohibition on taking game on the land they owned or rented, while the rural labourer saw no harm in taking the odd rabbit or pheasant for the pot. This defiance of what was an unjust law is central to the poacher's claim for candidacy as a social criminal: he did not merely break the law, but in doing so he asserted a set of attitudes to at least one form of property which was at variance with that of his social superiors. The thief, even if driven by necessity, usually broke the law in a way which he and those sharing his culture knew to be illegal. The poacher, on the other hand, could claim that he was merely exercising his right over a type of property which ought to have been common to all men: indeed, the poacher with a smattering of biblical knowledge could have buttressed his position by pointing out that Genesis declared that animals had been created for the use of mankind in general. The point was summed up neatly in 1816, by which time the game laws were attracting considerable criticism from many quarters, not the least of them the owners of commercial and industrial wealth. Game, it was declared,

> is viewed with peculiar jealousy, both by those who are precluded from taking it, and those to whom its enjoyment is secured. The former consider it as a common right of which they are unjustly deprived; the latter as more sacred than any other class of property, on account, not only of its intrinsic value, but the amusement it affords them.[21]

Such analyses have led many historians to see poaching as a uniquely important key to tensions in the countryside: Douglas Hay, for example, has claimed that 'the game laws cast a flood of light on class conflict in many parts of rural England'.[22]

Certainly Hay's work on poaching and the game laws of the estates of the Earls of Uxbridge at Cannock Chase, Staffordshire, suggests that poaching in this area at least showed all the characteristics of social crime. The poor poached game with some notion of a common right to such property in their heads. Indeed, it is no accident that Hay's description of the endemic poaching on the Chase should culminate in a description of a riot in 1753 in which the local commoners, headed by the more prosperous of their number, spent two weeks pillaging Uxbridge's rabbit warrens. This sense of their rights gave the commoners a feeling of solidarity and an idea of shared values within which poachers were often tolerated. Gamekeepers were generally hated, and informers hardly less so, while at least some villagers near the Chase were willing to swear false witness in defence of those on trial for infringements of the game laws. Above all, the poaching described by Hay would have been meaningless outside the context of an overwhelmingly unjust social system which the laws on poaching both reflected and reinforced. The game laws were manifestly unfair (or, in eighteenth-century parlance, 'irrational') in a sense that laws against (for example) rape and murder obviously were not. At first glance, poor people breaking such laws, and hence defying the ascendancy of a peculiarly unappealing set of rich people, the English landed orders, deserve a good deal of sympathy, perhaps even some admiration.

Hay's portrayal of poaching is, therefore, very persuasive. It does not, however, completely assuage the doubts that linger over treating poaching, *all* poaching, as social crime throughout the whole of the period 1550–1750. The initial problem is, of course, to determine whether the characteristics delineated so expertly by Hay in one area around 1750 were equally prevalent in other regions enjoying a high level of poaching in earlier periods. Certainly, surviving Elizabethan and early Stuart records provide numerous, if scattered, examples of figures who would have felt very much at home among Uxbridge's tenants on Cannock Chase. In Worcestershire, for example, a steady trickle of countrymen were indicted between 1591 and 1643 for minor infringements of the game laws: keeping a greyhound and coursing hares, hunting with a hawk or dog, using setting nets called 'hayes' to take hares, or shooting at partidges.[23] Records for Elizabethan Essex portray much the same situation, as well as rare evidence of an early example of the persistent poacher. In 1598 Francis Harvey JP complained to the county bench of the depredations of the incorrigible poacher, Edward Tunbridge. 'He hath for more than twenty years continually', wrote Harvey, 'abused me and others, and yet doth, in stealing my conies, robbing my fishponds, and taking my partridges and pheasants.' As a consequence of the activities of Tunbridge and his accomplices, the justice continued, 'my conies are stolen so that I have not any served in my house, my ponds which I stored for provision of my house are robbed, most of my partridges and especially in the ground near his house are taken this year, and pheasants he hath not left any'.[24] Tunbridge's record, even if some allowance is made for hyperbole on the part of the offended gentleman, is impressive: the problem is to assess how far he and his confederates thought that they were indulging in social crime, for the opinions of the poachers themselves are only rarely recorded in this early period. When, for example, an Essex tanner declared in 1580 that he leased the land which he was accused of taking game on, 'wherefore he thought he might have lawfully done it, and so intends to do so still', we recognize that note of defiance which was so familiar to the eighteenth-century gamekeeper: such outbursts are, however, all too infrequently noted.[25]

Regrets about the rarity with which the views of poachers are recorded introduces another obstruction to our full understanding of the operation of the game laws: a lack of relevant court evidence. From an early date, poaching and related offences might be dealt with by summary conviction, records of which rarely survive before the late eighteenth century.[26] Indictment of a poacher at the assizes or quarter sessions could be an expensive and troublesome business, and it is therefore hardly surprising that infringements of the game laws were very infrequently prosecuted at these courts. At the Worcestershire quarter sessions, for example, less than 2 per cent of indictments from the late Elizabethan and early Stuart periods involved infringements of the game laws.[27] This was obviously an under representation of the frequency of the offence: poachers might also be dealt with by summary conviction, by binding over, or in the manorial courts, where poachers were still occasionally made the subject of presentment in the late sixteenth century. Evidence from the eighteenth century suggests that summary convictions of poachers could be very numerous. Douglas Hay calculates that the eighty poaching prosecutions brought by the Earl of Uxbridge between 1750 and 1765 were fifteen times more numerous than indictments of theft tried at the assizes and quarter sessions in the same period originating from the three relevant parishes.[28] But it is Hay's work which demonstrates the very limitation of legal records: his reconstruction of the poaching on Cannock Chase is founded on an unusually rich collection of estate papers. Court archives, in the absence of records of summary convictions, are much less useful for studying poaching in our period, while (despite some notable exceptions) the relevant type of estate record becomes rarer the further back in time the historian seeks it.

Despite such weaknesses, surviving court records, as well as other evidence, provoke a number of reservations about any simplistic equation of poaching and social crime. Firstly, although it is possible to accept the labourer or poor artisan poaching for his immediate needs as a social criminal, it is more difficult to apply this label to members of organized gangs of poachers. Such gangs were in operation from the beginning of our period, their most favoured target being deer parks. Enclosed animals were, of course, less obviously a form of common property than game in the more general sense of the word, and, legally, by the eighteenth century constituted something akin to ordinary private property.[29] Such legal niceties, however, were probably of little import to offenders. All sessions records from Elizabeth's reign contain references to nocturnal raids on deer parks, and these in many respects prefigured incidents in the 'poaching wars' of the late eighteenth century. Secondly, the deer-stealers, like the later poachers, were often well-organized. A report on an Essex gang in 1595 described them as 'a company consociate together for such ill purposes, having had now of late (and whether of long time before or not we know not) a very suspicious resort . . . in such sort as the neighbours of late became very fearful lest they would attempt robbery or some other violence'. The local landowners, it was feared, had been 'greatly abused this year by these ill-disposed companions and their confederates'.[30] Thirdly, violence between the landlord's keepers, warreners, and other servants on the one hand and gangs of poachers on the other was already present in the Elizabethan period, although this violence was, perhaps, neither as frequent nor as bitter as it was to become in the second half of the eighteenth century. In this latter period, the high profits to be derived from commercial poaching, and the more severe penalties imposed by the 1671 Act and later legislation gave the members of poaching gangs every incentive to fight their way out of trouble: as professor Munsche has put it, 'violence was part of their *trade*: they depended on it, more than on silence or skill, to protect them from capture'.[31] Things may have been less desperate at earlier periods, but there is evidence enough of violence between poachers and keepers. In Essex in the 1590s, for example, we find deer-stealers wounding a keeper with a bill and setting mastiffs on him, or setting on the keeper's men and wounding them 'very sore'.[32]

The mere existence of group poaching should not, necessarily, automatically disqualify poaching from the status of social crime:

indeed, given Tudor criticisms of the dire social consequences of emparkment for raising deer or conies, contemporary attacks on deer parks would seem to confirm that it should be so regarded. Two factors, especially relevant to group poaching, must, however, modify such a conclusion. The first of these is the continual involvement of the more affluent members of rural society in poaching. In the Elizabethan period, gentry were often accused of leading poaching expeditions (one group of nocturnal poachers were described in a contemporary deposition as 'gentlemen's sons of worship, the most part of them'[33]), while the yeomanry also figured frequently on indictments and other court records dealing with poaching. By the eighteenth century, gentry-led raids on deer parks were no longer common, yet more evidence, perhaps, of the spread of decorous conduct among the landed orders. Nevertheless, Hay tells us that of those poachers caught by Uxbridge's keepers about which we have occupational information, 15 per cent were qualified sportsmen, doubtless hoping for 'the customary indulgence extended to gentlemen sporting on others' property'.[34] Gentlemen poachers figures less prominently in indictments in the eighteenth century than they did in the sixteenth, whether through this 'customary indulgence' or because it might have been thought that a civil suit was a more appropriate method of dealing with the well-bred poacher than a criminal trial.[35] Even so, it is evident that the gentry and substantial farmers poached throughout our period, and this participation of social groups other than the rural poor means that we must be very cautious when describing poaching as a type of social crime.

Secondly, poaching's candidacy for inclusion as a social crime is seriously undermined when it is realized that a large amount of game was taken, not to ensure the immediate subsistence of the rural poor, but rather to supply a large black market in game.[36] From the reign of James I onwards, legislation ensured that the game trade existed in a 'legal twilight'. Making the game trade illegal in a period when game was a welcome sight on the dinner tables of fashionable townsfolk had an all too predictable result: not only would the poacher be able to find somebody willing to buy game from him, but the purchaser would often encourage the poacher to take yet more. This growth in poaching as a commercial proposition, and the concomitant intensification on the part of the qualified to preserve game which was ever more at risk, was largely responsible for the bitterness and violence which surrounded poaching in the late eighteenth century. Legislation did its best to circumscribe the trade: in 1707, for example, an Act forbade every 'higler, chapman, carrier, innkeeper, victualler and alehouse-keeper' from buying, selling or possessing game under penalty of heavy fines or three months imprisonment.[37] This, and subsequent, legislation proved ineffective, and the trade continued to grow. Rising population in the late eighteenth century, and the more sophisticated dietary expectations of the urban well-to-do, doubtless encouraged the development of the commercialization of poaching, but the phenomenon was hardly a new one. Middlesex sessions records of the Jacobean period suggest that there was already a lively trade in game between the capital and its rural hinterland in the early seventeenth century, while at about the same time the Privy Council was showing concern over the movement of poached game from the home counties to the capital.[38] A case from one of these counties suggests that commercial poaching already existed at the very beginning of our period: the gang of three or four men, led by a persistent offender called Edward Chevely alias Lacye, who took 896 rabbits in the course of six raids in south-eastern Essex during the winter of 1563/4, make very unconvincing subsistence poachers.[39]

It is, therefore, rather more difficult to consider poaching as a form of social crime than might at first sight appear. Justified indignation at the game laws, as well as one or two nineteenth-century biographies by poachers whose instinctive political radicalism would put them into the category of social criminal[40] have tended to distort our views on the reality of poaching in the two centuries before 1750. As we have argued, it was, from the start of this period, a category of crime in which almost all social groups participated, and it is difficult to see much evidence of conscious, almost political challenges to the prevailing social and political order in 'gentlemen's sons of worship' poaching in Elizabethan Essex. Also, the development of a commercial rationale for poaching makes it equally difficult to see the poacher as rejecting current notions on property. Without doubt many of the poor did poach for the pot, and, as we have seen, as far back as the reign of Elizabeth they could justify their so doing in terms of interpretations of their right to hunt game rivalling those enshrined in the game laws. This was not, however, the whole story, and poaching was evidently a very complex social phenomenon. Nevertheless, despite an initial sympathy with the notion of poaching as a form of social crime, we must finally agree with the conclusion of the writer of the most recent serious monograph on the subject: 'there is little evidence to support the traditional image of starving peasants snaring game in order to keep body and soul together'.[41]

Few general historians, given the evident iniquity of the game laws, have been other than sympathetic to the poacher. The same cannot be said of the treatment that mainstream history has generally given to the rioter and the urban mob. Historians of eighteenth-century England, confronted by the unusual ferocity of the Gordon Riots of 1780, have been especially prone to treat the riots of their period with some sort of intellectual reflex action rather than subject them to serious historical analysis. Hence J. H. Plumb commented that 'violence, born of despair, and greed, belonged to the poor alone . . . burning, looting, and destruction by the mob were commonplaces of life'. Sir Charles Petrie, in describing the early eighteenth century, could refer to 'the mob of the capital, composed of beings so degraded as to scarcely deserve the appellation of human'. On a more popular level, Christopher Hibbert informs his readers that at about the same time 'the reasons for riot were of little concern to the mob, which joined in for the fun or the looting, the chances of free drink or free women, or perhaps free food for starving families'.[42] Such opinions, which could be multiplied, fit neatly enough into that interpretation of the Hanoverian poor which is standard in the textbooks: numbed by drink and brutalized by harsh conditions and a low life expectancy, it is little wonder that they should break out into acts of irrational, mindless violence. That previous historians of the sixteenth and seventeenth centuries have not been given to expressing similar opinions is probably due to their not having been aware that riot was endemic in the periods they studied: had they been so, they would have presumably voiced sentiments identical to those of their colleagues working on the eighteenth.

Such an unsophisticated (not to say disobliging) view of the attitudes, aspirations and abilities of the early modern rioter is no longer tenable among serious historians. Scholarly treatment of the subject is one of the more fruitful aspects of that revolution in social history which has taken place over the last two decades or so. Previously, even historians sympathetic to the lower orders in the past were constrained by what might be described as the Whig interpretation of labour history: briefly, this has been affected by the modern notion that popular involvement in the political life of the nation is only comprehensible in terms of recognizable institutions, such as the labour party and the trades unions. Once the common people come together in sensible institutions of this sort, the historian can begin to treat them seriously, as they have obviously achieved political maturity in the terms he understands. This tendency has received scathing criticism from E. P. Thompson, who attacks the view which argues that

> the common people can scarcely be taken as historical agents before the French Revolution. Before this period they intrude occasionally and spas-modically upon the historical canvas, in periods of sudden social disturbance. These intrusions are compulsive, rather than self-conscious or self-activating: they are simple responses to economic stimuli. It is sufficient to mention a bad harvest or a down-turn in trade, and all requirements of historical explanation are satisfied.[43]

As the researches of Thompson and others have demonstrated, the actions of rioters were directed neither by that combination of gin and lust for plunder diagnosed by popular historians of the eighteenth century, nor by the response to outside stimuli which is seen as crucial by those who would attempt to explain the actions of the early modern poor in terms of some crass economic determinism. Rather, the actions of the crowd were probably most often directed by a cultural awareness of the forms of behaviour appropriate to popular disturbance, and by what Thompson has described as a 'legitimizing notion'. 'By the notion of legitimation', he tells us, 'I mean that the men and women in the crowd were defending traditional rights and customs; and, in general, that they were supported by the wider consensus of the community.'[44] We are reminded of the discussion of social crime: the idea that certain actions, although against the law, are legitimate when placed in the context of a set of values different from those of the lawmakers. The concept of the legitimizing notion, therefore, would seem to furnish us with a useful means of understanding a phenomenon which many historians have either ignored or written off as either senseless or beyond comprehension.

This previous neglect of riot and popular disturbance certainly cannot be attributed to lack of examples of the phenomenon. Evidence is, of course, very scattered, certainly before the Home Office papers of the eighteenth century, and such details of incidents as do survive, particularly from the first two-thirds of our period, are often very limited. Nevertheless, work completed and in progress has already suggested that rioting was an endemic feature of English life in the early modern era.[45] These disturbances continue, however, to provide several difficulties of analysis and typology. Under English law, riot occurred when three people gathered and broke the peace, or gathered with the intention of so doing. The term was, therefore, a very imprecise one, and many of the indictments for riot which survive in the assize or quarter sessions records of the period arose simply from group assaults. Other incidents were, obviously enough, much more serious affairs. The period we are discussing follows the massive risings of 1549, the most serious disturbances which England had experienced since 1381, and arguably the last of the medieval 'peasant' risings to occur in this country. The dimensions of the events of that year are staggering. Two complete regions, the West Country and East Anglia, passed under rebel control, while smaller risings, some of them abortive, were reported from Yorkshire in the north to Sussex in the south.[46] Nothing as serious as this was experienced again during the period 1550–1750, although some lesser regional risings must have seemed troublesome enough at the time. In the early seventeenth century, for example, parts of the Midlands experienced several years of rioting against enclosure, while the fenland to the east was the scene of a similar degree of unrest as local society attempted to defend its customary privileges against improvers.[47] The outbreak of the Civil War was likewise accompanied by continual rioting. In the capital, pro-puritan mobs appeared periodically, often at moments of peculiar political stress, while numerous disturbances broke out in provincial

133

towns and in the countryside. So serious were these disturbances, indeed, that it seems that they may have been responsible for driving many members of the political nation back into Charles I's camp: the many-headed monster seemed to offer a greater threat to the privileges of the possessing classes than did the monarch.[48]

These large-scale incidents are familiar enough, and some of them, notably the rebellions of 1549, have allowed the common people to enter the arena of mainstream history. Recent research, however, has demonstrated that there also existed an undercurrent of small-scale rioting, often affecting no more than a village or two, and often of little more than a day's duration. Enclosure riots, sometimes conducted in conjunction with attempts to seek redress against landlords by the more legal means of petitioning or litigation, occurred spasmodically in the late sixteenth and early seventeenth centuries. By the time of the Civil Wars enclosure riots were becoming less frequent, but changing socio-economic conditions in the countryside, together with the growth of towns, produced a rise in the number of grain riots. The poor of town and country alike showed a willingness to riot in times of dearth, and in bad years reports regularly reached the central government of popular action to stop movement of grain, and to impose traditional ideas about the just price of grain in the market-place. Taxation was less of a problem before 1660 than it was in most of the large continental states, and it is probably this which helps explain why the country did not experience the levels of rioting and the atrocities which afflicted France in the 1630s and 1640s.[49] The imposition of the excise in the Interregnum provoked some disturbances, as did the hearth tax after the Restoration. Popular opposition to this latter tax was very marked: initial attempts to collect it through the parish constables proved unworkable, and the subsequent decision to farm it out did not end opposition: indeed, a number of collectors were killed by mobs.[50] Another distinctive form of rioting was that involving industrial workforces. What would now be described as demonstrations or strikes were often described as riots in the early modern period, and studying these disturbances affords unique insights into contemporary perceptions of class conflict and class consciousness. The riot, therefore, was a common phenomenon, as characteristic of the pre-industrial world as the strike is of our own, and usually not much more threatening.

Obviously, something as frequent and as variegated as the riot, and something which would seem to offer so many insights into popular mentality, is worth serious analysis. Unhappily, such an analysis is very difficult for our period. Records of rioting are scattered throughout many courts: Star Chamber, King's Bench, assizes and quarter sessions, borough sessions, and are also to be found in central government archives and in such records of the sittings of special commissions of oyer and terminer as survive.[51] This, and the problematic nature of much of the evidence, makes it very difficult to attempt a statistical study of rioting before 1750. Such records as do exist manage to provide fascinating insights into popular consciousness and into the capacity of the common people to mobilize in defence of what they considered to be their interests.

Often the statements of the crowd in these disturbances carried an overtone of defiance which betokened (given that we are dealing with a pre-industrial society) what might be termed a 'pre-class' consciousness. In 1675, to take one of many examples, the apprentices of Sheffield rioted when new measures for grain were introduced in the market-place. A remarkable document was attached to the constable's evidence concerning the affair. It is worth quoting in full.

> This is to give notice to all apprentices for to come in a Tuesday next for to break all ye pecks yt sells oat meal by strike, w[hi]ch is not according to ye law. Ye gentlemen, & such as is called ye head men of ye towne are much to blame about it yt have not sought for to have it righted. If it had been for yere advantage, as 'tis for ye disadvantage of ye poor, they would have sought to have had it righted before now. But ye wild Asse, is still ye lyons prey, soe doth ye rich feed on ye poore each day.
> For wee will not have it told for shame, if we will be daunted w[i]th 3 or 4 rusty halbards & ye constable & his cain; for wee will either have it unheapt, or it shall cost us several. Finis.[52]

This note, written in a good hand, conveys much of what is typical in such protests: a defiant tone, but limited objectives, a feeling that the rich have fallen down on their duties, and an underlying assumption that the poor are acting 'according to ye law'. Despite the essentially limited aims behind such statements, it is plainly evident that the poor had a fairly sharp consciousness of their corporate identity in opposition to the rich.

Such cases could be multiplied, but it is difficult to see how the topic can be approached on the level of anything better than the scattered anecdote. One possible method might be to take one locality over a period of time, and let it serve as a case study. Exhaustive research might well provide comparable or better examples, but, for our immediate purposes, the borough of Colchester in Essex would seem to represent a location which enjoyed a reasonably well-documented history of riot over much of our period.

Colchester was, by English standards, a fair-sized town, with a population which probably stayed fairly stable at 10–12,000 over much of the period 1600–1750. A large proportion of this population was involved in textile production, and riots connected with problems in the cloth trade were not uncommon. The first serious incident of which we have information, indeed, was a weavers' rebellion of May/June 1566. A number of those selected as ringleaders were subsequently tried at the assizes, and their reported comments make interesting reading. 'Weaver's occupation is a dead science nowadays', declared one, 'and it will never be better before we make a rising.' Another declared that 'we can get no work and we have no money, and if we should steal we should be hanged, and if we should ask, no man would give us, but we will have a remedy one of these days, or else we will lose all, for the commons will rise, we know not how soon, for we look for it every hour'. A third commented that 'wool goeth over as fast as it did, it will cause the people to go together by the ears . . . if there come business it will come about harvest time, and that will make as hot a harvest as ever was'. Plans were evidently made to mobilize the population of other Essex weaving towns, and to make contact with the Suffolk textile belt. Little seems to have happened, but the bitterness of the sentiments expressed by those indicted is clear enough, even over a timespan of more than four centuries: four of them were hanged, an expression of the sensitivity of the Elizabethan state to such matters, in itself indicative, perhaps, of a fundamental sense of insecurity in high places.[53]

There is little evidence of rioting in the town for over seventy years after this incident. Detailed work remains to be done on the borough archives, which are extensive and still largely unworked before the 1620s. Nevertheless, it would seem that Colchester even escaped serious disturbances in those two most difficult of periods, the late 1590s and the years 1629–31. Even so, scattered if suggestive evidence indicates that all was not harmonious in the town. In February 1624, for example, a weaver was reported to have commented that 'if this hard weather continue' there would be a rising in those parishes inhabited by textile workers, adding that 'there be more pore than rich and if they do rise we will begynn first with the Bailiffs [i.e. Colchester's ruling oligarchy] and pull them out of their porches'.[54] As so often, little seems to have followed this isolated tavern-talk. Conversely, it adds to our suspicion that the pre-industrial poor did have a perception of the society in which they lived which, however imperfectly and temporarily, and however clouded by notions of deference or respect, was basically a perception based on notions of class. That our evidence on this point is scattered and anecdotal probably has much to do with the knowledge that voicing such notions might well lead to being reported to the authorities and, as in 1566, to being executed.

The years of political crisis, 1640–42, were marked by frequent rioting in the borough and in the surrounding area. These incidents are fairly familiar, and have been described elsewhere by the present writer and by others, so need not be rehearsed again here.[55] Minor disturbances, for the most part very ill-documented, occurred during the Interregnum and at the time of the Restoration. The next serious riot came in 1668, when the rioters chased two hearth-tax surveyors off to the borough justices, the mob following them 'hallowing and throwing stones & dirt as they went'. The speed with which the crowd assembled, and the fact that a boy was posted with a horn ready to sound the alarm, are suggestive of the capacity of the poor of a pre-industrial town to organize in defence of their interests.[56]

Further evidence on this point came in 1675, on this occasion in the form of a weavers' riot against attempts to cut their pay. The cloth owners attempted to cut the rate paid for weaving a bay from 10/- to 9/-, with predictable results. After about a week spent discussing their grievances, some 500 weavers gathered, demonstrated outside the houses of clothiers, and gave saucy answers when threatened with the calling in of the military. Matters took a more serious turn when a body of townswomen appeared, and urged the men to attack the house of John Furly, a Quaker corn-dealer. Whether or not any serious damage took place is unclear from existing documentation, but the incident was obviously taken seriously enough by the Privy Council, which intervened and gave several of the rioters a hard time before eventually releasing them with minimal punishment. What is striking, however, is the way in which the statements of several of those involved in the disturbances include an awareness of solidarity, albeit temporary, among the weavers. One rioter was reported to have exhorted his fellows to 'stande up for the trade for the company is up', and another declared his intent to 'stand for ye good of ye trade'. An elderly weaver was encouraged to join the rioters in his ward since he was 'an antient man & Magdalen Street is now fireing out & we hope this ward will not stand out'. Further evidence of organization is provided by a constable's assertion that the crowd was called together by the sounding of a horn.[57]

The most serious disturbances among the borough's textile workers, however, came in 1715. At the time, the long-term decline in the Colchester cloth trade was being intensified by the disruption of the export of cloth to the Iberian peninsula attendant upon the War of the Spanish Succession. Class antagonisms in the town sharpened, and all sections of the workforce, from master craftsmen to labourers, became bitter as conditions worsened. They expressed their grievances, as so often, by reference to supposed 'privileges'. Their demands included the cessation of truck payments; the restoration of cuts in piece rates; more open entry into the clothiers' corporation; the ending of a compulsory holiday in August, the time of harvest; and the reform of certain of the ways in which production was regulated. Colchester was paralysed for the best part of March, the climax coming towards the end of that month when 'many hundreds of them marched into Town all armed with Pistols, Swords or Clubs and several other weapons, Resolutely bent upon pulling down the Bay Hall and Houses of several persons, threatening the lives of many unless their demands within two hours were granted'. The town government collapsed, and order was not restored until four troops of guards were sent in on 1 April. The Privy Council, which once again intervened to help redress the balance of Colchester's affairs, showed considerable delicacy in its handling of the incident. The reimposition of stability was followed by both the weavers and their masters attempting to continue the dispute by petitioning, first the Privy Council and then the House of Commons. In the event, the affair ended with a victory for the workforce: in 1716 an Act of Parliament was passed which met some of their grievances.[58] The last point raises an important conclusion: rioting, especially when combined with agitation along other, legal, lines, was frequently successful. Once again, the alleged irrationality of rioting collapses when the phenomenon is subjected to serious analysis.

Despite the settlement of 1716, problems in the textile trade continued, and there seem to have been a number of incidents in the 1720s. This chronicle of popular disturbances, however, ends in 1740, with a grain riot. Colchester, like other towns, regularly experienced popular disturbances over the price of grain, and incidents of this type are known to have occurred in 1674 and 1692–93. A printed account gives us a clear picture of what happened in 1740. On 12 June of that year a George Mallard led a mob which was bent on plundering a vessel laden with corn intended for London. The owner of the vessel, William Frost, went down to the quay to argue with them. Frost apparently knew Mallard, and attempted to bargain with him. Mallard would have none of it: 'he had a naked sword flourishing in his hand, and said that he and the other poor people were come for Corn, for that they had neither victuals nor drink, nor broke their fast the whole day'. Frost, despite his modest claim that 'I knew not very well what to do on this occasion', kept his head and continued to try to negotiate. His offer of drink was refused by the mob, and he then offered them half a peck of corn each, explaining later that 'as they insisted on having meal, I thought it be the best way to give them some'. Mallard offered to help Frost to supervise the distribution, but the process was disrupted when the rioters began to cut the sacks open and help themselves.[59]

These records of riot and popular disturbances, culled from one town, must modify the conventional wisdom surrounding such matters. Firstly, they demonstrate the frequency and variety of riots: certainly few long-term residents of Colchester could have missed the opportunity to witness or participate in such an event, certainly after 1640. Secondly, the Colchester incidents demonstrate that many of these riots were not merely blind outbreaks of looting and plunder, but rather structured and coherent in their form, and limited in their objectives. Above all, despite manhandling and threats, there is no evidence that anyone was killed or seriously injured by the mob: the crowd appreciated the rules of the game. Thirdly, this catalogue of disturbances confirms the notion that riots provide a most important avenue into the mentality of the labouring poor of early modern England. Even when they were involved in tumult and disorder, it is evident that they were thinking men and women with the ability to formulate their grievances, to act in ways appropriate to gaining redress for them, and to combine together when so doing. The student of the early modern English riot is not confronting the doings of a drink-crazed sub-human poor, but is rather discovering rare evidence of something which looks very like an early form of class consciousness, of however unformed and temporary a nature.

Moreover, and more importantly for our immediate purposes, the study of riot in our period gives the impression that even when local authority is being defied, the mob rarely loses respect for all forms of hierarchy and order, for all forms of legality. Behind the menacing postures, the dark mutterings about there being more poor than rich, there usually lay a concern for the redress of specific grievances, not a desire to turn the world upside down. Rioters normally had a sense of justice, and a sense of restraint: indeed, they often possessed both these commodities in greater measure than the superiors they confronted. Thus the riot rarely posed any permanent threat to the structure of society, not least because few of the participants in riots, as far as we can see, had any very clear idea of an alternative social order. The riot was normally initiated in the hope that the legitimate feelings of the lower orders would be listened to, and that the authorities should practise those standards which their paternalistic rhetoric so often preached. The frequency with which the authorities handled riots cautiously supports the suspicion, so rapidly engendered by the words and actions of the mob, that both sides knew that they were participating in a social process which was governed by certain rules and conventions. The common people showed a surprising orderliness in their disorder: it is impossible not to interpret this as evidence that something very like Mr Thompson's legitimizing notions were in operation.

Sympathetic study of some of the relevant offences would, therefore, suggest that the concept of social crime is a far from valueless one. Rioting, certainly, can be understood in terms of collective actions in defence of what were perceived as rights, and informed by some set of cultural values often amounting to the legitimizing notions postulated by Thompson. Moreover, despite reservations, it would seem that ideas of social crime can be applied to at least some aspects of poaching, especially when it can be proved that poachers were acting in accordance with what they felt were their rights to hunt game. When, for example, the Waltham Blacks are portrayed as 'armed foresters, enforcing the definition of rights to which the "country people" had become habituated, and . . . resisting the private emparkments which encroached upon their tillage, their firing and their grazing',[60] we feel that we are confronting the essence of social criminality. Other offences, in certain contexts, seem to have been much the same, and even an historian unsympathetic to the idea of social crime tells us that eighteenth-century Yorkshire coiners were protected from the successful application of the law by 'the determined defence of the illegal business by its numerous practitioners and supporters'.[61] Contemporaries evidently did not regard all lawbreakers in the same way, and historians would do well to follow their example.

Nevertheless, a number of problems remain which make an uncritical acceptance of the concept of social crime impossible. The most crucial of these is determining exactly where social crime ends and normal crime begins. There is little unanimity on this point, although, as we have seen, social crime is meant to possess a number of distinctive attributes: an element of social protest; strong communal support; and divergent definitions between the interpretations placed on an activity by those participating in it and that of the law and its enforcers. Unfortunately, it is frequently difficult to make distinctions as clearcut as this: as E. P. Thompson has warned, 'one must draw the distinction cautiously and with reservations, and must handle the evidence with the greatest care'.[62] Some, indeed, might argue that the distinction is an impossible one: once more, we must return to the possibility that any crime *could* be portrayed as 'social'. Even Professor Hobsbawm, the scholar responsible for the classic formulation of the concept, admitted that all normal crime and delinquency 'can of course be defined as "social" in a wider sociological sense', and that 'non-social criminals may be a substitute for social protest, or be idealized as such a substitute'.[63]

Mention of idealization suggests another set of problems. Most historians who had studied social crime and legitimizing notions have done so from a left-wing perspective. Given the topics under consideration, and given that the assumptions that have governed both what was felt to be the appropriate subject matter of English history, and how that subject matter has been approached, have come overwhelmingly from the other end of the political spectrum, this is no bad thing. However, the students of social crime have, on occasion, cast their nets rather wide in their attempts to find recruits for their army of primitive class warriors: as one sceptic has commented, the search for 'social forms of resistance' can come 'perilously close to encompassing any plebeian act that can be interpreted as defiance towards authority'.[64] Yet more difficulties arise when closer examination reveals that many of the participants in social crime were far from plebeian. As we have argued, poaching's candidacy for social crime is hampered by the presence of the gentleman poacher: similar problems arise with other offences. Smuggling, for example, was often organized by and on behalf of people of property, and it is difficult to see anything very hostile to capitalism in the large smuggling networks of the mid-eighteenth century, or to interpret them as forms of social protest. Much the same is true of the Yorkshire coiners portrayed by Mr Styles: local values supported the coiners, but these values were as attractive to men of property as they were to the poor.

These reservations make it difficult to accept the concept of social crime in any other than a very circumscribed way. It does seem that communities would be more favourable to coiners, smugglers or poachers than they would be to thieves or murderers. However, we need much more information on attitudes to offenders and offences, and on the identity of those involved in the activities which have been described as social crime. Until such information is available, the historian would do well to avoid exaggerating the degree of solidarity with which such offences were greeted by the populace at large, and the degree of consciousness of the offender about the political or social aspects of what he was doing. Above all, the historian must be cautious in his claim that the social and the normal criminal were essentially different. Work on crime in early eighteenth-century London, as we have seen, has suggested that the social background of those hanged for felony at Tyburn was similar to those involved in food-rioting in the capital: the labouring poor in general, and youngish workers who had served out their apprenticeships in particular.[65] Once again, we find Edward Thompson offering a warning: 'there is not "nice" social crime and "nasty" antisocial crime.'[66]

The concept of social crime is, therefore, beset by a number of difficulties. On the other hand, investigation of poaching, coining, rioting and the rest has helped to raise some fundamental issues about the history of crime. As has been pointed out, 'the principal object of the "social" crime/"normal" crime distinction is, at its crudest, to isolate a group of activities as forerunners of popular political movements'.[67] This can, of course, lead to idealization, distortion, misinterpretation and exaggeration: it can also serve as an invaluable corrective to that view which writes off the common people of early modern England as 'beings so degraded as to scarcely deserve the appellation of human'. The poor of this period may not have been as easily digestible for the modern historian as those respectable workers and artisans of the nineteenth century who turned away from 'senseless' rioting to the 'sensible' world of Chartism, trades unions, and the labour party: but work on social crime, and rioting in particular, has made it impossible to deny that these people had coherent ideas about the society in which they lived and how it ought to operate.

Most relevantly, these ideas on how society ought to operate included fairly developed notions of what the law was about. As we have argued at an earlier point, participation in legal institutions reached far down the social scale, and the law was familiar enough to a surprisingly large number of the English. Above all, popular conceptions of government and the social order were intimately connected with popular experiences of the law, both in its operation and as an ideology. The law had a political nature, not least because the state used the courts as a chief means of exercising authority and enforcing regulations. As one recent work has reminded us: 'it was in the courtroom or, at least, in the presence of the justice of the peace and his clerk, that men were most aware of the powers that were wielded over them. Good governance was equated with justice, and the fair dispensation of the law with good government'.[68]

Investigation of social crime, by examining popular redefinitions of the law, or delineating popular attitudes on occasions when the law was not felt to be fair, has done much to emphasize this point. Study of crime in the past cannot ignore the law, but it must be remembered that the law was more than just what appeared on the statute book: it was a major component in the political culture of England, a culture in which the ruled, by definition, shared as much as the rulers. Ideas of legality, of however idiosyncratic a nature, therefore meant something to the ruled. As one study of the subject has remarked, although the common people were usually at a disadvantage when they clashed with their superiors over matters of legality, 'they knew that they were never merely the passive victims of a process that they were powerless to affect'.[69] The presence of such knowledge opens up a number of lines of enquiry into both popular mentalities and the nature of power in society. Ultimately, studying social crime and legitimizing notions emphasizes a fundamental truth, perhaps summarized most neatly by John Brewer and John Styles: 'the best social history is not the history of society with questions of politics and power omitted.'[70]

Chapter 7

ELITE PERCEPTIONS AND POPULAR IMAGES

As we argued in the last chapter, law was a cultural and ideological force so widely diffused in English society as to inform the notions and actions of the population at large. It would be idle, however, to deny that the law was more obviously an embodiment of the ideas and aspirations of the groups which ruled that population. Law was a means of expressing power. Statutes were made in parliament, theoretically the representative of the people as a whole, in fact essentially the representative of the landed orders: the peers who sat in the House of Lords, and the gentry who sat in the Commons. These statutes were, for the most part, administered and enforced by the gentry acting as justices in the countryside, or by men or urban wealth in the towns. Moreover, the men of property did not wield power only through the whipping post, the house of correction, and the gallows: they also controlled what would in modern parlance be described as the media, and hence were able to reinforce their economic and political power with an ideological one. Most obviously, apart from the years 1640–60, they had at their disposal a state church which not only preached the virtues of obedience, but which also attempted to enforce religious conformity and conformity to christian standards of behaviour through its courts. Superficially, therefore, the forces of authority, and the upper strata of society, would seem to have had overwhelmingly powerful resources in what some historians might portray as their struggle to assert their hegemony under the guise of maintaining law and order. The problem is to ascertain how far this superficial impression is a correct one.

Generally speaking, most educated Englishmen liked the English common law. As early as the fifteenth century, Sir John Fortescue was eulogising it, and this trend was to continue into the Elizabethan period, notably in the comments of such legal writers as Lambarde.[1] To Matthew Hale, the common law was 'not only a very just and excellent law in itself', but was also 'singularly accommodated to the frame of the English government and the disposition of the English nation'.[2] This tendency to regard respect for the common law as an essential part of being English was reinforced by the constitutional struggles of the seventeenth century, which placed the common law firmly on the side of the winners. After 1688, men of property, looking back at the pretensions of the early Stuarts, or at the inconveniences of Cromwell's ascendancy, or looking across the channel at the system of informers and arbitrary laws that were held to be mainstays of French absolutism, counted their blessings in living under a more agreeable regime. The common law, along with a respect for those property rights which it did so much to uphold, and attachment to the protestantism of the Anglican church, was a fundamental of English political culture. After the Glorious Revolution, accepting the constitution of England involved accepting the law of the land: as an apologist for that law commented a century after that revolution, 'the terms *constitutional* and *unconstitutional* mean legal and illegal'.[3]

Law was considered essential for the preservation of civil society. Humphrey Babington, preaching an assize sermon in Lincolnshire in 1678, reminded his listeners that 'without judgment and justice there can be no society. These are the bonds of all communities, which knit, and keep all the members of the body-politic together.'[4] A century later, Madan was to echo these sentiments: 'the honour and welfare of the kingdom in general, as well as the security and happiness of individuals, must depend on a due administration of the law.'[5] The law was there to restrain individuals whose wrongdoings might disrupt society. There was little optimism about human nature in our period, and hence little confidence in mankind's innate ability to resist evil. 'Man, if once he throws off the easy and advantageous yoke of law,' declared one preacher, 'is certainly the wildest animal in the world.'[6] The theme was a common one. Another preacher thought that 'it is government which is the hedge to keep in those men, who like wilde beasts would trample upon their neighbours', adding that 'stocks, and whips, pillories and ropes, the prison and the gallows are those engines upon which hangs the garland of peace'.[7] Above all, the law was the one certain method of ensuring that the masses remained obedient. John Fielding, after declaring that 'religion, education, and good breeding preserve good order and decency among the superior rank of mankind', went on to assert that 'good laws, therefore, are necessary to supply the place of education among the populace'.[8]

The importance of law in providing social cement, and in curbing the excesses of wicked individuals, is evident enough. It is difficult, however, for the modern observer to appreciate how important the law was in early modern culture. As we have argued, the system of law enforcement was characterized by a high level of popular participation, which must have ensured that numerous Englishmen had first-hand knowledge of how the law operated, albeit on a lowly level. Many other contacts with the law were made through litigation. Detailed information on this point is rare, but it seems likely that, in the first half of our period at least, almost every court in the country enjoyed a growth in business which far outstripped population growth. Cases at an advanced stage in the Courts of Common Pleas and King's Bench at Westminster, for example, numbered 2,100 in 1490, 13,300 in 1580, and 29,162 in 1640.[9] For the man of any more than middling property, both the major *rites de passage* of life, and most major business transactions, involved contact with the law and lawyers. Family and fortune were preserved when wills and marriage contracts were drawn up, while the increasing complexity of both landed property and commerce implied contact with the law via contracts, deeds, mortgages, and bills of sale.

The law was also of vital importance as an ideology. As we have seen, it was a commonplace that law was essential for curbing man's disorderly passions and thus preserving the body politic. It did not exercise control merely through physical repression, through the stocks, whips, pillory, ropes, prison and gallows. It also succeeded because, ultimately, a large proportion of the population accepted the idea of a rule of law. Class differences existed in early modern England and, ultimately, the law could be represented by the historian as an instrument of class oppression: however, it was a number of other things as well, while the historian does himself a grave disservice if he does not remember that it oppressed in a subtle fashion. As Douglas Hay has pointed out, much of the success of the law depended upon its being merciful as well as an object of terror. The system of pardons and reprieves ensured that a fair number of convicted felons left the courtroom feeling fortunate rather than aggrieved, and thus mercy ensured the acceptance of the rule of law more surely than festooning the gibbets after every assize would have done.[10] Defenders of the system could also demonstrate its fairness by reference to those celebrated, and well publicized, occasions when the great and famous suffered the law's full rigours as completely as the meanest felon in the land. Further support for the notion of the rule of law might come from those numerous occasions, perhaps more frequent at the beginning of our period than at the end, when poor men managed to obtain legal remedy against their social superiors in the courts. Most importantly, the authorities could be seen acting with due respect for legality and popular notions of legitimacy in times of stress: local justices' handling of grain riots were a frequent reminder on this point.[11] By the eighteenth century the law, it might be argued, had come to replace religion as the main ideological cement of society.

The importance of the law engendered and was then fuelled by a growth in the legal profession. In the mid sixteenth century, indeed, the term 'profession' is hardly applicable to the wide variety of legal practitioners existing in England. Obviously the Cokes, Bacons and Hales, leading judges and holders of high legal office, were respected men of considerable skill. In the localities, however, there were numerous country attorneys, forerunners of modern solicitors, whose skill in the law was probably in many cases analogous to that of contemporary cunning men in medicine. Gradually, professional standards asserted themselves, and by the late eighteenth century 'folk lawyers' of this type were much less common. First the barristers, heirs to the medieval serjeants-at-law, emerged as a skilled group with some sort of corporate consciousness. Then, in the second half of the eighteenth century, the attorneys demonstrated a similar increase in status and, ultimately, wealth. The society of Gentlemen Practitioners in the Courts of Law and Equity, founded in 1739, did its best both to enforce higher standards of professional conduct on attorneys and to improve their public reputation, and from 1770 this London-based society was followed by a number of provincial counterparts. By the end of our period, therefore, England possessed something like a legal profession in the modern sense of the term.[12]

Despite this improvement in professional standards, contemporaries continued to demonstrate that an affection for the law did not preclude a healthy dislike of lawyers. Anti-lawyer sentiment was a commonplace in both literary sources and in contemporary satirical prints. Lawyers, like most members of the professions, were regarded with suspicion. As with doctors and clergymen, it was difficult for contemporaries to find the correct niche for the lawyer in the commonly-held conception of the social hierarchy, not least because the practice of law was widely held to offer unique opportunities for upward social mobility. Moreover, contemporary comment criticized the way in which lawyers took advantage of the law's delays to extract money from their clients, and of arcane knowledge to swindle them. Behind specific criticisms there was a general feeling that lawyers, again like doctors and the clergy, were basically unproductive drones who made their living from the misfortunes of others. Thomas Scot, preaching an assize sermon in Norfolk, traditionally held to be the county most infested with lawyers, touched on a common theme when he pointed out that 'in this country where you most abound, most suites abound, as if you bred diseases and did not take care to cure them'.[13] Such criticism is hardly fair, and the historian must concur with the lawyers' defence that such a situation would have been unthinkable without a ready supply of eager litigants. This view would have found little support among contemporaries, few of whom had a good word to say for the men of law: Dr Johnson summed up several centuries of popular prejudice with his customary urbanity when he said of an acquaintance that 'he did not care to speak ill of any man behind his back, but he believed the gentleman to be an attorney'.[14]

If the cultural diffusion of the law, and the rise of a profession anxious to make money from it, had made it an important force in national life, it remained true that it was at parliament that individual laws first saw the light of day: as an MP put it bluntly in 1621, 'we sit in parliament to make laws, where our ancestors have sat who have made laws that we are governed by'.[15] The thinking that lay behind general trends in criminal legislation, and the motives that underlay individual acts, are, therefore, of some importance to the historian of crime. Unfortunately it is very difficult to find much evidence on such issues, certainly in the first half of our period. As a student of the Marian bail and committal statutes put it, 'it will come as no surprise to students of Tudor legislation that absolutely nothing is known about the drafting process which preceded the introduction of the two Marian Bills into parliament'.[16] Similar problems obtain in the early Stuart period. Attempts to find out anything about the origins of a Jacobean statute extending benefit of clergy to women convicted of small thefts, an interesting if minor episode in legal history, come to nothing if contemporary Parliamentary diaries are consulted. The Bill seems to have passed its various readings with little trouble, although some judges objected and some members thought the occasion a useful one to propose a general overhaul of the law on the subject. It is impossible, however, to discover very much more about either its origins or its proponents.[17]

When sufficient evidence is available to permit the reconstruction of the background to a piece of legislation, the picture which emerges is often a very confusing one. Certainly, any simplistic ideas of a 'ruling class' enacting 'class legislation' should be treated with extreme caution. In the last analysis, such ideas may well be tenable: but close examination of a number of case-studies suggests several complexities which must be confronted. The Elizabethan Statute of Artificers, to cite a notable example, was, taken in its entirety, a statement of a more or less coherent view of social and economic matters, and many of its clauses worked to the disadvantage of the poor. Nevertheless, the making of the statute involved accommodating different pressure groups and great men who had varying ideas on the correct nature of economic policy, and who were often at odds over the most appropriate methods of dealing with the immediate crises that had stimulated the statute.[18] On a slightly different tack, the making of the Privy Council's decision to reissue the Book of Orders in 1631 showed a similar lack of unanimity in policy-making circles: if anything, we are informed, this decision provided yet more evidence of 'the problem of confused objectives and faulty execution, which bedevilled many areas of social policy'.[19] If individual pieces of legislation or policy-making demonstrate confusion in high places, so do manifestations of more general attitudes. Investigation of the reactions of Elizabethan and early Stuart MPs to laws regulating personal conduct, for instance, shows that such laws were usually engineered by enthusiastic individuals or pressure groups, with the vast body of Members of the House being indifferent to such Bills or, indeed, absent while they were debated. The most striking unanimity shown by the Commons to laws regulating personal conduct was that the upper orders of society should be subjected to their penalties as little as possible.[20]

One suspects that a similar lack of concerted purpose lay behind that most celebrated of legislative trends, the extension of the death penalty by statute after 1688. Given that most of these statutes sought to use hanging to defend property, it might be expected that it is here, if anywhere, that we are to find a propertied class anxious to further its class interests consciously through use of the criminal law. The picture is, unfortunately, a little less clear. As Madan put it in 1786

> laws of this kind commonly pass as of course, without observation of debate. Having thus stolen into existence, they lie dormant on the statute book, till they are notified to the world by the execution of some unthinking wretch, who, to his utter astonishment, finds himself by law adjudged to die.[21]

Recent historians have similarly been struck by the insouciance with which this exceptionally bloody code was put together. Douglas Hay found that 'few of the new penalties were the product of hysteria, or ferocious reaction; they were part of the conventional wisdom of England's governors', and has also emphasized that the creation of such statutes was essentially haphazard. Typical, perhaps, was an act of 1764, which made breaking into buildings to steal or destroy linen, or the tools needed to make linen, or to cut linen in bleaching grounds, capital offences. This legislation was not a panic measure to combat an upsurge of wickedness on the part of linen-makers, but rather a clause in an act passed to incorporate the English Linen Company.[22] Even the Waltham Black Act, whose background has been subjected to such detailed analysis by E. P. Thompson, was passed through Parliament easily enough: 'at no stage in its passage does there appear to have been debate or serious division; a House prepared to debate for hours a disputed election could find unanimity at creating at a blow some fifty new capital offences.'[23]

The background to legislation is a subject which calls for detailed and sophisticated research, not least when dealing with the expansion of capital statutes after 1688. Most of these statutes were passed in defence of property, and it was no accident that it was the men of property in Parliament who passed them. Nevertheless, we are dealing with a facet of a 'conventional wisdom', rather than with more immediate manifestation of class consciousness among the propertied: indeed, as the previous paragraph has suggested, the eighteenth-century English Parliament created the bloodiest criminal code in Europe without any consciousness of so doing. If this conclusion is accurate, we are confronted by an interesting philosophical point: is a regime whose 'conventional wisdom' allows it to construct such a code in a series of fits of absence of mind morally better or worse than one which embarks on a policy of deliberate terror? Whatever our conclusions on this matter might be, it remains clear that further work is needed on the attitudes and objectives of MPs, and that any comments on what men of property or the ruling class might have had in mind when passing statutes should be treated as highly conjectural for the present.

Attempting to understand the parliamentary background to legislation is impeded by further complications. As Hay has reminded us, when discussing the extension of the death penalty, 'eighteenth-century lawyers were well aware that never before had the legislature passed a mass of capital statutes so quickly'.[24] It is worth remembering that the legislature had never passed *any* statutes so quickly as in the eighteenth century. The 45-year reign of Elizabeth I witnessed the passing of 438 Acts of Parliament. Another 45-year period, from the first regnal year of George I to the thirty-third of George II, 1760, witnessed the passing of 3,529. Elizabethan Parliaments were not noticeably coy about passing capital statutes, and one suspects that if length and regularity of sittings had given them the opportunity, they might have added as many capital statutes to the legal code as did their Hanoverian successors. This possibility raises interesting objections to the view which sees the later legislative trend as evidence of increasing use of the criminal law as a weapon of class warfare in defence of property.

Such a hypothesis is, of course, extremely speculative. Similar objections to another, essentially similar, interpretation of developments in the criminal code are, perhaps, better founded. Not only was Parliament sitting more frequently, and hence legislating more. It was also becoming the unique institution through which certain forms of governance could be carried out. In earlier periods, some types of control could be exercised by means other than Parliamentary statute. One such period was the late Elizabethan and early Stuart era, a period marked by a decline in Parliamentary government, when much regulation, especially of industrial production, was carried out by patent of monopoly. After 1640, of course, government no longer had this option, and industrial processes were regulated by statute rather than by the granting of patents. This has obvious implications for the argument which presents the criminalization of embezzlement by workers in putting out industries purely in terms of some sort of advance of capitalism. Before 1640, there might have been easier ways of preventing such abuses than by Act of Parliament. The processes by which such patents were generally granted are also instructive. Interested parties would present a petition to the Privy Council exposing a mischief and suggesting a remedy. This would be followed by an enquiry by the Council into the convenience and lawfulness of the proposed remedy. If this enquiry were favourable, a patent of monopoly would be granted to the person or group of persons from whom the proposal had come. One suspects that this is not dissimilar from the background to many of the Acts regulating industrial processes in the eighteenth century. This would suggest that the supposed connections between changes on the statute book and the onward march of capitalism need further scrutiny.[25]

One important shift is suggested by the general consensus that the law by the mid eighteenth century was concerned mainly with the defence of property. This is axiomatic to Hay, for whom the statutes extending the death penalty in the eighteenth century were 'the legal instruments which enforced the division of property by terror'.[26] Certainly there is no lack of contemporary opinion in support of the contention that, by 1750, the criminal law was primarily a bulwark of property. Locke's famous dictum that 'government has no other end but the preservation of property'[27] was taken all too literally by the generations that followed the Glorious Revolution: by 1702, indeed, the view that 'our laws are made to maintain property, not at all to keep up religion' was sufficiently widespread to be attacked from the pulpit.[28] If this insistence on the law's importance in protecting property is a correctly diagnosed one, it marks an important break with earlier concerns. In the century before the Civil Wars, concern was not merely with defence of property, but with much wider fears of disorder. As one recent historian has commented, during that period, what contemporaries 'admired most, the quality they sought most avidly in their own lives, was order, the establishment of control, the obliteration of chaos'.[29] A concern for the defence of property was, of course, a component of the wider *angst*: if the many-headed monster overturned the social hierarchy, property relationships would necessarily be inverted correspondingly. But the fear was more general, more cosmic, more apocalyptic. The desire of order and harmony among the lower orders may not have been as elaborately or forcefully expressed as among their book- or sermon-writing social superiors, but even on a village level it is possible to find evidence of a dislike of disruption. In 1601, for example, we find the inhabitants of Wearmouth, County Durham, complaining to the archdeacon about one of their number as 'an outrageous scholde and a disquieter of her neighbo[ur]s wherebie much disquietnes doeth arise'.[30] It is obvious that the complainants too had their own concepts of order, and were willing to use the law to reinforce it in their own narrow sphere. If our analysis is accurate, this transition from a general concern over order to a more limited one concentrating on the defence of property suggests some important changes in attitudes to the law, and possibly in the whole nature of social relations and perceptions of them, between 1550 and 1750.

The law was, therefore, of central importance in early modern England. Most contemporaries, however, would have considered that religion was the law's inseparable helpmate in the battle against disorder. They would have had some difficulty in differentiating sin from crime. Equally, they would have agreed that the civil and the religious authority was, and ought to have been, entwined. The Puritan William Perkins was pleased that 'magistrates in towns and corporations carry & draw the sword for the maintenance of peace and civill order: it is well done, for it is a worke of their calling', but he added that the ideal magistrate 'beares the sword specially for the good of men's souls . . . magistracy and government be necessary in the societies of Christians'.[31] Later writers endorsed these sentiments. In 1729 it was asserted that magistrates were essentially 'the ministers of God; his revengers to execute wrath upon him that doth evil',[32] while another early eighteenth-century commentator felt that law enforcement should go hand in hand with 'the good instruction of the pulpit'.[33] The supposedly close connection between religious and legal control is demonstrated further by the contemporary conceit of seeing the individual's conscience as some sort of court of law, as 'a private sessions prepatory to the general and grand assize' of the Last Judgement,[34] or as something God had installed in man 'in commission of the peace . . . to direct his action, and to curb his passions and extravagant desires'.[35] Moreover, religion was as essential a part of the constitution as was the law. A sermon of 1714 declared that 'they who are well affected to our constitution must needs be implicitly zealous for the church',[36] while to Hale Christianity was 'a parcel of the laws of England and therefore to reproach the Christian religion is to speak in subversion of the law'.[37] Human law was seen as something more than merely human: it was a reflection of divine will as to how the world should be ordered, and a set of precepts by which the Almighty informed men on how to tell right from wrong.

Such notions were considerably reinforced by the Reformation. On one level, this was a reflection of the needs of the state: after the Reformation, a greater stress was laid on the need to maintain religious conformity, not least because of the threat to order so obviously posed by disunity in religion. There was also a greater stress laid on the need to raise standards of Christian belief and Christian conduct: after all, the Reformation can be seen as a revolution of rising spiritual expectations. Central to these spiritual concerns was worry over sin. If the Christian's main concern was salvation of the soul, it was natural that sin, the main obstacle to that salvation, should loom large in his or her preoccupations. For the state, the clergy, and the godly laity alike, turning the population of England into good Christians involved not only getting the people into church to teach them true religion, but also made an all-out war against sin an immediate priority.

151

Certainly, late sixteenth-and early seventeenth-century writers were convinced that there was plenty of sin waiting to have war waged against it. Henry Goodcole, that early reporter of crime in London, felt that 'there is in the whole world a deludge of iniquity, more prone, swifter running after all manner of wickedness to perpetrate them, then willing to performe any of the least office, or intertaine such motion making unto God, or goodnesse'.[38] The Puritan Thomas Scot voiced a common concern that 'this nation of ours at this day, out-sinnes all the nations of the world, even in the proper sinnes for which they have beene infamous'.[39] On another occasion the same preacher bewailed 'such common, open, crying sinnes, such raigning, roaring, raging sinnes, such beaten roads, common high-wayes of sinnes and sinning, as if there were no king, no laws, no priest, no judge in England'.[40] Sin was, of course, bad enough in itself. It was made worse, however, by a widespread feeling that divine wrath would be unleashed upon the nation if sin went unpunished: a Jacobean MP expressed a commonplace when he opined that if sin went unchecked in England, the Almighty 'will lay his heavy hand of wrath and indignation upon this land'.[41]

The emergence of Puritanism in the late sixteenth century ensured that there was at least one group consciously striving to stave off such an eventuality. Puritanism was an extremely complex phenomenon which has engendered, and will doubtlessly continue to engender, considerable debate among historians. It is inevitable that much of this debate has so far been concentrated upon Puritanism's political aspects: after all, the events of 1640–60 have been labelled 'The Puritan Revolution'. Arguably, however, this concentration has tended to obscure the emphases that contemporaries would have put upon Puritanism. Recent research has suggested that, before the Arminian innovations of the 1630s forced traditionally-minded English Protestants to take defensive action, Puritanism was hardly a revolutionary or oppositionist ideology.[42] The part played by the godly in the Civil Wars and the eventual execution of Charles I should not obscure the earlier Puritan insistence on the need to preserve order and, in particular, to defend order from the consequences of man's sinfulness. If nothing else, the regenerate individual, whether godly monarch, godly magistrate, godly minister or even godly parish officer, had a duty to discipline the unregenerate masses. Accordingly, law enforcement in the first half of our period, in terms of both legislation and actual prosecutions, was marked by the impact of the Puritan desire to reform what contemporaries referred to as 'manners'.[43]

One manifestation of the Puritan attack on 'common country dis-orders' was their assault on some of the more *folklorique* aspects of popular culture. This is a familiar theme, although its importance has not, perhaps, been fully appreciated: indeed, it was part of a general

European movement to reform the culture of the common people along lines conducive to order and godliness. In England, this movement often took the form of court action against popular recreations, especially those connected with traditional 'medieval' ideas on the function of the church and the nature of religious festivals. In Devon, we find a stream of quarter sessions orders against church ales, parish ales, young men's ales, sexton's ales, all other revels, maypoles, 'cockmatches', and so on. Oxfordshire church court records for 1584 include the presentment of the churchwardens of Goring for allowing 'dauncyng and bowlinge' in the churchyard, and those of another parish for 'keeping enterludes and plays in the churche'. In Storrington, Sussex, the parson objected in 1623 to the ancient custom of his giving 'bread and cheese and a barrell of beere' in the church on Easter day immediately after evening prayer, while a remarkable presentment from the previous year involved the flock of another Sussex parish reporting their minister 'for not making our drincking at harvest . . . which is a custom in our parishe'. Resistance to the new standards of godliness could take other forms, as a Staffordshire curate of reforming tendencies discovered when he entered his church to find a parishioner attired in the guise of 'a lord of myssrule's foole in a pyde coote' in the pulpit. Such episodes only encouraged both lay and ecclesiastical authorities in their struggle against 'rush-bearing, bull-baitings, beare-baitings, may-games, morice dances, ales, or any such like prophane pastimes or assemblies'.[44]

The struggle against 'prophane pastimes and assemblies' constitutes a telling demonstration of the dimensions of control which the early modern state found both desirable and feasible. Equally important to the Puritan reformation of manners was the struggle against the more mundane sins of sexual immorality, drunkenness, swearing and idleness. Localized concern over such matters could have a dramatic impact on court records. The archives of the Cheshire Court of Great Sessions, for example, show a dramatic upsurge in the presentment of such cases in the middle years of James I: 'a seldom comer to church & a drunckard'; 'a drunckard & a great blasphemer'; 'for keepinge a lewd & disordered house'; 'for harbouring a fornicatrix'; 'for harbouring of whores'; 'for haveing duos bastards, the fathers unknowen'.[45] The force of the impressionistic impact of such presentments can be supported by statistical analysis of court archives. In Lancashire, the Puritan ascendancy after the Civil Wars saw a marked rise in the prosecution of regulative offences of this type at the quarter sessions. In Terling, Essex, the arrival of a Puritan minister, and the adherence of the better sort of the village to his doctrines, as we have seen, could cause a similar shift on a parish level. When, in 1620, we find the jurymen of that parish reminding the assize judges that 'the magistrate beareth not the sword for naught, but is ordained by God to take punishment on them that do evil', we are confronted with convincing evidence of the impact of Puritanism on law enforcement.[46]

The return of the Stuarts in 1660 meant the end of Puritanism as a political force, and the godly turned from active assaults on man's sinfulness to the more personal, if less taxing, ethos of non-conformity. Religion, of course, never retreated entirely from debate on crime, and writers can be found denouncing sin well into the eighteenth century. The writer who in 1775 complained that 'to trace the sons of Belial through all their turnings and windings, crooked and oblique paths, would be an endless thing', was obviously discussing social problems in terms which William Perkins, Thomas Scot, or the more substantial villagers would have found fully comprehensible.[47] One senses, however, that the problem of man's sinfulness, although still a matter of evident concern, is being discussed in less urgent terms by this date. Observers of the mid eighteenth century were less used to seeing sin in apocalyptic terms than their Elizabethan or early Stuart forebears. Less convinced of the imminence of the Second Coming, they were able to take a more detached view, and concentrate debate on the practical benefits to be derived from combating sin rather than the divine retribution likely to follow should it not be combated. This shift in emphasis is illustrated neatly by a tract of 1753 addressed to 'the drinkers of gin, brandy, and other distilled spirits', which stressed not the moral aspects of the problem, but rather the medical ones. Such familiar arguments as drink's effects on the liver were deployed, as well as more esoteric ones: in an appendix, a clergyman in Maryland described how red indian 'squaas' used spirit-drinking to induce abortions. Eighteenth-century rationality was triumphing over the godly enthusiasm of the pre-Civil War period.[48]

This process is well illustrated by the fortunes of the Societies for the Reformation of Manners of the late seventeenth and early eighteenth centuries.[49] The origins of these Societies confirm the suspicion that the picture of a nation being plunged into irreligion after 1660 are somewhat overdrawn. Concern over religion, much of it demonstrating continuities with earlier mainstream Puritan thinking, was still present. From about 1678, it is possible to discern religious societies formed for self-help in spiritual matters, and to encourage the practise of devotion, the extension of charity, and mutual self-help, all from an impeccably Anglican position. By the time of the Glorious Revolution, this concern over the need to foster religion became stronger, the most obvious evidence of this, perhaps, being the foundation of the Society for the Propagation of Christian Knowledge, founded expressly to counter 'gross ignorance of the principles of the Christian religion', in 1698. This desire to spread knowledge was, as in the earlier period, accompanied by a growth in concern over national sinfulness. Josiah Woodward, whose tracts and sermons mark him as a leading protagonist of this new godliness, referred to 'national sins, that bring national judgements',[50] and there was widespread concern that a wrathful Almighty would chastise the ungodly English with Louis XIV's dragoons in much the same way as earlier generations had feared Spanish *tercios* as instruments of divine vengeance. The immediate impetus toward combating sin was, however, local. In 1690, the officers and more substantial inhabitants of the London suburb of Tower Hamlets, an area notorious for its brothels, formed an association and made a private agreement to endeavour to suppress immorality. Their efforts proved successful, and, with the encouragement of clergymen and various London lawyers and justices, a Society for the Reformation of Manners was formed in 1691. Its main objective was to curb immorality through the better enforcement of existing secular laws, the church courts being regarded as too ineffective, and perhaps too contentious, for this purpose. This better enforcement was to be achieved primarily through private informations and more activity on the part of parish officers.

The movement had a fair degree of initial success. It attracted support from the city fathers, from the Archbishop of Canterbury, Tennison, and, at a later date, Queen Anne. Its backbone, however, was solid householders, master-craftsmen and the like, who had a stake in the survival of conventions of sobriety, honesty, and a respect for religion and order. Details of prosecutions were, from 1694, recorded in a publication known as the *Black Book* or *Black Roll*, and the willingness to prosecute bolstered by sermons, sixty of these being preached in the metropolis for the Societies between 1697 and 1715. Prosecutions, mostly for prostitution or sabbath-breaking, rose steadily. Three hundred and thirteen were brought in 1692, and a total of 2,645 in the three years ending December 1702, a figure which was reached annually by the 1720s. Despite murders of constables attempting to make arrests for moral offences in 1702 and 1709, the principles of the Societies spread. There was some support among justices in the countryside, and a number of provincial towns, notably Bristol, formed local Societies for the Reformation of Manners. The greatest success in the provinces, however, seems to have been in the diocese of Durham. There the bishop enjoyed a palatinate jurisdiction over both ecclesiastical and civil matters, and it was therefore much easier to co-ordinate the work of reformation. The Archdeacon of Durham, Robert Booth, was especially active, and was particularly successful in obtaining the active assistance of magistrates in the county.

The movement for the reformation of manners made a promising start in the capital, and was also influential in some other parts of the country: nevertheless the Societies had largely fallen into a decline by about 1730. There were a number of reasons for this development, most of them providing instructive insights into the problems of law enforcement in the period. Firstly, the whole idea of reformation could be ridiculed because the Societies were singularly unsuccessful in curbing the immorality of the rich. Secondly, the Societies attracted considerable support from dissenters, and acquired a generally Whig-gish tinge. The result was that their work, like that of so many later reform movements, became complicated by party politics. Another major problem was the dependence upon prosecution through infor-mation, since, so contemporary comment would have us believe, nobody liked informers. Swift commented on how informing had 'grown a trade to enrich little knavish informers of the meanest rank, such as common constables and broken shop keepers',[51] and others evidently shared his dislike. An early supporter, justice Ralph Hartley, was thrown off the Middlesex bench as 'a troublesome person' after prosecuting a knight for swearing, and reports came through at a later date that 'lewd villains' were directing naval press-gangs to places where they knew informers to be meeting.

The most striking problem confronted by the movement for the reformation of manners, however, was the lack of universal support from persons in authority. In York the foundation of a local Society was prevented by the hostility of the Archbishop, John Sharp. Even more surprising is the action of Sir John Holt, CJQB, who in 1709 directed the jury trying the killers of the reforming constable John Dent to acquit. Holt, like so many of those in authority, regarded the members of the Societies as enthusiastic zealots: this, combined with their Whiggish and dissenting tinge, was quite enough to make them suspect to Tory squires and justices. Such men disliked anything smacking of religious zealotry much more than they disliked the sins of the nation, and were unwilling to be tainted by it. Hence the renewed demand for 'Reformation' foundered in the 1730s: the godly ministers and godly parish officers were still there, but the memories of 1640–60, when earlier religious zealots were thought to have been given a free hand, meant that godly magistrates were in somewhat shorter supply than they had been a century earlier.

The history of the Societies for the Reformation of Manners, like our examination of the background to parliamentary legislation, re-inforces the suspicion that the exercise of authority in our period was a very complex process, and that simplistic analyses along the lines of the ruling class enforcing its will should be avoided. Further evidence on this point is forthcoming when we study the actual implementation of policy in the field. Information on this subject is difficult to obtain in the form of anything more than scattered anecdotes. There are, how-ever, a few justices' notebooks and collections of justices' papers surviving, and these can be supplemented by lucky survivals of unusual documents.

One example of this latter category is a remarkable collection of correspondence dealing with ecclesiastical discipline in the Arch-bishop of York's peculiar of Hexhamshire between 1705 and 1733.[52] Despite reservations that might be felt about the general applicability of evidence from early eighteenth-century ecclesiastical materials, this correspondence provides some vivid insights into many of the problems of law enforcement current in our period. Hexhamshire at this time must have represented the less appealing end of ecclesiastical jurisdiction. It lay in the north of Northumberland, two days ride over bad roads from York even in good conditions. It was very poor, the populace being mainly dependent on farming and a declining lead-mining industry. Any local minister had to confront both a decrepit church structure and the fruits of a long period of lack of close ecclesiastical control in what was an isolated, and to a large extent still a border, community. The parish church was 'ruinous . . . unfit for divine service in bad weather', and its lack of a sound roof created special problems, for example when it was reported that 'the abuse of o[ur] church by pidgeons was certainly very scandalous'. Church attendance, conformity, and discipline were in a similarly ramshackle state, not least because ecclesiastical authority in these matters was undergoing a serious decline. In such a context, the correspondence of George Ritschel, curate, lecturer, and commissary in Hexham, is of unusual interest in laying bare the complications of enforcing control.

Ritschel was a man with a north-eastern background, and apparently old-fashioned ideas on ecclesiastical discipline and pastoral care. In 1714 he claimed that 'I have been a long time concerned for this jurisdiction, & have a great desire to put every thing in order'. His actions, although entirely consistent with such sentiments, suggest that he had an idiosyncratic view of how things should be done. For Ritschel, church discipline was essentially an exercise in the art of the possible. He knew local people, and appreciated local needs. While never losing sight of the spirit of the church law, he was willing to adjust its letter to the circumstances of Hexhamshire. Hence, when discussing the amount a man should pay as commutation for fornication, he wrote 'considering his estate & family I think it high enough'. Another offender, a drunkard, although in line for appearance at the church court, was informally bound over by a creditor 'upon condition to send him im[m]ediately to jail again if or whenever he shall be drunk'. Ritschel thought this perfectly satisfactory, 'as probable a means to reform him as any we can use'. On another occasion he reported that he had failed to cite a Mrs Carnaby for a church cess of 6d. 'w[hi]ch I had rather pay 10 times out of my own pocket than be lickt with the rough syde of her tongue'. Some offenders were simply too much trouble: 'as to Mary Summers, I conceive it is not worth o[ur] time to enquire after such vagring Scots spinner husseys'. Above all Ritschel was conscious of the limits to what could be done. The church in the area could not be over ambitious, for 'if we strain it too farr we make nothing at all', while 'if we threaten people & do not do it, they do but laugh at us & despise o[ur] courts'. This rare insight into how an admittedly difficult jurisdiction might be exercised demonstrates the inherent weakness of any general statements about the structure and running of the machinery of coercion.

Yet more complications arise when we study the reactions of Ritschel's superiors. He was not popular, either at York or Durham, the basic problem being the familiar one of an old and experienced man in the field having to deal with younger and less experienced superiors. His local knowledge, he was not backward in pointing out, was more in touch with the realities of the situation than the tactics concocted by these superiors many miles to the south. Occasionally this attitude was evidently felt to be exasperating, as when he was unhelpful in implementing York visitation articles in the peculiar, on the grounds that they were inappropriate in Hexham. At one point, one of his superiors remarked dryly 'he's so forward & dexterous in business yt as he thinks he needs noe assistance'. On one occasion, the higher authorities reacted by giving Ritschel little backing when he had got himself into a very difficult situation. Following a case of commutation, in which Ritschel claimed he was acting on their instructions, he was threatened with an action at Durham assizes. The Archdeacon of Durham, who could have intervened at an early stage to ease matters for him, was at first willing to leave him to take the full consequences of the case. Thus to the picture of the local agent of law enforcement acting in a sometimes wayward manner and constantly bending rules to suit local circumstances, we can add a bureaucracy which was sometimes unwilling to give full support to subordinates. There is little reason to think that this situation was unique to Hexhamshire: the problems experienced there demonstrate that the implementation of law enforcement in this period could be a very complex matter.

The rule of law implied another complication: that of transmitting general notions of the beneficial nature of lawful behaviour, as well as information on new laws and new policies, to the population at large. Two methods were readily at hand. The first of these was the charge regularly given to local jurors and anybody else within earshot, either by one of the judges at the assizes or by a senior JP at quarter sessions. The main purpose of these charges was to refresh the jury's memory on the main points of the law relating to their immediate business, but it was customary to preface this recapitulation with a preamble which would either give details of recent changes in governmental policies or preoccupations, or make a more general effort at increasing sensitivity to law and order problems. These preambles therefore provide rare information on how authority attempted to present itself to local officers.

Perhaps the best surviving collection of such preambles was that written by William Lambarde in the late sixteenth century. Lambarde, that doyen of the Kentish bench, left his listeners in little doubt about either their responsibilities or the difficulties facing them.[53] As was altogether appropriate, many of the charges contained praise for the jury system, which Lambarde, in common with most other commentators, held to be one of the peculiar glories of the English legal system. The jurymen were, however, constantly reminded that even the best institutions were useless unless the men responsible for working them were diligent, and hence his charges were full of exhortations to jurors and other inferior officers to make presentments and generally be active in their duties. To this was added some interesting though unremarkable comments on the nature and benefits of the law and the dreadfulness of man's sinfulness and rebellious nature. Once more, this last subject was usually broached in tones of panic. Certainly in the difficult years of the 1590s, some of Lambarde's statements have an apocalyptic tinge, which, even if allowance is made for contemporary styles of rhetoric, is suggestive of a genuine underlying anxiety on the part of the speaker. He felt the authorities in Kent were combating 'infinite swarms of evils that of latter years (more than in former ages) have invaded the realm and overrun it', or 'such an inundation of wickedness in this last and worst age that . . . we are justly to fear that we shall every one be overwhelmed thereby'.[54] No comparable collection of later charges exists, although a reading of a sample of those which are extant suggests that by the end of our period much the same sentiments were being expressed, but in a rather more measured fashion. Henry Fielding, in his charge to the Westminster grand jury in 1749, might end by expressing the fear that 'the immoralities of the people', if unchecked, 'must produce a downright state of wild and savage barbarism': unlike Lambarde, however, he does not give the impression of being a man who is frequently convinced that he is sitting on a powder-keg.[55]

Another medium through which ideas on law and order were expressed was the assize sermon. These would be preached, usually by one of the more skilful or better-connected of the local clergy, before every assize, and a large number of them were subsequently printed. Dr White's exhaustive researches on assize sermons between the Restoration and 1720 have demonstrated that they were invariably extremely conformist in tone.[56] Obedience was the prime virtue, and most of the preachers found it impossible to envisage that a subject, after a careful and sincere search of his or her conscience, could disobey the orders of superior authorities without sinning. The rapid political changes in the sixty years studied by Dr White caused the preachers surprisingly few problems. Contentious issues were simply discussed in non-controversial ways, and obedience to the monarch currently in power advised, whether the monarch in question was a king notorious for his loose morals, a Roman Catholic, or a foreigner: little wonder that 'hackneyed metaphors and allegories abounded'.[57] Examination of earlier assize sermons suggest a greater liveliness in tone, rather more reference to brimstone, and a willingness to attack

159

the vices of the rich which would have probably given affront to polite audiences in the eighteenth century. As might be expected, however, these earlier sermons were similarly conformist.[58]

Charges and assize sermons were obviously intended to provide at least certain segments of the population at large with some general ideas on crime, law, and order, although it is doubtful if we shall ever know how far their message was comprehended, and how far it affected behaviour. There was another source which might give information on more popular images of crime: popular literature. From the early sixteenth century the availability of the printing press and a steady growth in literacy combined to produce a popular literature aimed at a market which included members of social groups far below the elite.[59] From its inception, much of this literature was concerned with crime. Obviously enough, it was the sensational and newsworthy case which normally attracted attention: as a Victorian ballad-seller put it, 'there's nothing beats a stunning good murder after all'.[60] From the early years of Elizabeth I the reading public was treated to a constant stream of pamphlets and ballads describing the life and eventual fate of notorious criminals. Reading large numbers of these productions, as one student of popular literature has pointed out, can be a tedious affair: 'for the most part these murder sheets possess for us all the dullness of sensational news that has passed into obscurity. The prose and verse are largely stereotyped, while the illustrations are scarcely credible.'[61] It is, nevertheless, this very stereotyped nature of much of this popular literature which makes it so useful for our purposes: examining this sort of stereotype can be very instructive.

Popular accounts of crime always involve a certain duality. On the one hand, the eventual defeat of the criminal, in our period in the very definite form of an execution, is central to the story. Good must triumph, and the irrational and disorderly world of the delinquent be overturned by the order and rationality of the law. On the other hand, accounts of crime are also often written with the additional purpose of exciting or titillating the reader. In 1696 indeed, the author of a piece of social reportage on prostitution found it necessary to state that 'the designs then of this undertaking is not to minister fuel to wanton thoughts, or to please the prophane pallats of the beaus and sparks of the town'.[62] Despite such disclaimers, by the end of our period it was accepted that fictional accounts of crime might encourage participation in the real thing, and in 1728 a pamphlet was written claiming that a previously honest young man had been seduced into becoming a highway robber after seeing the *Beggar's Opera*.[63] Such a case is extreme, but it remains clear that there was often a great temptation to romanticize the criminal. Dick Turpin's modern fame might well be largely the product of a nineteenth-century novel,[64] but other highwaymen were being portrayed as romantic figures in the eighteenth century. Perhaps the earliest example was Captain James Hind, 'the great robber of England', whose 'merry life and mad exploits' were commemorated in a number of ballads and chapbooks. Hind was the prototype cavalier highwayman, and his execution in 1652 was for treason to the republican regime, not highway robbery. Tradition tells us that he was especially fond of robbing Roundheads, and that his victims included Bradshaw and Cromwell.[65]

Ballads were generally more stereotyped than pamphlets or chapbooks, and typically laid considerable emphasis on the anguish of the offender in his or her last hours, with the story being rounded off with an edifying description of penitence. These 'last goodnights' or 'sorrowful lamentations' usually followed a set formula. They were almost invariably written in the first person, with the speaker claiming to be the convicted criminal, although they were in fact almost equally invariably the work of a hack writer. The criminal was usually portrayed as leaving the world full of contrition, and warning his audience against falling into those lewd courses which had occasioned his sad downfall. The general tone was set by an early example of the genre, a 'sorrowful sonnet' allegedly composed by a convicted criminal an hour before his execution in 1576. It opened with the immortal couplet 'I waile in wo, I plunge in pain/with sorrowing sobs I do complain', and went on recount a story of a slow drift into crime in tones of mawkish pathos.[66]

As such examples remind us, despite the titillation which popular literature's treatment of crime provided, and despite the occasional romanticization of the criminal, the central purpose of the ballads and pamphlets was to act as a caution or warning to their readers. Thus execution was central to the literature. As any reader of Defoe or Fielding will be aware, the shadow of the gallows lies over much English literature of the early eighteenth century, and popular literature was even more explicit in its treatment of the theme.[67] Much of our evidence on this subject has been drawn from the accounts of the ceremonies attending hangings at Tyburn, and these have been described by a number of scholars, notably Radzinowicz and Linebaugh.[68] Obviously, Tyburn cases were more likely to be reported: an odd sidelight on the cultural ascendancy of the capital is provided by an account of the hanging of Jack Witherington, one of five brothers from Blandford, Dorset. The other four had been hanged in the country, 'but Jack had the good fortune to be reserved for Tyburn, and by that means to have his name transmitted to posterity'.[69] Accounts of executions outside London are harder to come by, at least before the advent of provincial newspapers. Pamphlet accounts, however, suggest that, at least in the case of the more notorious crimes, they were similar in their basic components to the theatre of punishment that was Tyburn. There were often thousands of 'sorrowful spectators', frequently some sort of procession to the gallows, and usually a sermon by a local clergyman. Above all, the condemned was expected to make a 'good end', to show courage on the gallows. The frequency with which such courage was shown was commented on by a number of those witnessing executions, both English and foreign. Most English observers attributed the hardiness of the condemned to either the obduracy of the labouring classes or to drink: other evidence suggests that a minority of the condemned at least were fortified in their last hours by a sense that they had achieved reconciliation with the Maker whom they were about to meet.

One aspect of making a good end, according to the pamphlet writers, was being launched into eternity in a contrite and penitent frame of mind. Proof of this was frequently offered in the 'last dying speech' or 'last dying confession' which the criminal was often recorded as delivering. Such speeches, far from being used as the occasion to hurl a final defiance at the unkind world, were usually marked by an acceptance of the justice and deservedness of the sentence which was about to be carried out, a warning to those present to avoid a similar fate, and a confession not only of the crime which had brought retribution, but also of a career of past sinfulness. This insistence on penitence is, in many ways, the most remarkable feature of accounts of execution. When several criminals made the final journey to Tyburn in 1669, for example, it was reported that

> several of them were very penitent, and begged of the Lord for pardon . . . two of the women were very penitent, and were much wrought upon while they were in Newgate, and brought to a sense of their sins by some ministers which came to them in prison, and died very cheerfully with an assured hope of their salvation.[70]

Isabell Hall, executed in 1604 for murdering her husband, not only hoped that her fate might be 'as a looking glasse to all that eyther did see or heare of her fall', but also tried to convert her fellow prisoners to her own level of Christian awareness while awaiting execution.[71] An Anabaptist convicted of murder in 1643 made a good end, delivered a speech against man's sinfulness to the crowd, and led them in a rendition of the fifty-first psalm.[72] Most accounts suggest that prisoners were generally willing to assist in this process, and the few that were unwilling to co-operate were obviously regarded as odd by the pamphlet writers. It is noteworthy that similar co-operation was given to the ordinary of Newgate as he went about his task of compiling accounts of the prisoners' lives: only in 'a dozen or so cases in a thousand' was the request for biographical details refused.[73]

Above all, these expressions of penitence from the scaffold emphasized how committing small sins led inexorably to the commission of large ones. Thomas Savage, executed in 1668, made a very good end indeed. After pleading guilty at his trial, where 'his carriage and confession was such, that he much moved the honourable bench and jury, and most of the beholders', he delivered a dying speech to the crowds gathered at his execution that was a classic of its kind:

> The first sin I began with, was sabbath-breaking, thereby I got acquaintance
> with bad company, and so went to the ale-house, and from the alehouse to
> the baudy-house: there I was perwaded to rob my master, as also to murder
> this poor innocent creature, for which I am come to this shameful end.[74]

Others recounted a similar story of decline and fall. John Noyse,
convicted of murder in 1686, 'turning to the spectators, who came to
see him executed', warned them, 'especially the younger sort', against
profaning the sabbath, drunkenness, and keeping company with
women 'in a lascivious and unlawful manner'.[75] Such examples could
be multiplied: the story was usually much the same. A minor youthful
fault, such as disobedience to parents or sabbath-breaking, led
through a course of alehouse-haunting, gambling, consorting with
whores, robbery and murder, to an untimely death on the gallows. The
didactic purposes of such case-histories was obvious: those at the
execution, or reading about it subsequently, would be left in little
doubt as to the consequences of sin. The young in particular would be
encouraged by the ceremonies at Tyburn and provincial executions to
regard death on the gallows as a natural consequence of adolescent
unruliness.

The power of such moral tales is, perhaps, best illustrated by the
enduring popularity of the story of George Barnwell. Barnwell, as the
title page of an eighteenth-century chapbook puts it, was an apprentice
'who was undone by a strumpet that caused him to rob his master, and
murder his uncle'. The origins of the story are obscure, and the tale
might date back to the reign of Elizabeth I: certainly, there seems to
have been a ballad version of it in print by the mid seventeenth
century. The story really gained wide currency, however, when a
minor and hitherto unsuccessful playwright named George Lillo
dramatized it in 1731. It was put on by a young cast, the male lead being
played by Theophilus Cibber, manager of the summer company then
performing at Drury Lane. The piece was a massive success. The
first-night audience of London sophisticates who had come to scoff
were moved to tears, Alexander Pope, who was present, subsequently
commended the play warmly, and the royal family attended later
performances. The later history of the play was remarkable. The story,
entitled in the chapbook alluded to earlier *Youth's warning piece or the
tragical history of George Barnwell*, was obviously regarded as an
excellent source of edification for the young, and was regularly performed at the holidays of Boxing Night and Easter in hopes of attracting a large audience of apprentices. The last London performance was
in 1819, but the play was still frequently staged in the provinces well
into the nineteenth century: Lillo's historian in the *Dictionary of
National Biography* recorded that it had regularly been performed on
Shrove Tuesday at the Theatre Royal, Manchester, until shortly

before he wrote. By that time such writers as Charles Lamb could dismiss the play as 'a nauseous sermon', but its popularity is striking evidence that such morality tales were thought worthy of repetition. Above all, the basic truth of so much of the popular literature dealing with crime and punishment was summed up in the last scene: 'bleeding hearts and weeping eyes' at executions are useless unless it is realized that the wages of sin are, indeed, death.[76]

The epitome of the moral tale warning the young that early sin led to the gallows, however, must surely have been Hogarth's series of twelve plates illustrating the respective fruits of *Industry and Idleness*, dating from 1747. As ever with Hogarth's work, things are rarely as simple as they seem, and the theme is treated with irony and nuance. Even so, on an immediate level the tale of the two apprentices, Francis Goodchild and Tom Idle, is a visual equivalent of the tales recounted in the last speeches of condemned felons, with much the same morality. Goodchild is industrious, rises in life through the time-honoured combination of working hard and marrying the boss's daughter, and eventually becomes Lord Mayor of London. Idle follows that route to Tyburn with which the ballads and pamphlets have acquainted us: idleness at work; gambling in the churchyard rather than attending divine service; becoming a robber; and consorting with a whore who betrays him to the authorities. The last print dealing with his career shows him in a cart approaching the gallows at Tyburn, alone under a cloudy sky but for a methodist minister who exhorts him. Closer inspection might suggest that Hogarth did not see the moral divide between the two case-histories as being absolute, and that Goodchild's success, to some extent, contains its peculiar seeds of destruction. Nevertheless, one suspects that those employers who bought copies of the prints, and put them on the walls of their workshops for the edification of their apprentices, took a simpler view. As an art critic has reminded us, the immediate impression given by the series is its simplicity of visual impact and its crudity of image relative to Hogarth's earlier work. The idea seems to have been to present 'a simple pattern of morality – right and wrong, reward and punishment, strengthened by the blacks and whites of the design . . . the greys are largely absent visually as well as morally'.[77] Most of those viewing these prints were being told what they wanted to hear, what they already knew. The familiar tale of the drift to the gallows through early sinfulness was being recounted yet again; a set of stereotyped ideas about crime and its origins was receiving yet more reinforcement.

If the public was being offered a stereotype of what serious crime was about, it seems likely that popular literature had long since established a stereotype of what the underworld in general was like. As we have argued when discussing organized crime, there seems to be a distressing lack of correspondence between the impression given by the rogue literature of the Elizabethan and Jacobean periods and the reliability of vagrant or metropolitan crime as it appears in court records. There are, as ever, a number of problems involved in interpreting this material, but placing it in the context of other forms of popular literature dealing with crime does suggest that its representation of the criminal underworld is in many respects fictional, and essentially normative. One student of popular literature in the early eighteenth century has claimed that too much importance has been placed on the 'journalistic realism' of popular accounts of crime and criminals, and not enough on 'the ideological significance of popular literature, the social, moral and religious values which it implicitly communicates and depends upon'.[78] The objectives of this literature might include a desire to titillate or shock, but its underlying purpose is to reinforce the values of 'straight' society. It is very stereotyped, a defect which is worsened, in the Elizabethan and Jacobean rogue literature at least, by a readiness to plagiarize: the same anecdotes, expressed in much the same way, recur repeatedly. As we have argued, the rogue pamphleteers were apparently convinced of the existence of a complete sub-culture, with its own hierarchy, argot, skills, and a high degree of organization. If this picture was only a very imperfect reflection of reality, why did it enjoy such a wide market?

Much of the appeal of the rogue literature, and of later popular works on crime, lay in its entertainment value. From the start, the tricks and exploits described in the rogue pamphlets are recounted with evident relish and panache, and reading them can still be an enjoyable experience. On the other hand, behind the relish there lurks the conviction that the underworld is dangerous: it may in many ways be presented as a mirror image of straight society, but (and possibly because it is such a mirror image) it *threatens* it. Could it be that descriptions of the 'Elizabethan underworld', or of gangs, tell us more about the fears of society, and ultimately of the government, than they do of reality? Many of the ideas that crystallized in the rogue pamphlets as the genre developed were commonplace of governmental thinking, enshrined in numerous statutes and proclamations: above all, the danger of idleness, and the need to preserve order. Hence the literature which helped form popular ideas on crime must be understood largely as a popular expression of disquiet at some of the symptoms of the social disruption of the period, with morally and socially desirable remedies either prescribed or implied. Perhaps it did more: by constructing the concept of the underworld, it gave crime an identity which made it comprehensible, just as abstract fears of disruption in the early nineteenth century were given a more concrete form by the emergence of the concept of the 'criminal class'. Thus 'crime' is restricted to certain groups, and can emerge as a clearly defined 'problem' for which 'solutions' can be proposed. The development of stereotyped views on this point simplified a very complex phenomenon, and allowed contemporaries the luxury of reacting to crime with a stock response rather than thinking too deeply about the issues involved.[79]

Studying elite attitudes and criminal stereotypes leads us to the conclusion that these matters were much more complicated than might at first have been expected. Parliament enacted legislation against both minor and major crime, but with little unanimity of purpose, often at the instigation of pressure groups, and often in so haphazard a fashion as to make it difficult to argue that members of either house had a coherent or consistent policy. The English seemed happy to eulogize the law, but were equally happy to satirize lawyers. The actual implementation of the law was often deliberately adjusted by officials in the face of local circumstances, while the upper reaches of the relevant administrations were often unwilling to give inferiors their full support. Magistrates around 1700 might refuse to countenance godly informers' prosecutions of moral offences because they felt that to do so would aid Whiggery or dissenting enthusiasm. Popular literature constructed a stereotype of the criminal, and convinced the public at large of the dreadful consequences of sin for the individual and of the threat posed by the underworld to society at large, but the awareness of these dangers was already being muted by a tendency to romanticize the criminal. Ultimately, the law was a means of protecting the property of the upper strata of society. Ultimately, men of property would make a stand against disorder, crime and sin. These ultimate choices, however, were invariably surrounded by an extensive behavioural hinterland where sloth, partiality, personal feelings and individual circumstances would affect the processes of law and order. Studying attitudes to crime and the law involves the analysis of a complex variety of real historial experience, an analysis that has as yet barely begun. Until it has progressed considerably further, we must accept that our impression of how English society was ruled, of why English society cohered, must be very incomplete.

Such an analysis would also help illuminate a problem on which we have touched at various points in this chapter: how far attitudes to crime, law and order, and related matters changed. Obviously, there are a number of continuities in official thinking. Much comment on sin and crime merely entailed the repetition of commonplaces, while throughout our period officialdom could point to an established cause of crime: the innate sinfulness of man. Delineating changes in attitudes is also impeded by the tendency of observers of all periods to feel that their particular epoch is experiencing crime at its worst: as an early eighteenth-century writer put it, 'the depravity and corruption of human nature hath been the general complaint of almost all ages'.[80]

Despite the continuities in ideas on crime, it is possible to trace a number of shifts in emphasis. Again and again, the historian is struck by the panic-ridden tone of writers on sin, crime, and disorder before the Civil Wars, and the more measured, rational, treatment of such matters after the Restoration. By the eighteenth century, government and society seemed more secure, more stable. An important transition had occurred. In the late sixteenth century, the poor were seen as the many-headed monster which, left to itself, would act as an agent of universal chaos. By the mid-eighteenth century, the poor, in the form of the mob, were regarded essentially as an inconvenience rather than a threat.[81]

Our claims for such a transition are, of course, very tentative, and will be expanded in the following chapter. If nothing else, they remind us that crime, to a large extent, is defined by people in positions of power, and that pressure on the criminal, expressed in terms of the efficiency with which the law-enforcement system is run, is similarly affected by the decisions of the powerful. It is therefore logical that the reactions of such groups to changing circumstances, and the alteration which such reactions can make on existing circumstances, are of essential importance to the study of crime as an historical phenomenon.

Chapter 8

CONTINUITY AND CHANGE IN CRIME AND PUNISHMENT 1550–1750

In the previous chapters we have ranged freely over a number of areas, and have demonstrated, if nothing else, the variety of approaches that can be employed in studying the history of crime, and the multiplicity of issues involved in the subject. The point has now come at which these various threads must be pulled together, and an attempt made to understand the general developments and problems relevant to the study of crime in this period. These developments and problems are fairly numerous, and the avenues towards understanding them correspondingly diverse. There is, nevertheless, a central theme which must be addressed: that of the possible connections between patterns of crime, patterns of punishment, the attitudes of ruling groups to such matters, and broader socio-economic change. There is, after all, a general consensus that such connections exist: a student of crime in Victorian and Edwardian Britain, for example, could claim that 'it has become one of the more widely accepted axioms of our age that an increasing crime rate is the invariable price of material progress'.[1] Commentators on earlier periods have, generally speaking, been equally convinced of the presence of links of this sort. Hence we find a recent work on crime in early modern Europe informing us that 'although crime is usually seen as an index of social distress, it can also be appreciated as an index of social development'. This work goes on to claim that the pattern of European theft, if drawn up, would correlate in time and geography with economic development, and also suggests that within the timespan it covers Europe witnessed 'the emergence of new forms of criminality that reflected the ongoing transition to industrial life'.[2]

Such views, however admirable in their willingness to address broad issues, should not obscure the fact that those economic changes they presuppose are often more complex and ambivalent than has been thought: many general notions about developments in crime and punishment in the past have compounded oversimplification of the criminal aspects of life with a gross oversimplification of economic developments. It remains true, we must remind ourselves, that there exist a number of studies which attempt to interpret the main lines of change in crime and punishment in the early modern period, usually from a Marxist or neo-Marxist perspective which interprets the period from the early sixteenth to the late eighteenth centuries as the crucial phase of the transition from feudalism to capitalism.[3] The attractions of such an approach are obvious. Some forms of crime, such as theft, smuggling, and fraud, appear to be capable of connection with economic development. Moreover, if we accept that crime is to a large extent defined by groups in power, and if it is accepted that new social groups, representing the dominance of new social forces, 'rise' in a given period, logic would suggest that new forms of criminality would be defined. Proponents of the wide-ranging study connecting crime with economic development have accordingly claimed to have discovered the emergence of a number of important developments in, or by the end of, the early modern period. The second half of the eighteenth century, we are therefore informed, saw the culmination of various processes which produced Europe's first sustained debate on the nature of crime; the first serious revision of criminal law codes; the first rationalization of judicial and prosecutional activity; the development, again for the first time, of a rational system of punishment; and the arrival of police forces in something like the modern sense.[4] Such an analysis, if accurate, is at once reassuring and challenging: studying crime in the early modern period is obviously likely to involve contact with some important issues, although interpreting them may well be difficult.

There is a second major change, other than that in the socio-economic sphere, which must be confronted: the development of the state.[5] This phenomenon, which is obviously connected somehow to developments in society and the economy, has received little attention from English historians. In general terms, it is evident that 'the state', however cautious we must be in defining that entity, was impinging more closely on the population of Europe. The major concern was a military one, the recruitment of armies and the collection of taxes to finance them, and hence the impingement came later in England than in some of the great European states. The period also witnessed an attempt to extend state control, and hence state law, in more general terms. This has been held to have accelerated another transition, from the 'private' law of the Middle Ages, 'the sublimation of a vendetta',[6] to the 'state' law with which we are currently familiar. This transition, one of the fundamental developments of European civilization, was a lengthy process, described by a recent historian as

> the millenial transition from anomic violence to regulated violence, the
> passage from private vengeance, private warfare and makeshift
> compromises devoid of guarantee, to a gradual acceptance of the king's
> justice as the sole locus of arbitral power which delivers his subjects from the

scourge of the never-ending round of violence and private revenge.[7]

More specifically, as we have already argued at various points, understanding crime in early modern England is impossible unless the objectives of the state, and of the state church, are taken into account. Above all, the crucial importance of fear of disorder, compounded after the Reformation by fear of disunity in religion, must be reiterated. The growth of state power, expressed in terms of the growing impingement of state law on the individual, must therefore be added to the problems of socio-economic development when discussing the general issue of crime in our period.

At first sight, the combination of these two phenomena would suggest that such a discussion would revolve around obvious and decisive changes. Our initial task, however, must be to confront a surprising number of continuities. The first of these is the broad similarity in the pattern of serious crime obtaining between the late middle ages and the early modern period. As we have seen, outside London, prosecution of all felonies, and especially property offences, underwent a marked drop between the early seventeenth and the early eighteenth centuries: this is an important finding, and one to which we will return in due course. Even allowing for this trend, the similarity between the eighteenth and the fourteenth centuries is striking: a predominance of property offences, most of them simple larcenies, with homicide as the only other felony regularly prosecuted, and a virtual absence of such remaining felonies as rape or arson. There are a few exceptions to this pattern, most of them limited regionally or chronologically: witchcraft in Essex between 1560 and 1645, or coining in the north in the 1690s, while the rise of infanticide from the late sixteenth century does mark the emergence of a distinctive new offence. This pattern seems to hold true for all of the period we are concerned with, and is confirmed by studying a good sample of extant assize records: Essex, Sussex and Hertfordshire 1559–1625; Cheshire 1580–1709; Essex 1620–1680; Sussex and Surrey 1660–1800; Devon 1700–1709; Cornwall 1700–1749; Norfolk and Suffolk 1734–1737.[8] It could therefore be argued, as far as serious crime is concerned, that despite a change in the quantity of prosecutions there is little sign of any qualitative transition in our period, while the similarities with the widespread investigation of fourteenth-century crime made by Hanawalt is striking. There was maybe more robbery, and perhaps more violence used in the committing of crimes, but the broad pattern was much the same. Hanawalt's findings, based on 15,952 indictments from eight widely-scattered counties over the years 1300–48, are not dissimilar from those obtaining in many areas in the period 1550–1750. Homicide comprised 18 per cent of indictments, property offences and receiving roughly 80 per cent. Arson accounted for less than 1 per cent, and rape about 0.5 per cent.[9] Those attempting to relate changing patterns of serious crime with some preconceived notion of economic change must, therefore, confront the problem that the patterns of serious crime do not seem to have changed much between the fourteenth century and 1800.

Changes in the prosecution of petty crime might seem more fruitful: the impact of the state might be expected to show more clearly in the prosecution of regulative offences than in felony, which was still essentially a matter for private prosecution. The ambitions of the Tudor state, the increased premium on controlling personal conduct after the Reformation, and the Puritan reformation of manners did indeed combine, in some areas at least, to produce an increase in the amount of crime being prosecuted in the quarter sessions and the local ecclesiastical tribunals. On a local level the impact of these forces could be dramatic in both qualitative and quantitative terms. Detailed parish studies have shown how communities might experience both an absolute rise in prosecutions, and a move away from purely inter-personal crime to the presentment or indictment of regulatory offences in the period 1560–1660, and county studies have confirmed the trend on a wider level.[10] This 'increase in governance', it might be argued, is therefore one of the decisive influences in crime statistics in the first half of our period. In a much-governed county, such as Essex, prosecutions of petty crime rose dramatically. Even in supposedly 'isolated' or 'backward' counties, such as Cheshire or Yorkshire in the north, much the same process can be found taking place.[11] In times of crisis, or in other periods when control was intensified, the impact of regulatory prosecutions on crime statistics could be very marked: one is reminded of the Essex quarter sessions, 1629–31, with their 652 prosecutions connected with the drink trade compared to 93 thefts.[12] Such statistics provide local evidence of a major European trend. The state was anxious to control its subjects more effectively, hence new offences were created and old ones prosecuted more vigorously. At the same time, state churches on both sides of the religious divide set out to curb immorality in the hope of promoting godliness. In the rise of the regulatory offence, therefore, we may feel that we have found one of the distinctive forms of early modern crime.

In England, there was an undeniable increase in the prosecution of such offences at the quarter sessions and in the archdeaconry courts. The conclusion that this marked a new departure must, however, be modified by the possibility that this increase was the result of a shift in jurisdiction. There is certainly considerable evidence that conduct which was later to be decried by supporters of reformation of manners was being tried in the late middle ages at manorial and borough courts. Detailed work on a Worcestershire manor between 1270 and 1400 has shown that, under demographic pressure, poor bastard-bearers and gleaners were prosecuted more frequently at the manorial court. In the fifteenth century, jurors on a Sussex manor, when

171

regulating moral offences, revealed 'an ethos that we tend to equate with puritanism'. Study of local law enforcement in the reign of Henry VII demonstrates a pattern of 'sex and business as usual'.[13] There is, moreover, evidence that late medieval quarter sessions were already dealing with large amounts of non-felonious offences. Thus we find that at the Yorkshire sessions of the peace for 1361–64, there were tried 78 felonies, 165 non-commercial trespasses, 107 commercial trespasses, and 222 infringements of the labour law.[14] The increase in the prosecution of regulatory offences that has been traced in the Elizabethan and early Stuart periods might be evidence not so much of something totally new as of a more aggressive policy and a shift of emphasis in the courts used to curb such offences. It is also intriguing to speculate on whether the alleged decline in the prosecution of such offences from the late seventeenth century onwards might not also be partly the result of another shift in jurisdiction. By the late eighteenth century, such writers as Zouch could pass comment on the growth of the summary powers of the JP, which rendered that officer 'one of the most powerful ministers of justice in the known world'.[15] The tendency to deal with petty offenders by this 'mode of summary proceedings' would, of course, have a marked effect on the record of court prosecutions. Changes in patterns of crime must not be confused with changes in jurisdiction.

Mention of the medieval manorial court introduces another continuity, that of the dependence upon unpaid amateur local officials. As was discussed in chapter 4, one of the most important changes that has been postulated concerning law enforcement in this period has been the tendency for richer villagers, from whom such office-holders were drawn, to become more efficient, more attached to the values of the state, and, in some villages at least, attached to Puritan ideas on the need to discipline the ungodly multitude. Work on medieval rural society, however, has suggested that the underlying features of this process were hardly new. J. A. Raftis, in an early survey, identified 'main families' of richer peasants who held local office and played a leading role in running their villages. A later study claimed that in King's Ripton, Huntingdonshire, fourteenth-century manorial jurors were 'the voice of the community in maintaining village bylaws, maintaining the policing institutions of the tithing and hue and cry, and settling inheritance claims'. Such jurors were drawn from the upper ranks of village society and, when need arose, would use their local domination to control the poorer strata of the peasantry. On the Ramsey Abbey estates, once more in the fourteenth century, we find that 'the criminal justice system and the social system of the villages were bound closely together', and that 'manipulation of the judicial system through jury service gave the village oligarchs . . . a powerful weapon for dominating their villages'.[16] Such evidence suggests that the type of pattern traced by Wrightson and Levine in Terling in the late sixteenth and early seventeenth centuries was, at the most, an intensification of an existing situation.

This suggestion raises a fundamental question: how far is it possible to trace similarities between the reactions of English society to the demographic pressures of 1550–1640 and those experienced during that other great period of population growth, between 1250 and the advent of the Black Death? The details of such a comparison are, of course, best left to medievalists and historical demographers: the issue must at least be raised here if we are to obtain any very realistic impression of what was peculiar to the later period. Despite the difficulties of comparisons of this type, it does seem probable that in many villages pressure on resources would lead to a sharpening of social stratification, a marginalization of the poorer villagers, and an increased willingness to control them by the richer ones holding manorial office. Even if certain broad similarities obtained at the base of society, the presence of important differences on a national level meant that experiences in the two periods were very different. In the period 1550–1660 changes on a village level occurred within the wider context of an aggressive central and local governmental system, of the new perceptions of society provided by post-Reformation Protestantism, and of a higher degree of literacy, which allowed the ideas of the government to penetrate more deeply and more rapidly into local society. Rural society in the century before 1348 certainly experienced greater pressure on resources, which may well have had consequences very similar to those experienced in the hundred years before 1650. It did not, on the other hand, have a central government which was anxious and (within limits) capable of intervening to alleviate these problems, nor a religion which made the presence of a mass of potentially sinful poor comprehensible in theological terms. Above all, the fourteenth century did not witness the emergence of an institutionalized poor, such as followed the end of demographic growth in the seventeenth: the Black Death ensured that.

Despite the existence of a more purposeful state, most governmental administration remained fairly ramshackle by modern standards, while the criminal courts continued to be irrational in their running. The great distinguishing mark of the administration of the English criminal law throughout our period was the selectivity of its application. That it was to remain so for the best part of a century after the concluding date of this study implies that the claims that the early modern period experienced the 'beginnings of a logical system of punishment' or 'attempts to devise new and more rational systems of punishment' need careful scrutiny. Some English commentators were, by the late eighteenth century, convinced of the irrationality of the system: Romilly, for example, thought it incredible that 'this mode of administering justice is supposed by some persons to be a regular, matured, and well-digested system'.[17] What is most remarkable is that, as in the Middle Ages, the irregularities of the system worked most frequently to the advantage of accused criminals. Generations of preachers urged that justice should be mixed with clemency, and by the end of our period this had made the whole business of punishment for felony something of a lottery. One critic remarked sourly on how 'the various connections which the convicts have formed in life, as well as his natural friends' might be brought in to aid him, 'perhaps a brother who is servant to some member of parliament, or a sister who is mistress to such a one, or perhaps to some greater man: in short, the higher powers are got at'.[18] Punishment statistics and impressionistic evidence combine to suggest that by the late seventeenth century it was only the exceptionally wicked or unlucky criminal who suffered execution. In 1675, for example, when two murderers attemped to obtain pardon, 'the heinousness of the crime, the quality of the person kill'd, and many other circumstances prevented that indulgence'; more typically, some means would have been found to lessen their punishment.[19]

The traditional rationale for this selectivity was given by Paley: a theoretical power to impose a capital sentence was given over 'every crime which, under any possible circumstances, may merit the punishment of death', but in practice execution should only be the fate of 'a small proportion of each class . . . the general character, or peculiar aggravation of whose crimes, render them fit examples of public justice'.[20] This selectivity did not operate merely when the assize judge was deliberating on his sentence. Criminals, we must remind ourselves, found themselves in court as a result of decisions taken by people in society at large: as we have stressed, they often only experienced formal prosecution after a variety of settlements out of court had been attempted and had failed. The whole philosophy of the administration of the criminal law was, therefore, very different from that familiar to the citizen of the modern state, with its police forces, social services, and fully bureaucratized law-enforcement system. Nevertheless, the old system seems to have worked tolerably enough, and its sheer longevity and the fact that it attracted some passionate defenders when it came under criticism at the turn of the eighteenth and nineteenth centuries indicates that it deserves serious attention. One of the outcomes of the uncertainty of prosecution and conviction, however, was that criminals must often have adopted a sort of gambling mentality towards the possible fruits of their delinquencies. Thus Madan reported a convicted man telling him that 'there are so many chances *for* us, and so few *against* us, that I never thought of coming to this'. Fielding felt that 'the probability of escaping punishment' was one of the great encouragements to robbery.[21]

The application of the criminal law was in many ways irrational to the modern student. But it was the criminal law itself which, in many ways, constituted the greatest continuity of them all. One of the great peculiarities of England was the way in which, from the twelfth century at least, the criminal law was almost uniquely the king's law. This theoretical royal monopoly was modified by a few franchises, and by the idleness, partiality, inefficiency, or corruption of officers. Even so, it remained true that criminal courts, from the King's Bench to the manorial leet, were supposedly royal courts administering the royal law. Moreover, there is every indication that people liked royal justice. The English, if not exactly a law-abiding race, were by 1550 long accustomed to settling disputes by recourse to the law, and were familiar with the law as a component of their wider culture. Even as early as the twelfth century, the sheer complexity of the Anglo-Norman legal system is suggestive of a law that was sophisticated and flexible.[22] This is of some importance when considering the supposed changes of the early modern period, and the supposed replacement of private by state justice. Arguably, the English crown already had several centuries of relatively successful control behind it by 1550. It ran an effective legal system, in a sense centralized, which was generally accepted by the population at large.

Such a conclusion introduces another general problem: the degree to which early modern England differed from earlier and later periods in terms of lawlessness and violence. It is tempting to interpret this question in terms of an evolutionary progress moving away from some sort of state of nature towards twentieth-century values. Certainly, writers on the medieval period give the impression of a society that was more violent than that of the seventeenth or eighteenth centuries. A student of thirteenth-century homicide, for example, finds the experience of homicide widespread in his period, and remarks that 'in studying the patterns of homicide we are concerned with one of the major social phenomena of the age'.[23] Basing arguments on statistics is dangerous, and more work obviously needs to be done, but it does seem that there was a steady diminution in homicidal violence between the thirteenth and the mid twentieth centuries.[24] Nevertheless, it seems unlikely that the murder rates were really high enough in the early modern period to support the argument that England was a particularly lawless or violent place. As Alan Macfarlane has been at pains to demonstrate, even an 'isolated' or 'backward' area like seventeenth-century Westmorland was not especially bruted or unsafe. Disputes in this region were normally settled by persuasion or reasoning, and by legal means if these failed: physical violence was rarely resorted to.[25] Violence and lawlessness were probably high by modern English standards, but not sufficiently so to constitute a society which was qualitatively different. Certainly the portrayal of early modern (and, in all probability, late medieval) England as a brutal society, where life was cheap and might be easily taken, is vastly overdrawn.[26]

The student of crime in the early modern period must, therefore, confront a number of continuities from the medieval world, and be correspondingly wary in attempting to delineate any changes. None of this should be taken as implying that changes did not take place. The problem remains of determining the exact nature of such differences as did occur, and, in particular, of relating them to wider socio-economic developments.

One crucial innovation was the criminalization of the poor. In the middle ages occasional members of the nobility turned criminal, while the more mundane offenders were characteristically drawn from the village elite: 'the suspects were for the most part village worthies . . . who moved in and out of crime as need and opportunity dictated'.[27] Medieval records do reveal the existence of marginal poor criminals who were essentially similar to those brought to light by studies of Elizabethan and Stuart villages. Moreover, the middling sort and even the aristocracy in the early modern period were not as tame as has sometimes been suggested. Nevertheless, by the end of our period crime was regarded primarily as an activity of the poor. This development, an outcome of demographic growth rather than the development of capitalism *per se*, was one of the most important in our period.

As we have seen at various points, a generalized fear of the many-headed monster was one of the recurring themes of social debate, especially in the century before the Civil Wars. This generalized fear produced a mass of more specific legislation: the familiar statutes against vagrants, the equally familiar laws extending the death penalty in the eighteenth century, and a host of lesser known statutes against the likely delinquencies of 'idle disorderly persons'. The poor no longer simply had to be provided for: they now had to be controlled as well, and, over much of our period, this control involved taking them to court when they pilfered, got drunk, or engendered bastards. The poor were to remain the group most likely to be regarded as criminal. If the study of the middle ages produces striking evidence of continuities from earlier periods surviving into ours, so the records of the Victorian and Edwardian era apparently lead the historian to conclude that the criminal orders were very similar to those with which a Jacobean justice would have been familiar: indeed, one late Victorian editor of an early Stuart JP's notebook commented on how little the country magistrate's work seemed to have changed.[28] Recent work on Victorian and Edwardian crime has portrayed criminals in terms that are very similar to those which emerge from the study of early modern materials: largely unskilled and opportunistic, many of them people in employment who were willing to supplement their income by theft, modest in their criminal ambitions, limited in their horizons, in a non-technical sense somehow 'innocent'.[29] The crime they committed also seems to have been broadly similar to that of the early modern period. In the early Victorian Black Country, for example, we find that crime was essentially 'prosaic and undramatic, involving small amounts being stolen, squalid robberies, burglaries and assaults'.[30] After the mid seventeenth century, the ruling strata must have felt that the poor were not only always with them, but were also always destined to be criminous.

`The poor increased in number, then, and accordingly made the transition from being God's poor to being the Devil's. To that extent a broad connection between socio-economic change and change in crime seems to have been established. What is therefore extremely surprising is that the type of crime which might be felt most logically to reflect this situation, the property offence, fell so drastically: as we have seen, one English county experienced a drop from 507 prosecutions of such offences at its assizes in the 1620s to a mere 55 in the decade 1700–09, with executions for crime against property falling from 138 to 5. There were more poor, they had to a certain extent been criminalized, and parliament had passed a number of statutes defending the propertied with the death penalty. This was evidently happening, however, in a period when the actual level of prosecutions and executions for property offences was dropping rapidly, and the chronology of the drop precludes any assumption that the legislation had any deterrent effect. This trend makes nonsense of any attempts to make a simplistic connection between the rise of theft and the rise of commerce, or to apply arguments about a *violence/vol* transition on the French pattern to England. Given our presuppositions about what ought to have happened to patterns of property offences in early modern England, this dramatic fall in such offences, and the lessening of the severity with which they were treated, is extremely surprising.

Tracing the rise of a criminality more directly connected with the development of an increasingly complex business life is more problematic. There doubtless were prefigurations of what has come to be known as 'white-collar' crime, but very few of them appear in the criminal courts. The statute book indicates that certain forms of commercial malpractice were indeed criminalized. Forgery, for example, was an offence which was obviously likely to attract more attention as commerce developed. Characteristically the offence was treated in a piecemeal fashion by a series of statutes. In 1563 the forgery of certain deeds and documents, notably those relating to real property, was made misdemeanour on the first offences, and felony without benefit of clergy on the second. Other forms of forgery seem to have been dealt with by Star Chamber, and after the demise of that institution the common law courts simply treated all forgery as misdemeanour. The situation changed in the early eighteenth century, when a whole series of Acts, of which the most significant were passed in 1724, 1725 and 1729, made all types of forgery felony. The net result of this legislation was that by the time Blackstone wrote, there was 'hardly a case possible to be conceived, wherein forgery, that tends to defraud, whether in the name of a real or fictitious person, is not made a capital crime'.[31] All this is evidence of the criminal law adjusting to commercial change. The problem is that prosecutions under this legislation were exceedingly rare. Both the Old Bailey Sessions Papers and the records of provincial assizes in the mid eighteenth century are largely devoid of evidence of a rising tide of forgers.[32]

Patterns of crime were not, therefore, reflecting patterns of legislation, and there is little evidence of new forms of crime creating serious problems before 1750. Arguably, more marked changes were taking place in punishment. There was a move away from those old shaming punishments which had been used to inflict humiliation on offenders. Some of these, the stocks, the ducking stool, or even ecclesiastical penance, are familiar enough, and were in most circumstances fairly regularized. Less familiar is the way in which punishments might be devised or adapted to fit particular crimes. In Somerset in 1617 we find the bench ordering the reputed parents of a bastard to be whipped 'till their bodies shall be bloody', with two fiddles being played before them 'in regard to make known their lewdness in begetting the said base child upon the sabboth day coming from dancyng'. John Taylor, indicted at Chester in 1608 'For wearinge weomen's apparell', received the sentence that 'his clothes to be cut and breeches to be made of them & to be whipped thorowe the citie tomorrowe'. A Somerset woman, convicted of embezzling wool to the value of 4d. from her employer, was ordered to be put in the stocks at Shepton Mallet with a lock of wool hung before her on market-day. In London, William Stanton of Whitecross Street, carted for running a brothel in 1617, was ordered 'to be sett upon the uppermost parte of a carte there to be made fast and bare faced with a paper inscripted for a base and filthie bawdy-housekeeper and so to be carted through the streets of the cittye'. It seems probable that late medieval records would supply more numerous and more ornate cases to match these Jacobean examples. In 1504 during the Archbishop of Canterbury's visitation of Bangor diocese, a man cited for harrowing on the sabbath was ordered to ride the wheel of his machine, bare-headed and bare-footed, through Ruthin market-square in the presence of the visitor.[33] The process defies statistical analysis, but it seems likely that this sort of thing was much less likely to happen in the mid eighteenth than the early sixteenth century. The gradual decline of shaming punishments represents one area where traditional ideas on law enforcement gave way before more 'rational' notions.

There is also an impressionistic sense that local and traditional views on arbitration in criminal cases were similarly rationalized out by stricter ideas on the proper procedures in such matters. Arbitration was central to litigation in the middle ages, and probably continued to be so throughout the early modern period. The common law accepted it, while the ecclesiastical law, whose main objective was reconciliation and the restoration of Christian charity, was very willing to sanction such settlements.[34] What is more surprising is scattered evidence from the early years of our period of official countenancing of settlements in more strictly criminal matters. In Elizabethan Devizes the mayor on one occasion dismissed the two parties in what seems to have been a fairly serious assault case after he had 'p[er]swaded a unitie betweene them'. At Warwick, the town authorities in the 1580s seemed happy to allow theft accusations to be discontinued after the parties involved had made a settlement. A generation later, the Surrey JP Bostock Fuller was similarly happy to allow theft charges to be dropped if a settlement were reached: some idea of local adjustments of the letter of the law can be gained from one case where he allowed a charge of wood-theft to drop after the accused agreed that he was 'to doe twoo dayes worke for Pycknett & never he himselfe nor his servants to poll his hedges &c'.[35] Once more, changing attitudes defy quantification, and judgement must be impressionistic, but it is probable that a move away from such accommodations, on a level of policy-making at least, occurred over our period. Doubtless there existed, throughout the eighteenth century, justices who encouraged informal settlement: against them must be set such examples as that of Thomas Butcher, fined by the Buckinghamshire quarter sessions in 1705 for compounding with a man whom he had accused of theft.[36]

If the decline of shame punishments and a harder line against settling crimes out of court can be interpreted as possible tokens of a new 'rational' thinking on how crime should be treated, the house of correction provides an almost unique example of an institution which has been universally regarded as marking a new departure in such matters. The house of correction, of which the London Bridewell was the prototype, constituted an important shift in punishment policy. To the established notions of punishment as deterrence and retribution was added the idea that it might be possible to cure criminal instincts through a healthy dose of labour discipline. It is this aspect of the house of correction's purpose which has allowed it to be greeted with such enthusiasm by those seeking to link changes in crime and punishment with socio-economic change. Rusche and Kirchheimer, whose basic assumption was that 'every system of production tends to discover punishments which correspond to its productive relationships', provided the classic formulation of this theme. Looking at houses of correction in a European context (the London Bridewell was only one of a number of experiments in this direction) they declared

> its main aim was to make the labour power of unwilling people socially useful. By being forced to work within the institution, the prisoners would form industrious habits and would receive a vocational training at the same time. When released, it was hoped they would voluntarily swell the labour market.[37]

This idea has informed the work of a number of other writers, notably Melossi and Pavarini, and has much to recommend it. If the basic concern of government was to impose order on what was felt to be an increasingly disorderly population, the house of correction was obviously a weapon of considerable utility.

So far little detailed work has been done on the actual operation of the houses,[38] and it is probable that they were not the smooth-running schools of labour discipline that the general historians of crime and punishment would have us believe: Fielding's comment that it was inconceivable that those sent to houses of correction 'will not come out of those houses much more idle and disorderly than when they went in' encourages scepticism.[39] What is apparent is that, from their inception, the houses of correction were used as repositories for all types of petty offender. From the late sixteenth century, statutes provided that convicted criminals might have a spell in the house of correction added to their other punishments. By the 1610s it is possible to find persons acquitted of theft at the assizes being sent to the house for a short period, the intention obviously being that even if they had escaped punishment for felony, they were still felt to be reprehensible characters in need of some lesser punishment.[40] Occasional records provide a fuller impression of the work of the houses. A series of calendars from the house of correction at Barking, Essex, between 1664 and 1676, for example, provides evidence of those passing through a small house of correction in what was still essentially a rural area. The largest single category among those incarcerated was formed by vagrants, although there were many others: an idle disorderly fellow, who had assaulted his master; runaway apprentices; a disorderly person caught setting snares in Waltham Forest; an unlicensed beer-seller; a man found wandering at night who was suspected of felony; a runaway from the army; pilferers; two Dutch prisoners-of-war escaped from captivity in Colchester; and a girl suspected of infanticide, held temporarily before being passed on to the county gaol.[41] The house was obviously regarded as an excellent means of dealing with a very wide variety of petty criminals. Certainly JPs thought so: local justices regularly ordered that such persons should be sent to or released from the Barking house at their monthly meetings. Members of the population at large seem to have been equally willing to recommend that offenders should go to the house. A Liverpool man neatly summarized the transition in styles of punishment when he wrote in 1678 of one of his tenants who had offended him: 'I was glad to send her to the house of correction, since which she hath been much better. She hath been once bridled, twice carted, and once ducked.'[42]

By the early eighteenth century, therefore, the house of correction was obviously thought of as an appropriate means of punishing large numbers of petty offenders who might at earlier points have been dealt with by presentment or indictment. This raises some teasing questions about fluctuations in criminal statistics. It also complicates some of the standard interpretations of that most celebrated of historico-criminal themes, the rise of the prison. It has long been axiomatic that this development was symbolic of the triumph of capitalism, with the prison being equated with the factory. A dual analogy is pursued: 'prisoners must be workers, workers must be prisoners', the end product of all this being an intimate relationship between 'the coercive prison' and 'the coercive labour economy'.[43] This whole idea has been restated, and then developed into a more philosophical set of ideas about punishment, in a recent work by Michel Foucault which has attracted considerable attention.[44] The problem is that the house of correction, established as it was in the sixteenth century, severely modifies the chronology of the rise of the prison as a 'modern' form of punishment. The point has been well made by two Italian Marxist scholars:

> this type of institution was the first and most important example of secular detention involving more than mere custody in the history of the prison; its characteristic features, its social function, and its internal organization are, as far as the final form of the institution is concerned, already *to a large extent* those of the classic nineteenth-century model of the prison.[45]

As we have suggested, until more detailed research has actually been carried out on the running of houses of correction, such statements must be considered as, to some extent at least, conjectural. It is, nevertheless, evidence that if the prison as a reformatory or penitentiary form of punishment is thought of as an essentially 'modern' institution, the house of correction must be taken into account as an early example of modernity.

Any discussion of the rise of the prison must also incorporate the numerous occasions on which commentators within the early modern period expressed views that were extremely sceptical about the efficacy of that institution. Indeed, their perceptions were often more acute than those of 'modern' nineteenth-century reformers, and often seem surprisingly close to those of current critics of imprisonment. It was almost a commonplace that offenders left prison more wicked than when they went in. The point was made by the Book of Orders in 1631[46], which sought to remedy the situation by placing more petty offenders in the house of correction. Timothy Nourse echoed the sentiment in 1701. He argued that prisoners should be set to work, 'thus preserving them from being instructed in further roguries, and from being idle and talking only with their fellow prisoners of former pranks: so that once in gaol, and a rogue ever after'.[47] De Mandeville, two decades later, thought it 'wrong to suffer such numbers of them to be and converse together', adding that 'nothing but the utmost corruption can be expected from a company of forty or fifty people in a prison, who, every one of them, singly consider'd, were all the worst of thousands before they met'.[48] Perhaps the most remarkable statement on this theme came from a draft bill presented to Parliament in 1621, intending to set to work 'wicked and ungodly persons' given to stealing. The draft stated that

> long imprisonment in common gaoles rendreth such offenders the more obdurate and desperate when they are delivered out of the gaols, they being then poor, miserable, and friendless, are in a manner exposed to the like mischiefs, they not having means of ther owne, nor place of habitation nor likely to gaigne so much credite from any honest householder as to interteyn them.[49]

There seemed to be a widespread awareness in seventeenth and eighteenth-century England of that basic truth which seems to have eluded so many of the later proponents of prison schemes: imprisonment is as likely to create criminals as it is to cure them.

Arguments arising from the emergence of the prison, its supposed modernity, and its alleged connections with capitalist work discipline must, therefore, be handled with extreme caution. Reservations about the importance of new forms of punishment are further strengthened by another consideration: arguably, the most significant development in punishment was not the emergence of new methods, but the dramatic reduction in the levels of that most traditional form, hanging. We must return to the trend that we examined in chapter 3. Despite the increase of capital statutes from the late seventeenth century onwards, despite the increased aspirations of the state, despite the hardening of attitudes that is thought to have accompanied the development of capitalism and the rise of the bourgeoisie, executions fell. Evidence from the south-eastern counties, from Cheshire, and from Devon combines to demonstrate that this was a national trend, and that in some areas the number of persons executed for felony in the early eighteenth century may have been about a tenth of that current in the early seventeenth. This is an important change, not least because, as far as is known, it was not the result of any conscious policy. Again, one of the greatest conundrums of early modern English crime reasserts itself: the celebrated wave of capital statutes follows a considerable slackening of the severity with which the criminal code was applied. Hay's explanation, that terror works best when tempered with mercy, is central to our understanding of the essentially static situation that emerged in the eighteenth century after this massive change.[50] It is perhaps less useful in explaining why the change, so unexpected and so irrefutable, came about. To put it simply, a society which is executing only a tenth of the criminals it was executing a century previously is either experiencing considerably less crime, worrying less about the crime it is experiencing, or being affected by a combination of these factors. In any case, fluctuations in felony and capital punishment over the early modern period point to some very important changes in English life.

As was suggested in the introduction to this book, the period it covers, 1550 to 1750, can, for many purposes, be regarded as falling into two halves, with a neat bisection coming in the mid seventeenth century. There are, undeniably, many continuities: but it is the difference between these two sub-periods which is the most striking. Significantly enough, research on that most fundamental social fact of all, demographic movement, has demonstrated clearly a sudden transformation in population history: there was a long period of steady growth until about 1640, and then a period of stability until the next wave of demographic expansion began in the 1740s.[51] In many respects, the social history of England in the 200 years with which we are concerned has to be written within an inescapable demographic context, for the implications of this surge and subsequent stability of population were far-reaching. On the most basic level of all, agricultural production could barely keep pace with population increase, with resultant high mortality and fear of disorder in years of bad harvest. Even the years of average harvest were not comfortable for the poor. A rising population meant a buyer's market for labour, and real wages may have been lower in some trades c. 1590–1610 than at any time between the late fifteenth and the late nineteenth centuries.[52]

All this coincided with, and in large measure helped to sustain, a period of governmental and administrative energy. At the same time as problems increased, so did awareness of and sensitivity towards them. Parliament passed statutes against vagrants, many of them couched in panic-stricken terms, at least one of them so harsh as to be unenforceable.[53] Puritan writers, lay and clerical alike, expressed their fears of a rising tide of sinfulness and disorder. In the counties, many justices, aware that the times were out of joint, co-operated in the enforcement of burdensome new regulations. And in the parishes, many officers, some of them attached to the new religious and educational ideas of the minister and the justice, or at least as convinced that they were as likely to suffer from disorder as their social superiors, enforced the law at the grass roots. The change was slow and undramatic by twentieth-century standards, and the contemporary perception of it was confused and imprecise. Nevertheless, the crucial issue is clear enough: in the century before 1640 English society was, and felt itself to be, under pressure.

By the 1660s this pressure had waned, and the late seventeenth and early eighteenth centuries experienced a period of relative social stability. Changes and conflicts still occurred, of course, but they did so within the constraints of a new equilibrium. For the historian of crime, the most important component of this equilibrium was the emergence of the poor as an institutionalized presence. The poor were not now the occasional beggar, such legitimate objects of charity as the old widow or the sick man, nor were they the sturdy beggars of Elizabethan trauma. They were that third or so of the population who, despite work and good health, were unlikely to be able to support themselves from week to week without assistance. The propertied, however much they grumbled over the poor rates, and however much they despised the labouring poor, had learnt how to live with them, how to fit them into their concepts of how society functioned.[54] In such a context, the poor law or the house of correction was a handier means of controlling the poor than frequent presentment of their disorders and frequent executions. The massive fall in both prosecution of and execution for felony which we have traced is hardly surprising: pressure was off society, and the fear of disorder was lessened.

This is not to deny numerous complaints in the eighteenth century that crime was rising. Most periods are convinced that they are experiencing uniquely difficult levels of crime. Such convictions existed in the Middle Ages, and have led one scholar to observe that 'complaints about the prevalence of crime, its increase, and the failure of proper authorities to deal with it are part of the Western tradition of social griping'.[55] Moreover, the eighteenth-century writers, De Mandeville, Fielding, Colquhoun, and the rest, had sound reasons for claiming that crime was on the increase: they were, after all, proposing schemes of reform for dealing with it. It is also noteworthy that their interest was mainly with London crime, and it is probable that by the early eighteenth century the capital might have been presenting unique law and order problems. For whatever reasons, the eighteenth-century writers were approaching nineteenth-century notions about the possibility of identifying 'social problems' and 'solving' them. Colquhoun, with his measured prose, statistics, and claims to detailed social investigation represents an intellectual world far removed from that of a Puritan writer decrying the sin of idleness and the infinite swarms of beggars. Complaints of an increase in crime continued, but, we must reiterate, they were stated in less apocalyptic tones. In the 1750s that working justice Henry Fielding thought that rising crime would make it impossible for gentlemen to ride safely in London streets after dark. In the 1590s two other working justices, Edward Hext and William Lambarde, were convinced that both the society and the moral universe they lived in were on the point of collapse.[56] The difference between these two perceptions of a similar problem is indicative of a profound social transition.

The historian of crime can, therefore, point to a lower level of prosecution in the mid eighteenth century than in the late sixteenth, a lower level of executions, and, despite evident concern over crime, less worry about the collapse of law and order. These trends can be connected to suggestions that Western Europe as a whole went through a fundamental transition in the same period. Over twenty years ago, E. J. Hobsbawm, by popularizing the concept of the 'General Crisis of the Seventeenth Century', initiated a scholarly debate whose repercussions are still with us. If nothing else, this debate has provided some sort of focus for a widespread suspicion that some rather peculiar and perhaps rather important things happened around 1650. As the debate continued, the general crisis became considerably more general. Changes were discerned in government, the state, literature, music, political theory, religion, warfare, science, even family life. The end product of these changes, it is generally agreed, was an enhancement of stability. As one proponent of the broad view has put it:

> In all these cases the years around 1700 appear more ordered, more assured
> about accepted conventions, less divided, less prone to vast and
> uncontrolled strivings in new directions – in sum, more settled and relaxed –
> than in the preceding years.[57]

As the same writer points out, this change was relative, not absolute. Disorder and division were still present, but they were less menacing than they had been in, say, the 1630s, and, above all, they were *perceived* as being less menacing by contemporaries. Most arguments on this point have revolved around elite culture and elite reactions: our study of crime in early modern England would seem to add another dimension to this image of a 'settled and relaxed' world in the early eighteenth century. The falling off of prosecutions by local officers, and the drop in executions at the assizes, must both be regarded as symptoms of this massive shift. Behind it all, one suspects, there lies an unconscious psychological reaction as the great wave of demographic expansion levelled off.

This evidence of a greater stability at the base of English society helps provide an underpinning for that growth of political stability which at least some historians of English politics have traced in the late seventeenth and early eighteenth centuries. In terms of political theory, this is evident enough: the contrast between the *angst*-ridden concern for order of Thomas Hobbes and the soothing confidence of John Locke suggest both the nature of the transition and its rapidity. In terms of practical politics, Professor J. H. Plumb has argued forcefully for a similar shift:

> the contrast between political society in eighteenth and seventeenth century
> England is vivid and dramatic. In the seventeenth century men killed,
> tortured and executed each other for political beliefs; they sacked towns
> and brutalized the countryside. They were subjected to conspiracy, plot and
> invasion . . . by comparison, the political nature of eighteenth-century
> England possesses an adamantine strength and profound inertia.[58]

It is difficult not to see this 'profound inertia' as being in some way connected with that stability at the base of society of which our study of crime has provided so much evidence. It may be too much to claim that the social stability was in any way a cause of the political stability: it is undeniable that it provided a context.

Moreover, our impression of the period 1550–1750 – a century of strain, followed by a century of relative stability – has some intriguing parallels with the next period of social upheaval, and of upheaval in ideas on law and order: the first half of the nineteenth century saw a dramatic rise in prosecutions; between 1805 and 1842 these increased sevenfold in absolute terms, four-and-a-half times relative to the population. This rise in prosecutions was accompanied by increased tension over law and order: as Dr Gatrell has put it, 'it was not accidental that the rise in early nineteenth century prosecutions occurred in decades when law-makers were anxious about the many disorders which cried out for strong government'.[59] This anxiety expressed itself not only in fear of crime, but also in fears of revolutionary upheaval. Crime was conflated with political conflict, criminals with revolutionaries: at the same time as crime levels seemed to have been rising, the ruling groups were confronted with the traumas of Peterloo, Swing, and Chartism. The masses, to borrow a concept then current in France, were seen as a 'dangerous class' in terms which, with due allowance for the passage of time, were as strident as those in which the Elizabethans had discussed vagrants. It was no accident that the public order question constituted an underlying theme of contemporary debate on the police. But by the end of the nineteenth century things had altered and the Criminal Registrar could comment on 'a great change in manners . . . a decline in the spirit of lawlessness'.[60] It is no part of our purpose to suggest that the history of crime in the nineteenth century was in any way a repetition of the history of crime 1550–1750. It would seem, nevertheless, that in both periods rising crime rates and increased public fear of disorder were essentially products of an early, transitional phase of longer periods of socio-economic change. If nothing else, both periods demonstrate that the history of crime does not move in a straight line.

Moreover, the history of crime in the nineteenth century reminds us of another problem, one which has been confronted throughout this book: that of distinguishing between what was actually happening, and what contemporaries thought was happening. Solving this problem is probably impossible. To do so would involve breaking a self-sustaining process: crime increase; the authorities become more worried; crime increases more; and so on. Our reconstruction of long-term fluctuations in prosecution does, however, suggest that crime was less of a problem in the early eighteenth century than in the closing decades of the reign of Elizabeth I. A number of factors worked to ensure that less crime turned up in court records: petty offenders might be dealt with through the manipulation of poor relief, or through the house of correction, while a less aggressive attitude on the part of local officers would also create a decline in levels of prosecution. But these very factors, and especially this last one, point to a slackening of those tensions of which crime as a social phenomenon is meant to be symptomatic. The crime that reached the courts, generally speaking, was not the product of professional agents paid to catch criminals: if we may modify Douglas Hay's comments on statistics slightly, this would suggest that court records might provide a very accurate impression of just how far crime was perceived as a social problem by the population at large. On this index, and on that of the number of executions, it would seem that it was not regarded very seriously at the end of the early modern period.

Our study of crime has proved the subject to be not only of great intrinsic interest, but also one which informs our view of many other aspects of English history in the early modern period. If there are many questions still to be answered, and many loose ends still to be tied up, this is a fair reflection not only of the current state of research into the subject, but also, perhaps, of its very nature. Crime, we must never forget, is an extremely complex phenomenon. In the period under survey it could not only include 'crime' in the modern layman's sense, murder and so on, but also the resolution of interpersonal quarrels, or the prosecution of actions which would be regarded currently as infringements of the moral rather than the criminal code. This complexity is further reflected in the variety of possible approaches to the subject. As we have seen, these can include: a legal-historical approach; deriving statistics on crime and punishment from court records; studying interactions in the village community; studying popular literature; or studying the opinions of the elite. A phenomenon of such complexity, capable of being studied in such varied ways, is unlikely to yield all its secrets to historians after barely two decades of serious research. As our frequent suggestions for areas where future work may be fruitful have indicated, there are still many facets of crime, law and order, punishment, and attitudes to such matters which await detailed investigation by historians of early modern England. If we do not yet have all the answers, we at least now have a knowledge of what the sensible questions are: given some recent writing on the subject, this in itself is a major breakthrough.

Above all, we have proved that crime can no longer be regarded as a trivial, peripheral subject, deserving no fuller treatment than a few anecdotes and a routine nod at received wisdom about the brutality of past ages. It is a serious subject which amply repays scholarly attention, and one which opens some important avenues into understanding the past. Making this claim, of course, makes a wider bid for the importance of social history. The history of England is still dominated by concern over the constitution, over elite politics, and conventional religion. The habit of regarding the wider life of society as something unworthy of discussion above vague generalization is only beginning to seem redundant.

If nothing else, I hope to have demonstrated how one aspect of social history, the history of crime, can be brought in from the historiographical periphery to a position a little nearer the centre. The history of crime throws light on a number of themes, among them some which are familiar to the student of mainstream history: puritanism, for example, or the emergence of political stability around 1700. Its greatest importance consists in providing insights into the sphere of social relations, and of the relationship between authority and society at large. The second of these themes is a familiar one, and is, in a sense, central to early modern history. The first is less familiar, but is one to which historians of England, lagging sadly behind those of France and America, are beginning to turn. In so doing, they are discovering that court archives provide unique information about relationships between people, on their conflicts, and on how they perceived their world. Studying crime, if nothing else, shows us how power was expressed and conflicts were resolved at the very base of society. It therefore provides unique insights into the experiences and attitudes of the mass of the populace – matters so often hidden from our view – while, as we have seen, it also provides considerable illumination on how power was perceived and wielded among higher social groups. These factors alone would confirm the more general assertion that the history of crime is one of the most exciting and important subjects currently being studied by historians.

NOTES AND REFERENCES

CHAPTER 1. DEFINITIONS, METHODS, AND OBJECTIVES

1. Most of the relevant printed material will be introduced where appropriate in the course of this chapter. Attention should also be drawn to a number of review articles, among the most useful of which are: Victor Bailey, 'Bibliographical essay: crime, criminal justice and authority in England', *Bulletin of the Society for the Study of Labour History*, **40**, Spring 1980, pp. 36–46: E. W. Ives, 'English law and English society', *History*, **61**, 1981, pp. 50–60; and J. A. Sharpe, 'The history of crime in late medieval and early modern England: a review of the field', *Social History*, **7**, 1982, pp. 187–203. I am grateful to the editors of *Social History* for permission to reproduce many of the arguments used in that article in this chapter.

2. J. B. Black, *The Reign of Elizabeth 1558–1603*, Oxford UP, 1959, pp. 261–7; Sir George Clark, *The Later Stuarts 1660–1714*, (2nd edn), Oxford UP, 1955, pp. 418–20; J. H. Plumb, *The First Four Georges*, Batsford, 1956, pp. 14, 19; Charles Wilson, *England's Apprenticeship 1603–1763*, Longman, 1965, pp. 177, 369.

3. Keith Thomas, 'The tools and the job', and E. P. Thompson, 'History from below', *Times Literary Supplement*, 7 Apr. 1966.

4. The possible relationship between history and anthropology is discussed in E. E. Evans-Pritchard, *Anthropology and History: a lecture delivered in the University of Manchester*, Manchester UP, 1961; and Keith Thomas, 'History and anthropology', *Past and Present*, **24**, 1963, pp. 3–24.

5. For a good recent discussion of these sources, see Alan Macfarlane, in collaboration with Sarah Harrison and Charles Jardine, *Reconstructing Historical Communities*, Cambridge UP, 1977.

6. L. O. Pike, *A History of Crime in England*, 2 vols, London, 1873–76, although something of an old curiosity shop, is written with enthusiasm, and attacks a wide range of issues. A. H. A. Hamilton, *Quarter Sessions*

from Queen Elizabeth to Queen Anne, London, 1878, is an early example of the use of court materials in a more or less systematic fashion.

7. E.g., Jason Ditton, *Controlology: beyond the new criminology*, Macmillan, 1979.

8. For some comments on the difficulties of defining crime in the past see J. B. Post, 'Criminals and the law in the reign of Richard II, with special reference to Hampshire', Oxford University D.Phil. thesis, 1973, ch. 1, 'A definition of crime'; Barbara Hanawalt, *Crime and Conflict in English Communities, 1300–1348*, Harvard UP, 1979, pp. 3–4; and Timothy Curtis, 'Explaining crime in early modern England', *Criminal Justice History: an international annual*, 1, 1980, pp. 117–19.

9. G. R. Elton, 'Introduction: crime and the historian', in *Crime in England 1550–1800*, ed. J. S. Cockburn, Methuen, 1977, pp. 2–3.

10. E.g., John Dod and Richard Cleaver, *A Plaine and Familiar Exposition of the Ten Commandments*, London, 1610, p. 289, where it is claimed that 'the adulterer is a theefe, by intruding his child into another man's possession'.

11. Elton, 'Crime and the historian', op. cit., p. 4.

12. Ibid., p. 3.

13. This would certainly seem to be the case in modern Britain. There were, for example, 911,365 persons found guilty of non-indictable offences (690,168 for motoring offences) in England and Wales in 1961, compared with 110, 761 for indictable offences: F. H. McClintock and N. Howard Avison, *Crime in England and Wales*, Heinemann, 1968, p. 290, table II.2. Cf. the observations of Nigel Walker, *Crime and Punishment in Britain*, (2nd edn), Edinburgh UP, 1968, p. 36, that the crimes about which public concern is most frequently expressed – murder, violence, and sexual offences – are among the least frequently committed.

14. Keith Wrightson, 'Two concepts of order: justices, constables and jurymen in seventeenth-century England', in *An Ungovernable People: the English and their law in the seventeenth and eighteenth centuries*, eds John Brewer and John Styles, Hutchinson, 1980, table 2, pp. 302–3.

15. See Keith Thomas, 'The puritans and adultery: the Act of 1650 reconsidered', in *Puritans and Revolutionaries: essays in seventeenth-century history presented to Christopher Hill*, eds Donald Pennington and Keith Thomas, Oxford UP, 1978.

16. Public Record Office (hereafter PRO), CHES 21/4, f.316 (Chester Crown Book).

17. *The Sufferer's Legacy to Surviving Sinners: or, Edmund Kirk's dying advice to young men*, London, 1684 (single page broadsheet).

18. For two concise discussions of the law of defamation in our period see Theodore F. T. Plucknett, *A Concise History of the Common Law*, (5th edn), Butterworth, 1956, book 2, part II, ch. 5, 'Defamation'; and S. F. C. Milsom, *Historical Foundations of the Common Law*, Butterworths, 1969, ch. 13, 'The rise of the modern law of torts', especially pp. 332 ff.

19. M. J. Ingram, 'Communities and courts: law and disorder in early seventeenth-century Wiltshire', in *Crime in England*, ed. Cockburn, op. cit., p. 114.

20. A full bibliography on the legal history of this period would fill a substantial book in itself. Among the more useful short guides are: J. H. Baker, *An Introduction to English Legal History*, Butterworths, 1971; and Alan Harding, *A Social History of English Law*, Penguin, 1966. Greater detail is provided by W. S. Holdsworth, *A History of English Law*, eds A. L. Goodhart and H. G. Hanbury, 17 vols, Methuen and Sweet & Maxwell, 1903–72; and Leon Radzinowicz, *A History of English Criminal Law and its Administration from 1750*, 4 vols, Stevens, 1948–68.

21. See, for example, *Legal Records and the Historian: papers presented to the Cambridge Legal History Conference, 7–10 July 1975, and in Lincoln's Inn Old Hall on 3 July 1974*, ed. J. H. Baker, Royal Historical Society, London, 1978.

22. J. S. Cockburn, 'Early modern assize records as historical evidence', *Journal of the Society of Archivists*, 5, 1975, pp. 215–31, provides a forceful demonstration of the unreliability of this source in the early part of our period.

23. See the comments of Sidney and Beatrice Webb, *English Local Government from the Revolution to the Municipal Corporation Act: the manor and the borough, part 1*, Longmans Green, 1924, p. 27.

24. Conduct which was held to constitute a breach of the peace, or of good behaviour, was very widely defined: for two contemporary discussions of the point, see William Lambarde, *Eirenarcha: or the office of the justices of peace in four bookes. Gathered 1579: first published 1581: and now secondly revised, corrected and enlarged agreeably to the reformed commission of the peace* (7th edn), London, 1592, pp. 76–123; and Michael Dalton, *The Countrey Justice: containing the practice of the justices of the peace out of their sessions: gathered for the better help of such justices of peace, as have not been much conversant with the laws of this realm* (10th edn), London, 1677, pp. 263–93.

25. PRO, CHES 21/3, f.8v.

26. Black, *Reign of Elizabeth*, op. cit., p. 263.

27. J. B. Post, reviewing Gamini Salgado, *The Elizabethan Underworld*, Dent, 1977, in *The London Journal*, 4, 1978, p. 288.

28. *Middlesex County Records*, ed. J. C. Jeaffreson, 4 vols, Middlesex County Records Society, Clerkenwell, 1886–92.

29. C. L. Ewen, *Witch Hunting and Witch Trials. The indictments for witchcraft from the records of 1373 assizes held for the Home circuit AD 1559–1736*, London, 1929.

30. Joel Samaha, *Law and Order in Historical Perspective: the case of Elizabethan Essex*, Academic Press, 1974; J.S. Cockburn, 'The nature and incidence of crime in England 1559–1625; a preliminary survey', in *Crime in England*, ed. Cockburn, op. cit.; J. M. Beattie, 'The pattern of crime in England 1660–1800', *Past and Present*, 62, 1974, pp. 47–95; Alan Macfarlane, *Witchcraft in Tudor and Stuart England: a regional and comparative study*, Routledge & Kegan Paul, 1970; T. C. Curtis, 'Some aspects of crime in seventeenth-century England, with special reference to Cheshire and Middlesex', Manchester University Ph.D. thesis, 1973; J. A. Sharpe, 'Crime in the county of Essex, 1620–1680: a study of offences and offenders at the assizes and quarter sessions', Oxford University D.Phil. thesis, 1978. This thesis is to be published by

the Cambridge University Press as *Crime in seventeenth-century England: a county study.*

31.   James Buchanan Given, *Society and Homicide in Thirteenth-century England*, Stanford UP, 1977; Hanawalt, *Crime and Conflict*, op. cit., David Philips, *Crime and Authority in Victorian England: The Black Country 1835–1860*, Croom Helm, 1977; V. A. C. Gatrell, 'The decline of theft and violence in Victorian and Edwardian England', in *Crime and the Law: the social history of crime in western Europe since 1500*, eds V. A. C. Gatrell, Bruce Lenman and Geoffrey Parker, Europa Publications, 1980.

32.   Richard Cobb, *The Police and the People: French popular protest 1789–1820*, Oxford UP, 1970; and *Death in Paris: the records of the Basse-Geole de la Seine, October 1795–September 1801*, Oxford UP, 1978.

33.   The materials upon which such a study might be based are described in Macfarlane *et al.*, *Reconstructing Historical Communities*, op. cit.; some of Dr Macfarlane's further thoughts on the subject are given in 'History, anthropology and the study of communities', *Social History*, **5**, May 1977, pp. 631–52.

34.   J. A. Sharpe, 'Crime and delinquency in an Essex parish 1600–1640', in *Crime in England*, ed. Cockburn, op. cit.

35.   Keith Wrightson and David Levine, *Poverty and Piety in an English Village: Terling 1525–1700*, Academic Press, 1979.

36.   One relevant study based on these researches is Alan Macfarlane, *The Justice and the Mare's Ale: law and disorder in seventeenth-century England*, Basil Blackwell, 1981.

37.   *Albion's Fatal Tree: crime and society in eighteenth-century England*, eds Douglas Hay, Peter Linebaugh, John G. Rule, E. P. Thompson, and Cal Winslow, Allen Lane, 1975; E. P. Thompson, *Whigs and Hunters: the origin of the Black Act*, Allen Lane, 1975; John G. Rule, 'Social crime in the rural south in the eighteenth and early nineteenth centuries', *Southern History*, **1**, 1979, pp. 135–53. Cf. Terry Chapman, 'Crime in eighteenth-century England: E. P. Thompson and the conflict theory of crime', *Criminal Justice History*, **1**, 1980.

38.   *An Ungovernable People*, eds Brewer and Styles, op. cit.

39.   Douglas Hay, 'Property, authority and the criminal law', in *Albion's Fatal Tree*, eds Hay *et al.*, op. cit.; Thompson, *Whigs and Hunters*, op. cit., pp. 258–69.

40.   E.g., Michael R. Weisser, *Crime and Punishment in Early Modern Europe*, Harvester Press, 1979.

41.   *The Collected Papers of Frederic William Maitland*, ed. H. A. L. Fisher, 3 vols, Cambridge UP, 1911, vol. 2, p. 484.

42.   J. H. Hexter, *Reappraisals in History*, Longman, 1961, p. 44.

43.   Curtis, 'Explaining crime in early modern England', op. cit., p. 133.

44.   George Rusche and Otto Kirchheimer, *Punishment and Social Structure*, New York, 1939; Weisser, *Crime and Punishment*, op. cit.

45.   This point is examined in J. A. Sharpe, 'Enforcing the law in the seventeenth-century English village', in *Crime and the Law since 1500*, eds Gatrell, Lenman and Parker, op. cit.

46.   Hay, 'Property, authority and the criminal law', op. cit., pp. 40–9; J. M. Beattie, 'Crime and the courts in Surrey 1736–1753', in *Crime in England*, ed. Cockburn, op. cit., pp. 170–4. These two essays concen-

trate upon eighteenth-century evidence, but less explicit sources suggest that the situation they describe was already obtaining in the sixteenth and seventeenth centuries: Joel Samaha, 'Hanging for felony: the rule of law in Elizabethan Colchester', *The Historical Journal*, 21, 1978, pp. 763–82; and J. A. Sharpe, 'Le alterative alla pena capitale: uno sguardo all 'Inghilterra del seicento', *Chaeiron: materiali e strumenti di aggiornamento storiografico*, 1, 1982, pp. 109–19.

47. See, for example, William J. Bouwsma, 'Lawyers and early modern culture', *American Historical Review*, 78, 1973, pp. 303–27; and *Lawyers in Early Modern Europe and America*, ed. Wilfrid Prest, Croom Helm, 1981.

48. John H. Langbein, *Prosecuting Crime in the Renaissance: England, Germany, France*, Harvard UP, 1974.

49. Samaha, *Law and Order in Historical Perspective*, op. cit.

50. E.g., 5 Eliz. I, cap. 1 (sodomy, 1563); 5 Eliz. I, cap. 16 (witchcraft, 1563); 8 Eliz. I, cap. 4 (pickpockets and cutpurses, 1566); 1 Ed. VI, cap. 12 (horse-theft, 1547).

51. G. R. Elton, *The Tudor Revolution in Government: administrative changes in the reign of Henry VIII*, Cambridge UP, 1953. For a more recent discussion of the problem, incorporating the findings of later research, and giving full references to the relevant publications, see Penry Williams, *The Tudor Regime*, Oxford UP, 1979.

52. A major work proving the validity of this argument is G. R. Elton, *Policy and Police: the enforcement of the Reformation in the age of Thomas Cromwell*, Cambridge UP, 1972.

53. Ibid., pp. 336–9.

54. This is no place for a full bibliography of English social history of the period in question. For the late sixteenth and seventeenth centuries, Keith Wrightson, *English Society 1580–1680*, Hutchinson, 1982, supersedes anything yet written. R. W. Malcolmson, *Life and Labour in England 1700–1780*, Hutchinson, 1981, continues the story into the eighteenth century. Two other useful background books are J. D. Chambers, *Population, Economy and Society in Pre-industrial England*, Oxford UP, 1972; and D. C. Coleman, *The Economy of England 1450–1750*, Oxford UP, 1977.

55. Population trends in this period receive exhaustive analysis in E. A. Wrigley and R. S. Schofield, *The Population History of England 1541–1871: a reconstruction*, Arnold, 1981.

56. Even this 'familiar theme' is currently undergoing detailed re-evaluation: see, for example, *Faction and Parliament: essays on early Stuart history*, ed. Kevin Sharpe, Oxford UP, 1978; and Conrad Russell *Parliaments and English Politics, 1624–1629*, Oxford UP, 1979.

57. J. H. Baker, 'The dark age of English legal history', in *Legal History Studies 1972*, ed. D. Jenkins, University of Wales Press, 1975.

CHAPTER 2. COURTS, OFFICERS, AND DOCUMENTS

1. The best way for the student to grasp the nature of the system of courts and offices in our period is to read some of the excellent studies of county government which have been published, of which the present writer's favourite is T. G. Barnes, *Somerset 1625–1640: a county's government during the 'Personal Rule'*, Oxford UP, 1961. Other good county studies include Anthony Fletcher, *A County Community at Peace and War: Sussex 1600–1660*, Longman, 1975; and A. Hassell Smith, *County and Court: government and politics in Norfolk, 1558–1603*, Oxford UP, 1974, part II, 'Office-holding: its significance in the county'. Mention must also be made of B. W. Quintrell, 'The government of the county of Essex, 1603–1642,' London University Ph.D. thesis, 1965, a model doctoral dissertation which, sadly, has never been published. J. H. Baker, 'Criminal courts and procedure at common law 1550–1800', in *Crime in England*, ed. Cockburn, op. cit., is a good initial guide to the subjects in question.

2. Little detailed research has been carried out on the King's Bench 1550–1750. G. O. Sayles, *The Court of King's Bench in Law and History*, Selden Society Lecture, 1959, is a useful introduction to the subject, while Marjorie Blatcher, *The Court of King's Bench 1450–1550: a study in self-help*, University of London Legal Series, 12, 1978, is a scholarly study of the court's history in that period.

3. Essex County Record Office, typescript calendar of Elizabethan Queen's Bench cases; Essex cases found in the King's Bench Ancient Indictments, 1620–1677, PRO, KB, 9/757–931.

4. This account of the Court of Star Chamber is based on G. R. Elton, *The Tudor Constitution: documents and commentary*, Cambridge UP, 1965, pp. 90–1; and J. P. Kenyon, *The Stuart Constitution: documents and commentary*, Cambridge UP, 1966, pp. 117–20.

5. T. G. Barnes, 'Due process and slow process in the late Elizabethan and early Stuart Star Chamber', *American Journal of Legal History*, 6, 1962, pp. 221–49. For some earlier case histories, see G. R. Elton, *Star Chamber Stories*, Methuen, 1958.

6. The standard introduction to this court in the early modern period is J. S. Cockburn, *A History of English Assizes 1558–1714*, Cambridge UP, 1972.

7. Anthony Walker, *Say On: or, a seasonable plea for a full hearing betwixt man and man. And, a serious plea for the like hearing betwixt God and man, delivered in a sermon at Chelmsford in Essex, at the general assize holden for the same county, July 8 1678*, London, 1679, p. 13.

8. Numerous county record societies have published editions of quarter sessions records, and the editors' introductions to them often form very useful guides to the operations of the sessions. Two good examples are *Calendar of the Quarter Sessions Papers, 1591–1643*, ed. J. W. Willis Bund, 2 vols, Worcestershire County Records, division 1: documents relating to the quarter sessions, 1900; and *Minutes of Proceedings in Quarter Sessions Held for the Parts of Kesteven in the County*

of Lincoln, 1674–1695, ed. S. A. Peyton, 2 vols, Lincoln Record Society Publications, **25–6**, 1931.

9. *North Riding Quarter Sessions Records*, ed. J. C. Atkinson, 9 vols, North Riding Record Society, 1884–92, vol. 5, p. 158.

10. Fletcher, *A County Community at Peace and War*, op. cit., p. 137.

11. The relevant clause of this document is reprinted in Kenyon, *Stuart Constitution*, op. cit., p. 499.

12. Fletcher, *A County Community at Peace and War*, op. cit., p. 139.

13. For a review of work in this field see Zvi Razi, 'The Toronto school's reconstruction of medieval peasant society: a critical view', *Past and Present*, **85**, 1979, pp. 141–57.

14. Quoted in Perry Williams, *The Tudor Regime*, Oxford UP, 1979, p. 219.

15. For a recent appraisal of the importance of manorial courts see Walter J. King, 'Leet jurors and the search for law and order in seventeenth-century England: "galling persecution" or reasonable justice?', *Histoire Sociale: Social History*, **13**, 1980, pp. 305–23.

16. Idem., 'Untapped resources for social historians: court leet records', *Journal of Social History*, **15**, 1982, p. 699.

17. Two good regional studies of the church courts are provided by R. A. Marchant, *The Church under the Law: justice, administration and discipline in the diocese of York 1560–1640*, Cambridge UP, 1969; and Ralph Houlbrooke, *Church Courts and the People During the English Reformation, 1520–1570*, Oxford UP, 1979. Anecdotal insights into the business of the ecclesiastical courts are to be found in *Before the Bawdy Court: selections from church court and other records relating to the correction of moral offences in England, Scotland and New England, 1300–1800*, ed. P. E. H. Hair, Elek, 1972; and F. G. Emmison, *Elizabethan Life: Morals and the church courts*, Essex Record Office, 1973.

18. This opinion is based on cursory inspection of act books for the archdeaconry of Colchester, Essex Record Office, D/ACA 54–9; and Barry Till, 'The ecclesiastical courts of York 1660–1883: a study in decline', unpublished typescript deposited at the Borthwick Institute of Historical Research, York, 1963.

19. Little systematic use has been made of these sources for the years 1550–1750: for a stimulating study dealing with an earlier period see R. H. Helmholz, *Marriage Litigation in Medieval England*, Cambridge UP, 1974.

20. For a recent discussion of this subject see J. A. Sharpe, *Defamation and sexual slander in early modern England: the church courts at York*, Borthwick Papers, **58**, 1980.

21. The standard work on the justice of the peace for the first half of the period is J. H. Gleason, *The Justices of the Peace in England, 1558–1640: a later Eirenarcha*, Oxford UP, 1969. The justice's duties are set out in a number of contemporary handbooks, of which the most informative (and most republished) are Lambarde, *Eirenarcha*, op. cit.; Dalton, *Countrey Justice*, op. cit.; and John Burn, *The Justice of the Peace*, London, 1755. Details of the Sussex bench given in the text are drawn from Fletcher, *A County Community at Peace and War*, op. cit., pp. 127–34, 348–58.

22. *William Lambarde and Local Government: his ephemeris and twenty-*

> *nine charges to juries and commissions*, ed. Conyers Read, Cornell UP, 1962.

23. There is no recent discussion of the sheriff and his staff in print. Barnes, *Somerset 1625–1640*, op. cit., ch. 5, 'Shrievalty', is a useful introduction. See also T. E. Hartley, 'Under-sheriffs and bailiffs in some English Shrievalties c.1580 to c.1625', *Bulletin of the Institute of Historical Research*, **47**, 1974, pp. 164–185.

24. J. C. Cox, *Three Centuries of Derbyshire Annals as Illustrated by the Records of the County of Derby from Queen Elizabeth to Queen Victoria*, 2 vols, London, 1890, pp. 58–9.

25. Wallace Notestein, *The English People on the Eve of Colonisation 1603–1630*, Hamish Hamilton, 1954, p. 204.

26. Barnes, *Somerset 1625–1640*, op. cit., p. 140.

27. *Quarter sessions order book, Easter 1625, to Trinity 1637*, eds S. C. Ratcliffe and H. C. Johnson, Warwick County Records, **1**, 1935, p. 2.

28. Cockburn, *History of English Assizes*, op. cit., p. 53.

29. No detailed account of the early modern coroner has yet been published. For a general overview of the history of the office, see J. D. J. Havard, *The Detection of Secret Homicide*, Macmillan, 1960.

30. Sir Thomas Smith, *De Republica Anglorum*, London, 1583, p. 72.

31. *Quarter Sessions Records*, ed. J. C. Atkinson, (North Riding Record Society, 9 vols, London, 1884–92), vol. 1, p. 182.

32. Ibid., p. 183.

33. See, for example, the opinions expressed in what is generally thought of as a standard popular history of the police, T. A. Critchley, *A History of Police in England and Wales 900–1966*, Constable, 1967, pp. 11–12. Cf. Hugh C. Evans, 'Comic constables – fictional and historical', *Shakespeare Quarterly*, **20**, 1969, pp. 427–34.

34. Wrightson, 'Two concepts of order' in *An Ungovernable People*, eds. J. Brewer and J. Styles, Hutchinson, 1980; Joan Kent, 'The English village constable, 1580–1642: The nature and dilemmas of the office', *Journal of British Studies*, **20**, (2), 1981, pp. 26–49.

35. The importance of this official is demonstrated in T. G. Barnes, *The Clerk of the Peace in Caroline Somerset*, Occasional papers of the Department of English Local History, Leicester University, **14**, Leicester 1961.

36. J. S. Cockburn, 'Seventeenth-century clerks of assizes – some anonymous members of the legal profession', *American Journal of Legal History*, **13**, 1969, pp. 315–32.

37. Marchant, *The Church under the Law*, op. cit., *passim*, gives the impression of a court system that was handling a steadily increasing volume of business over this period.

38. For interesting selections of depositions and examinations, see *Depositions from the Castle of York Relating to Offences Committed in the Northern Counties in the Seventeenth Century*, ed. James Raine, Surtees Society, **40**, 1861; and *Kentish Sources, 6: Crime and Punishment*, ed. E. Melling, Kent County Archive Office, Maidstone, 1969, pp. 34–50.

39. For the procedures involved in taking recognizances, see Dalton, *Countrey Justice*, op. cit., pp. 457 ff.

40. For trial procedure see Baker, 'Criminal courts and procedure', op. cit., pp. 21–5; J. S. Cockburn, 'Trial by the book? Fact and theory in the

criminal process 1580–1625', in *Legal records and the Historian*, ed. J. H. Baker, Royal Historical Society, London, 1978; and Richard Bragge's 'Rules to be observed by the quarter sessions', in *Quarter Sessions Order Book 1642–1649*, ed. B. C. Redwood, Sussex Record Society publications, **44**, 1954, pp. 210–14. John H. Langbein 'The criminal trial before the lawyers', *University of Chicago Law Review*, **45**, 1978, pp. 263–316, delineates important changes in trial procedure towards the end of the early modern period, and has much of value to say on the subject in general.

41. J. S. Cockburn, 'Early modern assize records as historical evidence', *Journal of the Society of Archivists*, **5**, 1975, pp. 215–31.

42. Ibid., p. 226.

43. *A Calendar of Assize Records*, ed. J. S. Cockburn, HMSO, 1974 (in progress).

44. Cockburn, *History of English Assizes*, op. cit., p. 122.

45. Several of these notebooks have been published. Examples which provide the basis for investigating changes over time in the period with which we are concerned are Granville Leveson-Gower, 'Note Book of a Surrey Justice', *Surrey Archaeological Collections*, **9**, 1888, pp. 161–232; *Deposition Book of Richard Wyatt JP, 1767–1776*, ed. Elizabeth Silverthorne, Surrey Record Society, **30**, 1978; and *Manchester Sessions. Notes of proceedings before Oswald Mosley, 1616–1630, Nicholas Mosely, 1661–1672, and Sir Oswald Mosley, 1734–1739, and other magistrates*, ed. Ernest Axon, Manchester Record Society, **42**, 1901.

CHAPTER 3. MEASURING CRIME, MEASURING PUNISHMENT

1. Douglas Greenberg, *Crime and Law Enforcement in the Colony of New York, 1691–1776*, Cornell UP, 1976, p. 14.

2. J. M. Beattie, 'The pattern of crime in England 1660–1800', *Past and Present*, **62**, 1974, pp. 47–95; Samaha, *Law and Order in Historical Perspective: the case of Elizabethan Essex*, Academic Press, 1974; cf. J. S. Cockburn, 'The nature and incidence of crime in England 1539–1625: a preliminary survey', in *Crime in England 1550–1800*, ed. J. S. Cockburn Methuen, 1977: J. A. Sharpe, 'Crime in the county of Essex 1620–1680: a study of offences and offenders at the assizes and quarter sessions', Oxford University D. Phil. thesis, 1978, ch. 18 'Overall patterns of crime'.

3. J. J. Tobias, *Crime and Industrial Society in the Nineteenth Century*, Batsford, 1967, p. 21.

4. Ibid., p. 15.

5. Quoted ibid., *loc. cit.*

6. For a standard discussion of this point by two modern criminologists see T. Sellin and M. Wolfgang, *The Measurement of Delinquency*, John Wiley & Sons, 1964.

7. The concept of the moral panic is discussed in Stanley Cohen, *Folk Devils and Moral Panics: the creation of the mods and rockers*,

MacGibbon & Kee, 1972. For an historical example of something very like this phenomenon, see Jennifer Davis, 'The London garotting panic of 1862: a moral panic and the creation of a criminal class in mid-Victorian England', in *Crime and the Law since 1500*, eds Gatrell, Lenman and Parker, Europa Publications, 1980.

8. Douglas Hay, 'War, dearth and theft in the eighteenth century: the record of the English courts' *Past and Present*, **95**, 1982, pp. 117–160.

9. Wrightson, 'Two concepts of order: justices, constables and jurymen in seventeenth-century England', in *An Ungovernable People*, eds Brewer and Styles, Hutchinson, 1980. Cited by Hay in 'War, dearth and theft', op. cit., p. 153, n. 96.

10. A number of relevant issues are outlined in T. C. Curtis, 'Quarter sessions records and their background: a seventeenth-century regional study', in *Crime in England*, ed. Cockburn, op. cit.; and Sharpe, 'Enforcing the law in the seventeenth-century English village', in *Crime and the Law since 1500*, eds Gatrell, Lenman and Parker, op. cit.

11. *Tudor Economic Documents*, eds R. H. Tawney and Eileen Power, 3 vols, Longman, London, 1924, vol. 2, p. 340; Patrick Colquhoun, *A Treatise on the Police of the Metropolis: explaining the various crimes and misdemeanours which at present are felt as a pressure upon the community: and suggesting remedies for their prevention*, London, 1796, p. 31.

12. J. S. Cockburn, *A History of English assizes 1558–1714*, Cambridge UP, 1972, p. 72.

13. *Tudor Economic Documents*, eds Tawney and Power, op. cit., vol. 2, p. 340.

14. W. J. Jones, *The Elizabethan Court of Chancery*, Oxford UP, 1967, pp. 266–7.

15. For some general comments on this point, see M. J. Ingram, 'Communities and courts: law and disorder in early seventeenth-century Wiltshire', in *Crime in England 1550–1800*, ed. J. S. Cockburn, op. cit., pp. 125–7. Arbitration also forms one of the main themes of J. A. Sharpe, 'Litigation and human relations in early modern England – ecclesiastical defamation suits at York', *Past and Present Society conference*, 1980.

16. Sir William Blackstone, *Commentaries on the Laws of England*, 4 vols (4th edn), 1771, vol. 4, pp. 356–7.

17. *Collections for a History of Staffordshire: the Staffordshire quarter sessions rolls*, ed. S. A. H. Burne, 5 vols, William Salt Archaeological Society, 1929–40, vol. 4, p. 34.

18. *The Book of John Fisher, Town Clerk and Deputy Recorder of Warwick, 1580–1588*, ed. Thomas Kemp, Warwick, 1900, p. 10.

19. Ibid., p. 12.

20. PRO, ASSI 5/19, file for Gloucester assizes, Hilary 1698/9.

21. *Quarter Sessions Records for the County of Somerset, vol. 3: Commonwealth*, ed. E. H. Bates, Somerset Record Society, **28**, 1912, p. 328.

22. *Hanging not Punishment enough for Murtherers, High-way Men, and House-breakers*, London, 1701, p. 4.

23. Richard Gough, *The History of Myddle*, ed. Peter Razzell, Caliban Books, 1979, p. 46.

24. *Collections for a History of Staffordshire*, ed. Burne, op. cit., vol. 3, p. 136.

25. Cockburn, 'Nature and incidence of crime', op. cit., pp. 53–6.
26. Wrightson, 'Two concepts of order', op. cit., table 2, pp. 302–3.
27. *County of Buckingham. Calendar to the sessions records*, ed. William le Hardy, 3 vols, Aylesbury, 1933–9.
28. North Humberside County Record Office, typescript calendar of sessions records.
29. For an interesting, if non-statistical, study of the operation of the church courts around 1700, see M. G. Smith, *Pastoral Discipline and the Church Courts: the Hexham Court 1680–1750*, Borthwick Papers, **62**, 1982.
30. J. A. Sharpe, 'Crime and delinquency in an Essex parish 1600–1640', in *Crime in England 1500–1800*, ed. Cockburn, op. cit., p. 109
31. R. A. Marchant, *The Church under the Law: justice, administration and discipline in the diocese of York 1560–1640*, Cambridge, UP, 1969, table 32, p. 219.
32. *Court Rolls of the Manor of Acomb*, ed. H. Richardson, Yorkshire Archaeological Society, **131**, 1969, *passim*.
33. Hence T. G. Barnes, 'Star chamber litigants and their counsel', in *Legal Records and the Historian*, ed. J. H. Baker, Royal Historical Society, London, 1978, p. 12, finds that 55 per cent of a large sample of plaintiffs in Star Chamber suits were also involved in other litigation.
34. These figures are based on a preliminary count of the cases detailed in *List and Index to the Proceedings in Star Chamber in the Reign of James I (1603–1625) in the Public Record Office, London, class STAC 8*, ed. T. G. Barnes, 3 vols, Chicago, 1975.
35. K. Wrightson and D. Levine, *Poverty and Piety in an English Village: Terling 1525–1700*, Academic Press, 1979, especially ch. 5, 'Conflict and control: the villagers and the courts'.
36. Cockburn, 'Nature and incidence of crime', op. cit.; J. A. Sharpe, 'Crime in the county of Essex 1620–1680'; op. cit., ch. 18, 'Overall patterns of crime in Essex 1620–1680'; Beattie, 'Pattern of crime' op. cit.
37. These materials form the basis for A. Macfarlane, *The justice and the Mare's Ale: law and disorder in seventeenth-century England*, Basil Blackwell, 1981, which contains useful illustrative extracts from the Northern circuit records.
38. PRO, PL 26, 27, respectively.
39. T. C. Curtis, 'Some aspects of crime in seventeenth-century England', Manchester University Ph.D. thesis, 1973, although based partly on Cheshire quarter sessions materials, does not claim to be an exhaustive study.
40. The files constitute PRO, CHES 24; the Crown Books PRO, CHES 21.
41. A. Macfarlane, *Witchcraft in Tudor and Stuart England: a regional and comparative study*, Routledge & Kegan Paul, 1970, for Essex witchcraft. Coining cases accounted for the slight rise in indicated felonies recorded in Chester in the 1690s, PRO, CHES 21/5, ff.306–69. Consultation of the relevant depositions for Lancashire (PRO, LANC 27/1), and the Northern circuit of the assizes (PRO, ASSI 45/15/4–/17/4), suggests that the authorities in the 1690s uncovered a network of coiners which extended over much of the north of England.
42. C. L. Ewen, *Witch Hunting and Witch Trials. The indictments for witchcraft from the records of 1373 assizes held for the Home circuit AD 1559–1736*, London 1929, p. 99.

43. *Middlesex County Records*, ed. Jeaffreson, 4 vols, 1886–92, vol. 2, pp. 245–314.

44. Peter Linebaugh, 'Tyburn: a study of crime and the labouring poor in London during the first half of the eighteenth century', Warwick University Ph.D. thesis, 1975, p. 18.

45. Catherine M. F. Ferguson, 'Law and order on the Anglo-Scottish border 1603–1707', St Andrews University Ph.D. thesis, 1980, pp. 78–80, for the late seventeenth century. Evidence for the earlier period can be found in the Northumberland gaol calendars for 1628 and 1629 printed in *Archaeologica Aeliana*, 1, 1822, pp. 149–53, 156–61.

46. Cockburn, 'Nature and incidence of crime', op. cit.; Beattie, 'Pattern of crime', op. cit.; Essex files for 1700–09 in PRO, ASSI 35/141/1/–/149/2.

47. For Devon, Cockburn, *History of Assizes*, op. cit., p. 100; and Devon cases for 1700–09 recorded in the relevant Western circuit gaol book, PRO, ASSI 23/4 ff.70–240. The impression that indictments in London rose is based on a comparison of the figures given in *Middlesex County Records*, ed. Jeaffreson, op. cit.; and Linebaugh, 'Tyburn', op. cit., p. 327.

48. Bruce Lenman and Geoffrey Parker, 'The State, the Community and the Criminal Law in early modern Europe', in *Crime and the Law since 1500*, eds Gatrell, Lenman and Parker, Europa Publications, 1980 p. 38.

49. B. Boutelet, 'Etude par sondage de la criminalité dans le bailliage de Pont de L'Arche (XVIIe–XVIIIe siècles), *Annales de Normandie*, 12, 1962, pp. 235–62; J. C. Gegot, 'Etude par sondage de la criminalité dans le bailliage de Falaise (XVIIe–XVIIIe siècles)', ibid., 16, 1966, pp. 103–64; M. M. Champin, 'La criminalité dans le bailliage d'Alençon de 1715 a 1745', ibid., 22, 1972, pp. 47–84; and A. Margot, 'La criminalité dans le bailliage de Mamers, 1695–1750', ibid., 22, 1972, pp. 185–224.

50. Cockburn, 'Nature and incidence of crime', op. cit., pp. 68–9; Sharpe. 'Crime in Essex', op. cit., pp. 341–4; PRO, ASSI 35/141/1–/149/2.

51. Beattie, 'Pattern of crime', op. cit.; *A Calendar of Assize Records*, ed. J. S. Cockburn, HMSO, 1974 (in progress), vols. covering Elizabethan and Jacobean Surrey and Sussex.

52. This is the impression given by an initial investigation of the topic, P. E. H. Hair, 'Deaths from violence in Britain: a tentative secular survey' *Population Studies*, 25, 1971, pp. 5–24. Cf. the comments of Beattie 'Pattern of crime', op. cit., p. 61, where a drop of two-thirds in the homicide rate between 1660 and 1800 is postulated.

53. 21 James I cap. 27. The background of this statute and the subsequen history of infanticide is discussed in Peter C. Hoffer and N. E. H. Hull *Murdering Mothers: infanticide in England and New England, 1558–1803*, New York UP, 1981.

54. Cockburn, 'Nature and incidence of crime', op. cit., pp. 68–70.

55. Hay, 'War, dearth and theft', op. cit., pp. 135–146; Beattie, 'Pattern of crime', op. cit., pp. 93–5.

56. Some typical examples are given in *Kentish Sources, 6: Crime and Punishment*, ed. E. Melling, Kent County Archive Office, Maidstone, 1969, pp. 35–6, 38–9, 44–5.

57. Bodleian Library, Oxford, MS. Firth c.4 (Essex Lieutenancy letter-book, 1608–1639), *passim*.

58. PRO, CHES 21/7, *passim.*
59. Samaha, *Law and Order in Historical Perspective*, op. cit., pp. 125–132; L. Radzinowicz, 'A History of English Criminal Law and its Administration from 1750, 4 vols. Stevens, 1948–68, vol. 1, p. 149.
60. Cockburn, *History of Assizes*, op. cit., pp. 94–5; PRO, ASSI 23/4, ff.70–240.
61. *Middlesex County Records*, ed. Jeaffreson, op. cit., vol. 2, p.xxi; Radzinowicz, *History of English Criminal Law*, op. cit., vol. 1, pp. 147, 157, 159.
62. Samaha, *Law and Order in Historical Perspective*, op. cit., p. 171; *Middlesex County Records*, ed. Jeaffreson, op. cit., vol. 2, pp. 245–314; PRO, CHES 21/3, ff.46–193.
63. PRO, ASSI 31/1, Norfolk circuit gaol book, 1734–7, *passim.*
64. PRO, ASSI 23/4, ff.70–240; PRO, CHES 21/3, ff.46–193.
65. Samaha, *Law and Order in Historical Perspective*, op. cit., p. 171; Cockburn, *History of Assizes*, op. cit., p. 96.
66. The standard work on the subject is A. E. Smith, *Colonists in Bondage: white servitude and convict labour in America, 1607–1776*, Chapel Hill, 1947.
67. Andrew Zysberg, 'Galères et galériens en France à la fin du XVIIe siècle', *Criminal Justice History*, 1, 1980. For a general discussion of the move away from reliance on the death penalty from the late seventeenth century, see John H. Langbein, *Torture and the Law of Proof: Europe and England in the ancien règime*, Chicago UP, 1977, part 2, 'The transformation of criminal sanctions'.
68. 4 Hen. VII, cap. 13.
69. PRO, ASSI 23/4, ff. 70–240; Samaha, *Law and Order in Historical Perspective*, op. cit., p. 171; *Middlesex County Records*, ed. Jeaffreson, op. cit., vol. 2, pp. 245–314.
70. 21 Jac. I cap. 6.
71. PRO, CHES 21/3, f. 45v; PRO, ASSI 23/4, f.149. For comments on the frequency of mention of the military in sessions records in the early eighteenth century, see the introduction to *Hertfordshire County Records. Calendar to the sessions books, sessions minute books and other sessions records, with appendixes, vol. VII, 1700 to 1752*, ed. William le Hardy, Hertford, 1930, pp.xv–xvii.
72. PRO, Northern circuit gaol book, ASSI 42/1, ff.27, 41, 249v.
73. John Bellamy, *Crime and Public Order in England in the Later Middle Ages*, Routledge & Kegan Paul, London, 1973, p. 194.
74. J. H. Langbein, 'The criminal trial before the lawyers', *University of Chicago Law Review*, 45, 1978, pp. 288–9.
75. 2 Jac. I, cap. 8.
76. Hay, 'Property, authority and the criminal law', in *Albion's Fatal Tree: crime and society in eighteenth century England*, eds D. Hay *et al.*, Allen Lane, 1975.
77. PRO, CHES 21/7, f.8.
78. Cockburn, 'Nature and incidence of crime', op. cit., p. 68.
79. Ibid., p. 71.

CHAPTER 4. CONTROLLING THE PARISH

1.   W. G. Hoskins, *The Midland Peasant: the economic and social history of a Leicestershire village*, Macmillan, 1957.
2.   A. Macfarlane *et al.*, *Reconstructing Historical Communities*, Cambridge, UP. 1977. Other important recent village studies include: David G. Hey, *An English Rural Community: Myddle under the Tudors and Stuarts*, Leicester UP, 1974; Margaret Spufford, *Contrasting Communities: English villagers in the sixteenth and seventeenth centuries*, Cambridge UP, 1974; and K. Wrightson and D. Levine, *Poverty and Piety in an English Village: Terling 1525–1700*, Academic Press, 1979.
3.   Macfarlane *et al.*, *Reconstructing historical communities*, op. cit., pp. 1–4.
4.   This is one of the major themes of his 'Aspects of social differentiation in rural England c. 1580–1660', *Journal of Peasant Studies*, **5**, pp. 33–47.
5.   For a strenuous denial of the existence of a classic peasantry in England at any stage in the country's development, see Alan Macfarlane, *The Origins of English Individualism: the family, property and social transition*, Basil Blackwell, 1978.
6.   Wrightson and Levine, *Poverty and Piety*, op. cit., *passim*; Hey, *English Rural Community*, op. cit., pp. 53–5.
7.   R. H. Hilton, *The English Peasantry of the Later Middle Ages*, Oxford UP, 1975, p. 53, ends a discussion of the implications of social stratification within the medieval village by commenting that 'nor was the gulf between employer and labourer profound. The social gulf that was still the most important was that between the peasant and the lord'.
8.   This theme figures prominently in the work of Keith Wrightson. For an early statement of it, see 'Aspects of social differentiation', op. cit., pp. 38–43.
9.   Hoskins, *Midland peasant*, op. cit., pp. 205–11; Wrightson, 'Two concepts of order', in *An Ungovernable People*, eds Brewer and Styles, Hutchinson, 1980, pp. 40–4; Sharpe, 'Crime and delinquency in an Essex parish 1600–1640', in *Crime in England 1550–1800*, ed. J. S. Cockburn, Methuen, 1977, pp. 94–5; Wrightson and Levine, *Poverty and piety*, op. cit., pp. 104–6; J. Kent, 'The English village constable, 1580–1642', *Journal of British Studies*, **20**, (no. 2), 1981, pp. 28–9.
10. *Quarter Sessions Records, Trinity 1682 to Epiphany 1690*, ed. H. C. Johnson, Warwickshire County Records, **8**, 1953, pp. 30, 31, 183, 184, 215, 227, 257.
11. *Before the Bawdy Court: selections from church court and other records relating to the correction of moral offences in England, Scotland and New England 1300–1800*, ed. P. E. H. Hair, Elek, 1972, pp. 85, 219.
12. Wrightson, 'Two concepts of order', op. cit., p. 24.
13. Kent, 'English village constable', op. cit., pp. 30–1.
14. Ibid., p. 38.
15. Sharpe, 'Enforcing the law in the seventeenth-century English village', in *Crime and the Law*, eds Gatrell, Lenman and Parker, Europa Publications, 1980, pp. 107–8.
16. Kent, 'English village constable', op. cit., p. 47.
17. Ewen, *Witch Hunting and Witch Trials. The indictments for witchcraft*

from the records of 1373 assizes held for the Home circuit AD 1559–1736, London, 1929, p. 292; Essex Record Office Quarter Sessions Bundles, Q/SBa 2/60; *Depositions from the castle of York Relating to Offences Committed in the Northern Counties in the Seventeenth Century*, ed. J. Raine, Surtees Society, **40**, 1861, p. 83; Macfarlane, *Witchcraft in Tudor and Stuart England*, Routledge & Kegan Paul, 1970, p. 7.

18. Ewen, *Witch Hunting and Witch Trials*, op. cit., p. 296.
19. Macfarlane, *Witchcraft in Tudor and Stuart England*, op. cit., p. 86.
20. Ibid., ch. 7, 'Informal counter-action against witchcraft'.
21. R. Gough, *The History of Myddle*, ed. Peter Razzell, Caliban Books, 1979, p. 78; cf. Hey, *English Rural Community*, op. cit., p. 225.
22. Sharpe, 'Crime and delinquency', op. cit., pp. 97–8; Macfarlane *et al.*, *Reconstructing Historical Communities*, op. cit., pp. 143–8.
23. Sharpe, 'Crime in the County of Essex 1620–1680', Oxford University D.Phil. thesis, 1978, ch. 17, 'The criminal and the community'; C. B. Herrup, 'The common peace: legal structure and legal substance in East Sussex 1594–1640', North Western University Ph.D. thesis, 1982.
24. *Quarter Sessions Order Book, Easter 1625 to Trinity 1637*, eds S. C. Ratcliff and H. C. Johnson, Warwick County Records, **1**, 1935, p. 271.
25. *Before the Bawdy Court*, ed. Hair, op. cit., pp. 86, 155, 167–8, 189; *Quarter Sessions Order Book, Easter 1625 to Trinity 1637*, eds Ratcliff and Johnson, op. cit., pp. 191–2.
26. *Kentish Sources, 6: Crime and Punishment*, ed. E. Melling, Kent County Archive Ofice, Maidstone, 1969, pp. 35–6, 40–1.
27. M. J. Ingram, 'Communities and courts', in *Crime in England 1550–1800*, ed. J. S. Cockburn, op. cit.. pp. 132–3.
28. Lawrence Stone, *The Family, Sex and Marriage in England 1500–1800*, Weidenfeld & Nicolson, 1977, p. 98.
29. *Court Rolls of the Manor of Acomb*, ed. H. Richardson, Yorkshire Archaeological Society, **131**, 1969, *passim*.
30. Ibid., pp. 120, 126–7, 131, 135, 141.
31. Ibid., p. 97.
32. Ibid., p. 143.
33. Ibid., pp. 94, 103.
34. J. P. Kenyon, *The Stuart Constitution: documents and commentary*, Cambridge UP, 1966, p. 500.
35. R. A. Marchant, *The Church under the Law: justice, administration and discipline in the diocese of York 1560–1640*, Cambridge UP, 1969; M. J. Ingram, 'Ecclesiastical justice in Wiltshire 1600–1640, with special reference to cases concerning sex and marriage', Oxford University D.Phil. thesis, 1976; Robert Peters, *Oculus episcopi: administration in the archdeaconry of St Albans 1580–1625*, Manchester UP, 1965; R. Houlbrooke, *Church Courts and the People during the English Reformation, 1520–1570*, Oxford UP, 1979.
36. Quoted in G. R. Quaife, *Wanton Wenches and Wayward Wives: Peasants and illicit sex in early seventeenth-century England*, Croom Helm, 1979, p. 52.
37. Essex Record Office, D/ACA, 54–9; B. Till, 'The ecclesiastical courts of York 1660–1883: a study in decline', unpublished MS, Borthwick Institute of Historical Research, York, 1963.
38. Keith Thomas, *Religion and the Decline of Magic: studies in popular*

Crime in early modern England 1550–1750

beliefs in sixteenth and seventeenth-century England, Weidenfeld & Nicolson, 1971, pp. 502–12.

39. Ibid., p. 505.
40. Borthwick Institute of Historical Research, York, Archbishop of York's Consistory court cause papers, CP H/758; G/3233, respectively.
41. For an attempt to study defamation in its social context, see J. A. Sharpe, *Defamation and sexual slander in early modern England: the church courts at York*, Borthwick Papers, **58**, 1980.
42. F. G. Emmison, *Elizabethan Life: disorder*, Essex Record Office, 1970, pp. 71–2.
43. Ingram, 'Ecclesiastical justice in Wiltshire', op. cit., ch. 9, 'Defamation causes'; Sharpe, *Defamation and sexual slander*, op. cit. For a somewhat different perspective on defamation, see C. A. Haigh, 'Slander and the church courts in the sixteenth century', *Transactions of the Lancashire and Cheshire Antiquarian society*, **78**, 1975, pp. 1–13.
44. *Quarter Sessions Records for the County of Somerset, vol. 3: Commonwealth*, ed. E. H. Bates, Somerset Record Society, **28**, 1912, p. 296.
45. *Collections for a History of Staffordshire: the Staffordshire quarter sessions rolls*, ed. S. A. H. Burne, 5 vols, William Salt Archaeological Society, 1929–40, vol. 4, p. 133. Jackson was to be the subject of a similar complaint five years later: ibid., vol. 5, p. 101.
46. University of Durham, Department of Palaeography and Diplomatic, Durham diocesan records, Archdeacon of Durham's act book 1600–19, ff. 25, 51v, 52v.
47. B. Dale, *The Annals of Coggeshall, otherwise Sunnedon, in the County of Essex*, London, 1863, p. 272.
48. Timothy Nourse, *Campania Foelix: or, a discourse of the benefits and improvements of husbandry*, London, 1700, pp. 166–7.
49. Metropolitan house of correction materials sampled include Greater London Record Office, MJ/SR/1751, 2143 (City of Westminster sessions rolls); and the numerous eighteenth-century house of correction calendars contained in Greater London Record Office, MJ/CP/P/3–89.
50. Sharpe, 'Enforcing the law', op. cit., pp. 112–14, discusses these matters at greater length.
51. Hence Wrightson, 'Aspects of social differentiation', op. cit., p. 45, argues that 'in the administration of the now fully institutionalized poor laws and in the parish vestry, local notables regained effective instruments of local control'.
52. K. Thomas, 'The puritans and adultery: the act of 1650 reconsidered', in *Puritans and Revolutionaries: essays in seventeenth-century history presented to Christopher Hill*, eds Pennington and Thomas, Oxford, UP, 1978, p. 258. For a rare capital conviction under the 1650 ordinance see PRO, CHES 21/4, f.245v.
53. In this respect, our findings would seem to coincide with the general trend away from 'community' towards state law postulated in a number of general interpretative surveys of changes in crime and the law in early modern Europe: see Alfred Soman, 'Deviance and criminal justice in western Europe, 1300–1800: an essay in structure', *Criminal Justice History*, **1**, 1980; Bruce Lenman and Geoffrey Parker, 'The state, the community and the criminal law in early modern Europe', in *Crime and the Law since 1500*, eds Gatrell, Lenman and Parker, op. cit.; and

Michael R. Weisser, *Crime and Punishment in Early Modern Europe*, Harvester Press, 1979.

CHAPTER 5. THE CRIMINAL ORDERS OF EARLY MODERN ENGLAND

1. J. J. Tobias, *Crime and Industrial Society in the Nineteenth Century*, Batsford, 1967, ch. 4, 'The criminal class'. For some initial comments on the applicability of the concept of the criminal class to the early modern period, see J. A. Sharpe, 'Was er een "criminal class". in het vroegmoderne Europa? Enig Engels materiaal', (trans. Pieter Spierenburg), *Tijdschrift voor Criminologie*, 20e jargaang, pp. 211–22.
2. See, for example, Dennis Chapman, *Sociology and the Stereotype of the Criminal*, Tavistock Publications, 1968. Two representative examples of the more traditional approach to the subject are T. Morris, *The Criminal Area: a study in social ecology*, Routledge & Kegan Paul, 1958; and Barbara Wootton, *Social Science and Social Pathology*, Allen & Unwin, 1959.
3. Joel T. Rosenthal, *Nobles and the Noble Life 1295–1500*, Allen & Unwin, 1976, p. 74.
4. John Bellamy, *Crime and Public Order in the Later Middle Ages*, Routledge & Kegan Paul, 1973, pp. 55–7.
5. Barbara A. Hanawalt, 'Fur-collar crime: the pattern of crime among the fourteenth-century English nobility', *Journal of Social History*, **8**, 1975, pp. 1–17.
6. E. L. G. Stones, 'The Folvilles of Ashby-Folville, Leicestershire, and their associates in crime, 1326–1341', *Transactions of the Royal Historical Society*, 5th series, **7**, 1957, pp. 117–36.
7. Lawrence Stone, *The Crisis of the Aristocracy 1558–1641*, Oxford UP, 1965, p. 223.
8. D. Hay, 'Property, authority and the criminal law', in *Albion's Fatal Tree*, eds Hay *et al.*, Allen Lane, 1975, pp. 33–4.
9. The duel is a subject which awaits detailed scholarly attention. For a useful preliminary survey, see Stone, *Crisis of the Aristocracy*, op. cit., pp. 242–50.
10. Buckingham and his circle are described in John H. Wilson, *The Rake and his Times: George Villiers, 2nd duke of Buckingham*, New York, 1954.
11. *A True Account of a Bloudy and Barbarous Murder, Committed on the Body of John Sparks, Waterman, by John Hutchins, in Fleet Street, near Serjeants-Inn, London*, London, 1684, p. 1.
12. *Strange and Bloody News from Fleet-Street. Being a true relation of the murder of Sir William Estcourt*, London, 1684.
13. *The Cry of Blood, or, the horrid sin of murder display'd*, London, 1692.
14. E.g., *Bloody News from Covent Garden: being a true relation, how one Mr Bulger, an Irish gentleman, who [sic] committed a horrible and bloody murther near the Three Tuns tavern in Chandos Street*, London, 1683.

15. *The Cry of Blood*, op. cit., p. 2.
16. *A True Account of a Bloudy and Barbarous Murder*, op. cit., p. 5.
17. *Depositions from the Castle of York Relating to Offences Committed in the Northern Counties in the Seventeenth Century*, ed. J. Raine, Surtees Society, **40**, 1861, p. 89.
18. Ibid., pp. 249–50.
19. Ibid., p. 125.
20. The best introduction to the position of labour in the early modern economy is still D. C. Coleman, 'Labour in the English economy of the seventeenth century', *Economic History Review*, 2nd series, **8**, 1956, pp. 280–95.
21. R. H. Tawney, *The Agrarian Problem of the Sixteenth Century*, London, 1912, p. 268.
22. For two collections of contemporary popular literature dealing with vagrancy and related forms of deviance, see *The Elizabethan Underworld*, ed. A. V. Judges, London, 1930; and *Cony-catchers and bawdy baskets*, ed. Gamini Salgado, Penguin, 1972. For recent criticisms of the portrayal of vagrants given in this literature, see P. A. Slack, 'Vagrants and vagrancy in England 1598–1664', *Economic History Review*, 2nd series, **27**, 1974, pp. 360–79; and A. L. Beier, 'Vagrants and the social order in Elizabethan England', *Past and Present*, **64**, 1974, pp. 3–29.
23. *The Book of John Fisher, Town Clerk and Deputy Recorder of Warwick, 1500–1588*, ed. T. Kemp, Warwick, 1900, pp. 5, 6–7, 178, 103, 66, 29.
24. Ibid., p. 3.
25. *The Book of Examination and Depositions 1622–1644*, ed. R. C. Anderson, Southampton Record Society Publications, 4 vols, 1929–36, vol. 4, pp. 1, 30.
26. *The Book of John Fisher*, ed. Kemp, op. cit., pp. 7–8.
27. Harman, for example, described among his typology of vagrants the 'autem-mort', or married female vagrant, who was characteristically 'as chaste as a cow I have, that goes to bull every moon, with what bull she careth not': *Cony-catchers and bawdy baskets*, ed. Salgado, op. cit., p. 128. Cf. The Book of Orders of 1631, which declared of vagrants that 'these people live like savages, neither marry, nor bury nor christen, which licentious liberty makes so many delight to be rogues and wanderers': J. P. Kenyon, *The Stuart Constitution: documents and commentary*, Cambridge UP, 1966, p. 501.
28. *The Book of John Fisher*, ed. Kemp, op. cit., p. 107.
29. *Quarter Sessions Order Book Easter 1625, to Trinity 16 ', eds S. C. Ratcliff and H. C. Johnson, Warwick County Records, I, 1935, p. 8.
30. *The Book of John Fisher*, ed. Kemp, op. cit., pp. 88, 104.
31. *Collections for a History of Staffordshire: the Staffordshire quarter sessions rolls*, ed. S. H. Burne, 5 vols, William Salt Archaeological Society, 1929–40, vol. 3, p. 226.
32. *Kentish Sources, 6: Crime and Punishment*, ed. E. Melling, Kent County Archive Office, Maidstone, 1969, pp. 38–9.
33. J. A. Sharpe, 'Crime and delinquency in an Essex parish 1600–1640', in *Crime in England 1550–1800*, ed. J. S. Cockburn, Methuen, 1977, pp. 98–9.
34. *Cony-catchers and bawdy baskets*, ed. Salgado, op. cit., p. 129.

35. This may well have been an element in the general exacerbation of attitudes towards the labouring poor which some historians have traced for this period: e.g. R. W. Malcolmson, *Life and Labour in England 1700–1780*, Hutchinson, 1981, pp. 146-53.

36. *Quarter Sessions Records for the County of Somerset, vol. 3: Commonwealth*, ed. E. H. Bates Harbin, Somerset Record Society, **28**, 1912, p. 285

37. *Quarter Session Order Book, Easter 1625 to Trinity 1637*, eds Ratcliff and Johnson, op. cit., pp. 181–2.

38. *Collections for a History of Staffordshire: the Staffordshire quarter sessions rolls*, ed. Burne, op. cit., vol. 3, p. 136; vol. 4, pp. 25–6, 313, 456–7.

39. John Fielding, *An Account of the Origin and Effects of a Police Set on Foot by His Grace the Duke of Newcastle in the year 1753, upon a Plan Presented to His Grace by the Late Henry Fielding, Esq. To which is added a plan for preserving those deserted girls in this town, who become prostitutes from necessity*, London, 1758, pp. x–xi.

40. *Quarter Sessions Records for the County of Somerset, vol. 2: Charles I*, ed. E. H. Bates Harbin, Somerset Record Society, **24**, 1908, pp. 42–3.

41. Cal Winslow, 'Sussex smugglers', in *Abion's Fatal Tree*, eds Hay *et al.*, Allen Lane, 1975.

42. Ibid., p. 165.

43. John Styles, ' "Our traitorous money makers": the Yorkshire coiners and the law, 1760–83', in *An Ungovernable People*, eds. Brewer and Styles, Hutchinson, 1980.

44. A. Macfarlane, *The Justice and the Mare's Ale*, Blackwell, 1981, p. 65.

45. PRO, PL 27/1; ASSI 45/15/4–/17/4, *passim*.

46. *The Book of John Fisher*, ed. Kemp, op. cit., pp. 116–17.

47. 1699 'Comit Glous' roll in PRO, ASSI 5/19 (Western circuit assize files).

48. *Staffordshire Quarter Sessions Rolls*, ed. Burne, op. cit., vol. 6, pp. 27–9.

49. This account is based on that given in *The Complete Newgate Calendar*, eds J. L. Rayner and G. T. Crook, 5 vols, London, 1926, vol. 3, pp. 88–97.

50. Macfarlane, *The Justice and the Mare's Ale*, op. cit.

51. Two important early surveys are Carol Z. Weiner, 'Sex-roles and crime in late Elizabethan Hertfordshire', *Journal of Social History*, **8**, 1975, pp. 18–37; and J. M. Beattie, 'The criminality of women in eighteenth-century England', ibid., pp. 80–116.

52. E.g. the statement that in 'the dark ages' (which apparently means the early modern period) 'nine million people, nearly all women, were put to death in a 300 year period' in Europe for witchcraft: *The Victimization of Women*, eds Jane Roberts Chapman and Margaret Gates, Sage, 1978, p. 23.

53. Beattie, 'Criminality of women', op. cit., p. 90.

54. Weiner, 'Sex-roles and crime', op. cit., p. 39.

55. Beattie, 'Criminality of women', op. cit., 96–101.

56. Connections between contemporary misogyny and witch accusations have not been fully explored for England, although Macfarlane, *Witchcraft in Tudor and Stuart England: a regional and comparative study*, Routledge & Kegan Paul, 1970, ch. 11, 'Witchcraft prosecutions and

social phenomena (1): personality, sex, age and marriage', suggests that the whole issue should be treated with caution. The problem receives scholarly attention in Christina Larner, *Enemies of God: the witch-hunt in Scotland*, Chatto & Windus, 1981.

57.   This is another subject which demands more serious research. P. C. Hoffer and N. E. H. Hull, *Murdering Mothers: infanticide in England and New England 1558–1803*, New York UP, 1981, establishes the importance of the subject, but is based on a comparatively narrow range of materials. R. W. Malcolmson, 'Infanticide in the eighteenth century', in *Crime in England 1550–1800*, ed. J. S. Cockburn, Methuen, 1977, is focused a little late for our purposes, although his conclusions about the background of infanticidal mothers and the circumstances attending infanticide are probably broadly relevant to the earlier period. Keith Wrightson, 'Infanticide in earlier seventeenth-century England', *Local Population Studies*, **15**, 1975, pp. 10–22, is short but suggestive.

58.   G. R. Quaife, *Wanton Wenches and Wayward Wives: peasants and illicit sex in early seventeenth-century England*, Croom Helm, 1979, pp. 146–58.

59.   F. G. Emmison, *Elizabethan Life: morals and the church courts*, Essex Record Office, 1973, p. 21.

60.   Quaife, *Wanton Wenches and Wayward Wives*, op. cit., p. 150.

61.   For estimates of London's population between the mid-sixteenth and late eighteenth centuries see C. Wilson, *England's Apprenticeship 1603–1763*, Longman, 1965, pp. 45–7, 229, 273; and M. Dorothy George, *London Life in the Eighteenth Century*, Penguin, 1966, pp. 318–20.

62.   Henry Fielding, *An Enquiry into the Causes of the Late Increase of Robbers, &c with some proposals for remedying this growing evil*, London, 1751, p. 116.

63.   Bernard de Mandeville, *An Enquiry into the Causes of the Frequent Executions at Tyburn: and a proposal for some regulations concerning felons in prison, and the good effects to be expected from them. To which is added, a discourse on transportation, and a method to render that punishment more effectual*, London, 1725, p. 21.

64.   The best introduction to Wild's career is G. Howson, *Thief-taker General: the rise and fall of Jonathon Wild*, Hutchinson, 1970.

65.   Sheppard's career was celebrated in a number of contemporary accounts and has been further described in a number of popular books, among them Christopher Hibbert, *The Road to Tyburn: the story of Jack Sheppard and the eighteenth-century underworld*, Longmans, Green & Co., 1957. The account given here is based on that of *The Dictionary of National Biography*.

66.   For a work which adopts these assumptions, and is founded on an uncritical acceptance of contemporary literary sources, see G. Salgado, *The Elizabethan Underworld*, Dent, 1977. A more stimulating, if not entirely satisfactory, approach to London crime in our period is provided by Mary McIntosh, 'Changes in the organization of thieving', in *Images of Deviance*, ed. Stanley Cohen, Penguin, 1971. The fullest recent treatment of London crime in the first part of the early modern period is John L. McMullan, 'Aspects of professional crime and criminal organization in sixteenth and seventeenth-century London: a sociological analysis', London University Ph.D. thesis, 1980. Professor

McMullan is currently preparing his thesis for publication.
67. 8 Eliz. I cap. 4.
68. Henry Zouch, *Hints Respecting the Public Police*, London, 1786, p. 1; Fielding, *An enquiry*, op. cit., pp. 3–4.
69. Ibid., p. 105; de Mandeville, *An enquiry*, op. cit., p. 8.
70. *Middlesex County Records*, ed. J. C. Jeaffreson, 4 vols, 1886–92, *passim*.
71. *Tudor Economic Documents*, eds R. H. Tawney and E. Power, 3 vols, Longman, London, 1924, vol. 2, pp. 337–9.
72. John Disney, *An Essay upon the Execution of the Laws Against Immortality and Prophaness*, London, 1708, pp.xx–xxi.
73. John Dunton, *The Night Walker or Evening Rambles in Search of Lewd Women with the Conferences Held with them &c.* The cases cited come from the issues of September and October 1696.
74. *The Arraignment & Burning of Margaret Ferne-seede, for the Murther of her Late Husband Anthony Ferne-seede, found dead in Peckham Field neere Lambeth, having once before attempted to poyson him with broth, being executed in S. Georges-field the last of Februarie 1608*, London, 1608. The indictment dealing with this case survives, PRO, ASSI 35/50/7/17.
75. Henry Goodcole, *Heaven's Speedie Hue and Cry Sent After Lust and Murther, manifested upon the suddaine apprehending of Thomas Shearwood, and Elizabeth Evans, whose manner of lives, deaths, and free confessions are heere expressed*, London, 1635.
76. City of London Record Office, 236D/30, unfoliated, 15/16 June 1729; 25 June 1729; 17 September 1729; 13 June 1729 (Mansion House Justice Room charge books).
77. Ibid., /13, unfoliated, 4 January 1683; 7 January 1683; /30, 9 September 1729; 13 March 1729.
78. Ibid., 25 June 1729; 3/4 August 1729; 14/15 September 1729.
79. Ibid., /13, 15 November 1683.
80. Greater London Record Office, MJ/SR/1751, 2143 (City of Westminster sessions rolls). The Middlesex authorities also made extensive use of the houses of correction within that county in the early eighteenth century, as a search of committals of petty criminals between 1711 and 1745 indicates: Greater London Record Office, MJ/CP/P/3–89.
81. PRO, CHES 25/92/7/–/94/4; Essex Record Office, Q/SR1–7.
82. *Wiltshire Quarter Sessions and Assizes, 1736*, ed. J. P. M. Fowle, Wiltshire Archaeological and Natural History Society records branch, **9**, 1955; *Deposition Book of Richard Wyatt JP, 1767–1776*, ed. E. Silverthorne, Surrey Record Society, **30**, 1978,; North Humberside Record Office, DDGR 34/11/–/175 (Grimston Papers).
83. B. Hanawalt, *Crime and Conflict in English Communities, 1300–1348*, Harvard UP, 1979, ch. 6, 'Criminal associations and professional crime'.
84. For a good popular account of border troubles see George MacDonald Fraser, *The Steel Bonnets: the story of the Anglo-Scottish border reivers*, Barrie & Jenkins, 1971.
85. C. M. F. Ferguson, 'Law and order on the Anglo-Scottish border 1603–1707', St Andrews University Ph.D. thesis, 1980, p. 95.
86. E. P. Thompson, 'Eighteenth-century crime, popular movements and social control', *Society for the Study of Labour History bulletin*, **25**,

Autumn 1972, p. 10; idem., *Whigs and Hunters: the origin of the Black Act*, Allen Lane, 1975, p. 194.
87.   North Humberside Record Office, DDGR 34/86.
88.   Doncaster Borough Records, DB/5/53–4 (quarter sessions examinations).

CHAPTER 6. SOCIAL CRIME AND LEGITIMIZING NOTIONS

1.   E.g. *Elizabethan Underworld*, ed. Judges, 1930 pp. 201–5, where brokers are put on a moral plane with cony-catchers.
2.   The classic formulation of the concept of 'social crime' can be found in E. J. Hobsbawm, 'Distinctions between socio-political and other forms of crime', *Society for the Study of Labour History bulletin*, **25**, Autumn 1972, pp. 5–6.
3.   *Albion's Fatal Tree: crime and society in eighteenth-century England*, eds Hay *et al.*, Allen Lane, 1975, p. 14.
4.   E. P. Thompson, 'Eighteenth-century crime, popular movements and social control', *Society for the Study of Labour History bulletin*, **25**, Autumn 1972, p. 11.
5.   Ibid., *loc. cit.*
6.   Essex Record Office, Q/SR 399/100.
7.   *Notes and Extracts from the Sessions Rolls, 1581 to 1698*, ed. W. J. Hardy, Hertford County Records, **1**, 1905, p. 35; Essex Record Office, A/SBa 2/81, respectively.
8.   R. W. Bushaway, ' "Grovely, Grovely, and all Grovely": custom, crime and conflict in the English woodland', *History Today*, **31**, May 1981, pp. 37–43.
9.   7 James I cap. 7. I am grateful for this reference to Mr John Styles, who has worked extensively on embezzlement in seventeenth- and eighteenth-century industries.
10.   22 George II cap. 27, 'An act for the more effectual preventing of frauds and abuses committed by persons employed in the manufacture of hats, and in the woollen, linnen, fustian, cotton, iron, leather, furr, hemp, flax, mohair, and silk manufactures; and for the preventing unlawful combinations of journeymen dyers and journeymen hot pressers, and of all persons employed in the said several manufactures; and for the better payment of their wages.' As the title of the act suggests, this was a fairly comprehensive attempt to reform abuses in a wide variety of industries. In particular, it prescribed whipping for workers convicted of embezzling and heavy fines or whipping for those buying or otherwise receiving embezzled goods.
11.   P. Colquhoun, *A Treatise on the police of the Metropolis*, London, 1796, pp. 77–82.
12.   Hobsbawm, 'Distinctions between socio-political and other forms of crime', op. cit., p.6.
13.   The most recent scholarly introduction to the subject is P. B. Munsche,

Gentlemen and Poachers: the English game laws 1671–1831, Cambridge UP, 1981. This develops a number of themes raised earlier by Munsche in 'The game laws in Wiltshire 1750–1800', in *Crime in England 1550–1800*, ed. J. S. Cockburn, Methuen, 1977. For a detailed case study, see Douglas Hay, 'Poaching and the game laws on Cannock Chase', in *Albion's Fatal Tree*, eds Hay *et al.*, op. cit., and E. P. Thompson, *Whigs and Hunters: the origin of the Black Act*, Allen Lane, 1975. For a wider ranging account of the laws, see C. and E. Kirby, 'The English game law system', *American Historical Review*, **38**, 1931, pp. 239–54.

14.   Quoted in Munsche, 'Game laws in Wiltshire', op. cit., p. 210.
15.   Sir William Blackstone, *Commentaries on the Laws of England*, 4 vols (4th edn), 1771, vol. 4, p. 175.
16.   22 and 23 Car. II, cap. 25. The text of the act is given in J. P. Kenyon, *The Stuart Constitution: documents and commentary*, Cambridge UP, 1966, pp. 503–5.
17.   Blackstone, *Commentaries*, op. cit., vol. 4, p. 174.
18.   13 Rich. II, stat. 1, cap. 13.
19.   Quoted in Hay, 'Poaching and the game laws on Cannock Chase', op. cit., p. 191.
20.   Blackstone, *Commentaries*, op. cit. vol. 4, pp. 174–5.
21.   J. Chitty, quoted in Hay, 'Poaching and the game laws on Cannock Chase', *loc. cit.*
22.   Ibid., p. 192.
23.   *Calendar of the Quarter Sessions Papers 1591–1643*, ed. J. W. Willis Bund, Worcester County Records: division 1. Documents relating to quarter sessions, 2 vols, 1900, vol. 1, pp. lxix–lxxi.
24.   F. G. Emmison, *Elizabethan Life: disorder*, Essex Record Office, 1970, p. 250.
25.   Ibid., p. 244.
26.   A point discussed by Munsche 'Game laws in Wiltshire', op. cit., pp. 224–7.
27.   *Calendar of the Quarter Sessions Papers*, ed. Willis Bund, op. cit., vol. 1, p. lviii.
28.   Hay, 'Poaching and the game laws on Cannock Chase', op. cit., p. 251.
29.   Munsche, *Gentlemen and Poachers*, op. cit., pp. 4–5.
30.   Emmison, *Elizabethan Life: disorder*, op. cit., p. 238.
31.   Munsche, *Gentlemen and Poachers*, op. cit., p. 71.
32.   Emmison, *Elizabethan Life: disorder*, op. cit. p.239.
33.   Ibid., p. 236.
34.   Hay, 'Poaching and the game laws on Cannock Chase', op. cit., p. 200.
35.   Launching a civil suit was, by the eighteenth century, a possible alternative to criminal prosecution for the game preserver. As might be expected, however, the costs involved meant that recourse was only very rarely had to civil actions: Munsche, *Gentlemen and Poachers*, op. cit., p. 91.
36.   Ibid., ch. 3, 'Poachers and the black market'. Cf. the comments of Hay, 'Poaching and the game laws on Cannock Chase', op. cit., pp. 203–5.
37.   5 Anne cap. 14.
38.   *Middlesex County Records*, ed. J. C. Jeaffreson, 4 vols, 1886–92, *passim*; PRO, SP 14/48/23 (State Papers).
39.   Emmison, *Elizabethan Life: disorder*, op. cit., p. 246.

40   E.g. *A Victorian Poacher: James Hawker's Journal*, ed. Garth Christian, Oxford UP, 1978.
41.   Munsche, *Gentlemen and Poachers*, op. cit. p. 62.
42.   J. H. Plumb, *England in the Eighteenth Century*, Penguin, 1950, p. 13; Sir Charles Petrie, *The Four Georges, a Revaluation of the Period from 1714–1830*, Eyre & Spottiswoode, London, 1935, p. 81; C. Hibbert, *The Road to Tyburn: the story of Jack Sheppard and the eighteenth-century underworld*, Longmans, Green & Co., 1957, p. 20.
43.   E. P. Thompson, 'The moral economy of the English crowd in the eighteenth century', *Past and Present*, **50**, 1971, p. 76.
44.   Ibid., p. 78.
45.   For an early survey of the topic, see C. S. L. Davies, 'Les révoltes populaires en Angleterre (1500–1700)', *Annales ESC*, 1969, pp. 24–60. Two detailed local studies of popular disturbances are provided by Buchanan Sharp, *In Contempt of All Authority: rural artisans and riot in the West of England, 1586–1660*, University of California Press, 1980; and Keith Lindley, *Fenland Riots and the English Revolution*, Heinemann, 1982. Other regional evidence is to be found in Peter Clark, 'Popular protest and disturbance in Kent, 1558–1640', *Economic History Review*, 2nd series, **29**, 1976, pp. 365–82; and John Walter, 'Grain riots and popular attitudes to the law: Maldon and the crisis of 1629', in *An Ungovernable People: the English and their law in the seventeenth and eighteenth centuries*, eds J. Brewer and J Styles, Hutchinson, 1980. An important aspect of the early modern popular disturbance, the grain riot, is discussed in John Walter and Keith Wrightson, 'Dearth and the social order in early modern England', *Past and Present*, **71**, 1976, pp. 22–42. Max Beloff, *Public Order and Popular Disturbances 1660–1714*, Oxford UP, 1938, is very dated but still of use. John Stevenson, *Popular Disturbances in England 1700–1870*, Longman, 1979, is a good review of the field, but at its strongest in the period after 1750.
46.   More work needs to be done on the risings of 1549, despite their familiarity to the general historian. Julian Cornwell, *The Revolt of the Peasantry 1549*, Routledge & Kegan Paul, 1977, although idiosyncratic in its approach, is the nearest thing to a general survey yet to appear, while Anthony Fletcher, *Tudor Rebellions*, Longman, 1968, contains a chapter on the events of 1549. S. T. Bindoff, *Kett's Rebellion*, Historical Association pamphlet, 1949, is still regarded as standard, although Diarmaid MacCullock, 'Kett's Rebellion in context', *Past and Present*, **84**, 1979, pp. 36–59, demonstrates just how much close study of relevant local sources would help deepen our understanding of the risings.
47.   Sharp, *In Contempt of All Authority*, op. cit.; Lindley, *Fenland Riots*, op. cit.
48.   For the background to this rioting, see Brian Manning, *The English People and the English Revolution, 1640–1649*, Heinemann, 1976.
49.   For a discussion of this point see C. S. L. Davies, 'Peasant revolt in France and England: a comparison', *Agricultural History Review*, **21**, 1973, pp. 122–34.
50.   These problems are described in L. M. Marshall, 'The levying of the hearth tax, 1662–1688', *English Historical Review*, **51**, 1936, pp. 628–46.
51.   A commission of oyer and terminer was a special commission sent out

by the central government to examine and judge (oyer et terminer) specified offences. It was frequently used to try participants in large-scale riots, and was usually welcomed by the county JPs, whose track record in dealing with serious disturbances was not a very good one. Records of these commissions, so far little investigated, might, if available in sufficient bulk, be invaluable in casting light on popular disturbances in our period.

52. Sheffield City Central Library, CD 509/18 (Copley Deeds).
53. Emmison, *Elizabethan Life: disorder*, op. cit., pp. 62–4.
54. Colchester Borough Archives, Examination and Recognizance Book 1619–1645, unfoliated, 8 February 1624.
55. Much of the material relating to rioting in and around Colchester in this period is to be found in Manning, *English People and English Revolution*, op. cit. pp. 171–8. Cf. J. A. Sharpe, 'Crime in the county of Essex 1620–1680', Oxford University D.Phil. thesis, 1978, pp. 157–62.
56 Colchester Borough Archives, Examination and Recognizance Book 1647–1684, unfoliated, 1 March 1668.
57. Ibid., 13–14 October 1675; PRO, P C 2/65, f.20.
58. This incident is described in K. H. Burley, 'A note on a labour dispute in early eighteenth-century Colchester', *Bulletin of the Institute of Historical Research*, **29**, 1956, pp. 220–30.
59 *The Proceedings at the Assizes for the County of Essex held at Chelmsford 17th, 18th and 19th Days of July*, London, 1740.
60. Thompson, *Whigs and Hunters*, op. cit., p. 194.
61. J. Styles, 'Our traitorous money makers', in *An Ungovernable People*, eds Brewer and Styles, op. cit., p. 243.
62. Thompson, 'Eighteenth-century crime, popular movements and social control', op. cit., p. 9.
63. Hobsbawm, 'Distinctions between socio-political and other forms of crime', op. cit., p. 6.
64. John Styles, 'Criminal records', *The Historical Journal*, **20**, 1977, p. 981.
65. This emerges from P. Linebaugh 'Tyburn: a study of crime and the labouring poor in London during the first half of the eighteenth century', Warwick University Ph.D. thesis, 1975.
66. Thompson, 'Eighteenth-century crime, popular movements and social control', op. cit., p. 10.
67. Styles, 'Our traitorous money makers', op. cit., p. 245.
68. 'Introduction' to *An Ungovernable People*, eds Brewer and Styles, op. cit., pp. 13–14.
69. Ibid., pp. 19–20.
70. Ibid., p. 11.

CHAPTER 7. ELITE PERCEPTIONS AND POPULAR IMAGES

1. Sir John Fortescue, *De Laudibus Legum Anglias*, ed. S. B. Chrimes,

Cambridge UP, 1948; the most accessible location for examining Lambarde's views on the law is in the collection of his jury charges in *William Lambarde and local government*, ed. Conyers Read, Cornell UP, 1962.

2.   Matthew Hale, *The History of the Common Law of England*, ed. Charles M. Gray, Chicago UP, 1971, p. 30.

3.   *The Works of William Paley, DD*, ed. James Paxton, 5 vols, London, 1838, vol. 2, pp. 365–6.

4.   Humphrey Babington, *Mercy & Judgement: a sermon preached at the assizes held at Lincolne, July 15 1678*, Cambridge, 1678, p. 18.

5.   Martin Madan, *Thoughts on Executive Justice, with respect to our criminal laws particularly on the circuits*, London, 1785, p. 1.

6.   Richard Millechamp, *The Unreasonableness and Danger of Grudging: a sermon preach'd at Gloucester before Mr Justice Powell, and Mr Justice Gould: at the assize held there by Mr Justice Gould, March the 7th, 1707/8*, London, 1708, p. 7.

7.   Nathaniel Hardy, *The Apostolical Liturgy Revived: a sermon preached at the assizes held at Chelmsford in the county of Essex, March 18, 1660*, London, 1661, p. 32.

8.   John Fielding, *An Account of the Origin and Effects of a Police Set on Foot by His Grace the Duke of Newcastle in the Year 1753, upon a Plan Presented to His Grace by the Late Henry Fielding, Esq.; to which is added a plan for preserving those deserted girls in this town, who become prostitutes from necessity*, London, 1758, p. viii.

9.   C. W. Brooks, 'Litigants and attorneys in King's Bench and Common Pleas 1560–1640', in *Legal Records and the Historian: papers presented to the Cambridge Legal History Conference 7–10 July 1975, and in Lincoln's Inn Old Hall on 3 July, 1974*, ed. J. H. Baker, Royal Historical Society, London, 1978, pp. 43–4.

10.   See the comments of D. Hay, 'Property, authority, and the criminal law', in *Albion's Fatal Tree*, eds Hay *et al.*, Allen Lane, 1975, pp. 40–9.

11.   See J. Walter and K. Wrightson, 'Dearth and the social order in early modern England', for a *Past and Present*, **71**, 1976, pp. 22–42, for a discussion of this point.

12.   For general discussions of the legal profession in this period see *Lawyers in Early Modern Europe and America*, ed. W. Prest, Croom Helm, 1981; and Bouwsma, 'Lawyers and early modern culture', *American Historical Review*, **78**, 1973, pp. 303–27. A more specialized description of one section of the legal profession is provided by Robert Robson, *The Attorney in Eighteenth-Century England*, CUP, 1959.

13.   Thomas Scot, *The Proiector: teaching a direct, ¡sure and ready way to restore the decayes of the church and state both in honour and revenue, delivered in a sermon before the Iudges in Norwich, at summer assizes there holden, anno 1620*, London, 1623, p. 23.

14.   Quoted in M. Dorothy George, *Hogarth to Cruikshank: ¡social change in graphic satire*, Allen Lane, 1967, pp. 98–9.

15.   *Commons Debates 1621*, eds Wallace Notestein, Frances Helen Relf, Hartley Simpson, 7 vols, New Haven, Yale UP, 1935, Yale Historical Publications, Manuscripts and Edited Texts, **14**, vol. 2, p. 120.

16.   Langbein, *Prosecuting Crime in the Renaissance: England, Germany, France*, Harvard UP, 1974, p. 55.

17. *Commons Debates 1621*, eds. Noestein, Relf, and Simpson, op. cit., vol. 2, pp. 68, 117, 203, 236; vol. 3, p. 87; vol. 4, pp. 45, 89; vol. 5, pp. 254, 305.

18. S. T. Bindoff, 'The making of the Statute of Artificers', in *Elizabethan Government and Society*, eds S. T. Bindoff, J. Hurstfield, and C. H. Williams, London UP, 1961; and D. M. Woodward, 'The background to the Statute of Artificers: the genesis of a labour policy 1558–63', *Economic History Review*, 2nd series, **33**, 1980, pp. 32–44.

19. Paul Slack, 'Books of Orders: the making of |English social policy, 1577–1631', *Transactions of the Royal Historical Society*, 5th series, **30**, 1980, p. 13.

20. Joan R. Kent, 'Attitudes of members of the House of |Commons to the regulation of "personal conduct" in late Elizabethan and early Stuart England', *Bulletin of the Institute of Historical Research*, **44**, 1973, pp. 41–71.

21. Madan, *Thoughts on Executive Justice*, op. cit., 'Appendix', p. 43.

22. Hay, 'Property, authority, and the criminal law', op. cit., pp. 19, 21.

23. E. P. Thompson, *Whigs and Hunters: the origin of the Black Act*, Allen Lane, 1975, p. 21.

24. Hay, 'Property, authority, and the criminal law', op. cit., pp. 19–20.

25. For a discussion of the alternatives to legislation, see R. W. K. Hinton, 'The decline of parliamentary government under Elizabeth I and the early Stuarts', *Cambridge Historical Journal*, **13**, 1957, pp. 116–32.

26. Hay, 'Property, authority, and the criminal law', op. cit., p. 21.

27. John Locke, *Two treatises of government*, ed. Peter Laslett, Cambridge UP, 1963, p. 347.

28. White Kennet, quoted in A. G. Craig, 'The movement for the reformation of manners, 1688–1715', Edinburgh Ph.D. thesis, 1980, p. 196.

29. Carol Z. Wiener, 'The beleaguered isle: a study of Elizabethan and Jacobean anti-catholicism', *Past and Present*, **51**, 1971, p. 41.

30. University of Durham, Department of Palaeography and Diplomatic, Archdeacon of Durham's Act Book 1600–19, f.95.

31. *The Workes of that Famous and Worthy Minister of Christ in the Universitie of Cambridge, Mr William Perkins*, ed. J. Legatt, 2 vols, London, 1616–17, vol. 1, p. 764; vol. 2, p. 266.

32. Richard Coleire, *Kings and Judges the Viceregents of God. A sermon preach'd July 31, 1729 at the assizes holden at Kingston upon Thames in the county of Surrey*, London, 1729, p. 17.

33. J. Disney, *An Essay upon the Execution of the Laws Against Immorality and Prophaness*, London, 1708, pp. xxi-xxii.

34. Anthony Walker, *Say On: or, a seasonable plea for a full hearing betwixt man and man. And, a serious plea for the like hearing betwixt God and man, delivered in a sermon at Chelmsford in Essex, at the general assize holden for the same county, July 8 1678*, London, 1679, pp. 43–4.

35. T. Nourse, *Campania Foelix: or a discourse of the benefits and improvements of husbandry*, London, 1700, p. 277.

36. Jean Armand Dubourdicis, *Ely Trembling for the Ark of God: or, the religious duty of being concerned for the present state of the protestant religion, incumbent upon all, but chiefly incumbent upon the clergy and the magistracy. A sermon preach'd at the assizes held at Chelmsford in*

Essex, on July 15, 1714, London, 1714, pp. 11–12.
37. Hale, *History of the Common Law*, ed. Gray, op. cit., p. 31.
38. Henry Goodcole, *London's Cry Ascended to God, and entered into the hearts and eares of men for revenge of bloodshedders, burglaires and vagabonds*, London, 1620, sig. A.5.
39. Scot, *The Proiector*, op. cit., p. 31.
40. Idem, *The High-waies of God and King, wherein all men ,ought to walke in holinesse here to happinesse hereafter. Delivered in two sermons preached at Thetford in Norfolk, Anno, 1620*, London, 1623, p. 73.
41. Kent, 'Attitudes of members', op. cit. p. 43.
42. For a preliminary statement of this important revision of accepted views, see Nicholas Tyacke, 'Puritanism, Arminianism, and Counter-revolution', in *The Origins of the English Civil War*, ed. Conrad Russell, Macmillan, 1973. Puritan social thought is discussed at length in C. H. and K. George, *The Protestant Mind of the English Reformation 1570–1640*, Princeton UP, 1961.
43. The problem is discussed, and some more detailed regional evidence offered, in Keith Wrightson, 'The Puritan reformation of manners, with special reference to the counties of Lancashire and Essex, 1640–1660', Cambridge University Ph.D. thesis, 1973.
44. A. H. A. Hamilton, *Quarter Sessions from Queen |Elizabeth to Queen Anne*, pp. 73, 99, 115, 116, 139, 161; *Before the Bawdy Court*, ed. Hair, Elek, 1972, pp. 46, 55, 70, 37; *Collection for a History of Staffordshire: the Staffordshire Quarter Sessions Rolls*, ed. J. A. H. Burne, 5 vols, William Salt Archaeological Society, 1929–40, vol. 2, p. 92; *Articles to be Enquired of in the Metropolitcall Visitation of the Father in God, Samuel, by the providence of God Archbishop of York, Primate of England and Metropolitan*, London, 1629, p. 9.
45. PRO, CHES 21/2, f. 106; 21/3, f.29.
46. K. Wrightson, 'Two concepts of order', in *An Ungovernable People*, eds J. Brewer and J. Styles, Hutchinson, 1980, pp. 34–5, 304, 306–7; K. Wrightson and D. Levine, *Poverty and Piety in an English Village: Terling 1525–1700*, Academic Press, 1979, p. 140.
47. James Ellesby, *A Caution Against Ill Company: or, a discourse shewing the danger of conversing familiarly with bad men* (5th edn), London, 1775, p. 11.
48. Stephen Hales, *A Friendly Admonition to the Drinkers of Gine, Brandy and other distilled spiritous liquors*, London, 1734,. This approach to the subject should be contrasted with that of such earlier books as Richard Younge, *The Drunkard's Character*, London, 1638.
49. The standard work on the Societies remains Garnet V. Portus, *Caritas Anglican, or, an historical enquiry into those religious and philanthropical societies that flourished in England between the years 1678 and 1740*, London, 1912. More recent work includes T. C. Curtis and W. A. Speck, 'The societies for the reformation of manners: a case study in the theory and practice of moral reform', *Literature and History*, 3, 1976, pp. 45–64; Tine Isaacs, 'The Anglican Hierarchy and the reformation of manners 1688–1738', *Journal of Ecclesiastical History*, 33, 1982, pp. 391–411; and Craig, 'Movement for the reformation of manners', op. cit. For a statement of the principles of the socieites from a contemporary supporter, see Josiah Woodward, *An Account of the*

Progress of the Reformation of Manners on England, Scotland and Ireland, and Other Parts of Europe and America. With some reasons and plain directions for our hearty and vigorous prosecution of this glorious work, London (12th edn), 1724.

50. Woodward, *An Account*, op. cit., p. 23.
51. Quoted in Portus, *Caritas Anglicana*, op. cit., p. 90.
52. Borthwick Institute of Historical Research, York, HEX 2. This material figures prominently in M. G. Smith, *Pastoral Discipline and the Church Courts: the Hexham court 1680–1750*, Borthwick Papers, **62**, 1982.
53. *William Lambarde and Local Government*, ed. Conyers Read, Cornell UP, 1962, *passim*.
54. Ibid., pp. 130, 143–4.
55. Henry Fielding, 'A charge delivered to the grand jury, at the sessions of the peace held for the City and Liberty of Westminster &c., on Thursday the 29th of June 1749', in *Works*, ed. Arthur Murphy, 14 vols, London, 1808, vol. 12, p. 276. For other examples of eighteenth-century charges, see *The Charge of Whitlocke Bulstrode, Esq., to the Grand-Jury, and Other Juries, of the County of Middlesex. At the general quarter sessions of the peace, held April 21st 1718, at Westminster Hall*, London, 1718; and *The Charge of William Cowper Esq., to the Grand Jury of the City and Liberty of Westminster &c, at the general quarter sessions of the peace, held October the 7th, 1719, in Westminster Hall*, London, 1719.
56. Barbara White, 'Assizes sermons 1669–1720', CNAA Ph.D., Polytechnic of Newcastle upon Tyne, 1980.
57. Ibid., p.xxx.
58. This is not the place for an exhaustive bibliography of pre-1660 assize sermons, along the lines of that constructed by Dr White for her period. Typical examples, however, include: [N]ath: [B]ownd, *Saint Paul's Trumpet, Sounding an Alarme to Judgement. Warning all men to prepare themselves against their appearing before Christ's tribunall. delivered in two sermons, commanded by publique authoritie to be preached: the one at Paul's Crosse: the other at the assizes at Chelmsford in Essex July 24 1615*, London, 1615;[L]ancelot [D]awes, *Two Sermons Preached at the Assizes Holden at Carlisle, Touching Sundry Corruptions of These Times*, Oxford, 1614; Samuel Garey, *A Manuall for Magistrates or a Lanterne for Lawyers: a sermon preached before Iudges and Iustices at Norwich assizes, 1619*, London, 1623; Scot, *The Proiector*, op. cit. and idem. *High-waise of God and the King*, op. cit.
59. This literature is only beginning to attract serious attention. For a preliminary survey, see Victor E. Neuberg, *Popular Literature: a history and guide*, Penguin, Harmondsworth, 1977, while another stimulating introduction to the subject is provided by Leslie Sheperd, *The History of Street Literature*, David & Charles, 1973. Joseph H. Marshburn, *Murder and Witchcraft in England, 1550–1640, as recounted in pamphlets, ballads, broadsides and plays*, Norman, Oklahoma, 1971, is based on the types of popular literature used in the present study. Much of value on popular literature is to be found in Margaret Spufford, *Small Books and Pleasant Histories*, Methuen, 1982, while some remarks on this literature on a European level are to be found in Peter Burke, *Popular Culture in Early modern Europe*, Temple Smith, 1978, pp. 250–9.

60. Neuberg, *Popular Literature*, op. cit., p. 139.

61. Ibid., loc. cit.

62. J. Dunton, *The Night Walker or Evening Rambles in Search of lewd Women with the Conferences Held with them &c*, September 1696, sig. B1.

63. *Thievery à la Mode: or the fatal encouragement*, London, 1728. One senses that the author of this anonymous piece had his tongue firmly in his cheek.

64. Despite the appearance of a number of pamphlets and ballads dealing with Turpin which appeared shortly after his death, he owes his unique status as the prototype highwayman of popular imagination to William Ainsworth Harrison, *Rookwood: a romance*, 3 vols, London, 1834. Harrison, a novelist who wrote a number of widely-read historical romances, described Turpin as 'the *ultimus romanorum*, the last of a race which (we were almost about to say we regret) is now altogether extinct. . . with him expired the chivalrous spirit which animated sucessively the bosoms of so many knights of the road': ibid., vol. 2, p. 307. Near-contemporary sources suggest that Turpin, like most highwaymen, was fundamentally a nasty thug: see, for example, *The Complete Newgate calendar*, eds J. L. Rayner and G. T. Crook, 5 vols, London, 1926, vol. 3, pp. 88–97.

65. Ibid., vol. 1, pp. 92–105; *Chap-Books of the Eighteenth Century*, ed. John Ashton, London, 1882, pp. 433–6.

66. *The Viking Book of Folk Ballads of the English-speaking World*, ed. Albert B. Friedman, Viking Press, 1963, p. 218.

67. For a useful introduction to this subject see J. J. Richetts, *Popular Fiction Before Richardson*, Oxford UP, 1969, ch. 2, 'Rogues and whores, heroes and anti-heroes'. The social environment of the writers of popular fiction in the eighteenth century is described in Pat Rogers, *Grub Street: studies in a subculture*, London, 1972. For a more critical appraisal of the use of at least one type of literary source, the rogue literature of the Elizabethan and Jacobean periods, see T. C. Curtis and F. M. Hale, 'English thinking about crime, 1530–1620', in *Crime and Criminal Justice in Europe and Canada*, ed. L. A. Knafla, Wilfred Louvier UP, 1981.

68. Radzinowicz, *A History of English Criminal Law and its administration from 1750*, 4 vols, Stevens, 1948–68, vol. 1, ch. 6, 'Execution of capital sentences'; Peter Linebaugh, 'The Tyburn riot against the surgeons', in *Albion's Fatal Tree*, eds Hay *et al.*, op. cit.

69. *The Complete Newgate calendar*, eds Rayner and Crook, op. cit., vol. 2, p. 59.

70. *An Exact Narrative of the Bloody Murder and Robbery Committed by Stephen Eaton, Sarah Swift, George Rhodes and Henry Pritchard upon the Person of Mr John Talbot, Minister*, London, 1669, pp. 8–9.

71. Gilbert Dugdale, *A True Discourse of the Practices of Elizabeth Caldwell, Ma. Ieffrey Bownd, Isabell Hall, Widdow, and George Fernely, on the Person of Ma. Thomas Caldwell, in the County of Chester*, London, 1604, sig. B3.

72. *The Arraignment, Tryall, Conviction and Confession of Francis Deane, a Salter, and Iohn Faulkner a Strong-water Man (both Anabaptists, and Lately Received into that Sect) for the Murther of one Mr. Daniel a*

solicitor, London, 1643, single sheet broadside.

73. Peter Linebaugh, 'The ordinary of Newgate and his *Account*', in *Crime in England 1550–1800*, ed. J. S. Cockburn, Methuen, 1977, p. 260.

74. Robert Franklin, *A Murderer Punished and Pardoned: or, a true relation of the wicked life and shameful happy death of Thomas Savage, imprisoned, justly condemned, and twice executed at Ratcliffe, for his bloody fact, in killing his fellow servant, on Wednesday, Octob. 28, 1668* (12th edn), London, 1669, pp. 21, 33.

75. *A Full and True Account of a Most Barbarous and Bloody Murther Committed by Esther Ives, with the assistance of John Noyse a cooper: on the body of William Ives, her husband, at Rumsey in Hampshire, on the fifth day of February 1686*, London, 1686, p.8.

76. *Dictionary of National Biography*; *Chap-Books of the Eighteenth Century*, ed. Ashton, op. cit., pp. 429–32; George Lillo, *The London Merchant*, ed. William H. McBurney, Edward Arnold, 1965.

77. Ronald Paulson, *Emblem and Expression: meaning in English Art in the eighteenth century*, Harvard UP, 1975, p. 59. Pictorial representations of crime are among the subjects discussed in J. A. Sharpe, *Crime and the Law in English Satirical Prints 1600–1832*, Chadwyck-Healey, forthcoming.

78. Ritchetts, *Popular Fiction*, op. cit., pp. 23–4.

79. This argument is put forward in Curtis and Hale, 'English thinking about crime', op. cit.

80. Ellesby, *A Caution Against Ill Company*, op. cit., p.9.

81. Thus E. P. Thompson, 'Patrician society, plebeian culture', *Journal of Social History*, 7, 1974, p. 387, comments that

> one never feels, before the French Revolution, that the rulers of England conceived that their whole social order might be endangered. The insubordination of the poor was an inconvenience; it was not a menace. The styles of politics and of architecture, the rhetoric of the gentry and their decorative arts, all seem to proclaim stability, self-confidence, a habit of managing all threats to their hegemony.

For an exploration of upper-class perceptions of the poor in the first half of the period covered by this book, see Christopher Hill, 'The many-headed monster in late Tudor and early Stuart political thinking', in *From the Renaissance to the Counter Reformation: essays in honour of Garrett Mattingley*, ed. C. H. Carter, Cape, 1966.

CHAPTER 8. CONTINUITY AND CHANGE IN CRIME AND PUNISHMENT, 1550–1750

1. V. A. C. Gatrell, 'The decline of theft and violence in Victorian and Edwardian England', in *Crime and the Law: the social history of crime in Western Europe since 1500*, eds V. A. C. Gatrell, Bruce Lenman and Geoffrey Parker, Europa Publications, 1980, p. 238.

2. M. R. Weisser, *Crime and Punishment in Early Modern Europe*,

Harvester Press, 1979, pp. 1, 3, 17.

3.   G. Rusche and O. Kirchheimer, *Punishment and Social Structure*, New York, 1939; Melossi and Pavarini, *The Prison and the Factory origins of the penitentiary system*, Macmillan, 1981; Weisser, *Crime and Punishment*, op. cit.

4.   Ibid., pp. 1–2.

5.   For an introduction to this topic, which unfortunately has little to say about the impact of the state at a grass-roots level, see J. H. Shennan, *The Origins of the European State 1450–1725*, Hutchinson, 1974.

6.   Melossi and Pavarini, *The Prison and the Factory*, op. cit., p.2.

7.   A. Soman, 'Deviance and criminal justice in western Europe, 1300– 1800: an essay in structure', p. 5. *Criminal Justice History*, **1**, 1980, Cf. Lenman and Parker, 'The state, the community and the criminal law in early modern Europe', in *Crime and the Law since 1500*, eds Gatrell, Lenman and Parker, op. cit.

8.   J. S. Cockburn, 'The nature and incidence of crime in England 1559– 1625: a preliminary survey', in *Crime in England 1550–1800*, ed. Cockburn, Methuen, 1977; PRO, CHES 21/1–5; J. A. Sharpe, 'Crime in the county of Essex, 1620–1680: a study of offences and offenders at the assizes and quarter sessions', Oxford University D.Phil. thesis, 1978 (to be published by Cambridge UP as *Crime in Seventeenth-century England: a county study*); J. M. Beattie, 'The pattern of crime in England 1660–1800', *Past and Present*, **62**, 1974, pp. 47–95; PRO, ASSI 23/4–6; ASSI 31/1.

9.   B. Hanawalt, *Crime and Conflict in English Communities, 1300–1348*, Harvard UP, 1979, table 3, p. 66.

10.   K. Wrightson and D. Levine, *Poverty and Piety in an English Village: Terling 1525–1700*, Academic Press, 1979, ch. 5, 'Conflict and control: the villagers and the courts'; K. Wrightson, 'Two concepts of order: justices, constables and jurymen in seventeenth-century England', in *An Ungovernable People*, eds Brewer and Styles, Hutchinson, 1980, p. 34.

11.   PRO, CHES 21/2–3, *passim*; R. A. Marchant, *The Church Under the Law: justice, administration and discipline in the diocese of York 1560– 1640*, Cambridge UP, 1969, table 32, p. 219.

12.   Wrightson, 'Two concepts of order', op. cit., table 2, pp. 302–3.

13.   Zvi Razi, *Life, Marriage and Death in a Medieval Parish. Economy, society and demography in Halesowen 1270–1400*, Cambridge UP, 1980, pp. 37, 38, 66, 137–8; Eleanor Searle, *Lordship and Community: Battle Abbey and its banlieu 1066–1538*, Toronto Pontifical Institute of Medieval Studies, 1974, p. 415; DeLloyd J. Guth, 'Enforcing late-medieval law: patterns in litigation during Henry VII's reign', in *Legal Records and the Historian*, ed. Baker, Royal Historical Society, London, 1978, p. 96.

14.   J. Bellamy, *Crime and Public Order in England in the Later Middle Ages*, Routledge & Kegan Paul, London, 1973, p. 34.

15.   Henry Zouch, *Hints Respecting the Public Police*, London, 1786, p. 1.

16.   J. A. Raftis, 'The concentration of responsibility in five villages', *Medieval Studies*, **28**, 1966, pp. 92–118; Anne DeWindt, 'Peasant power structures in fourteenth-century King's Ripton', ibid., **38**, 1976, pp. 236–67; Hanawalt, *Crime and Conflict*, op. cit., pp. 32, 52. For a

critical review of recent writing on peasant communities in medieval England, see Zvi Razi, 'The Toronto school's reconstitution of medieval peasant society: a critical view', *Past and Present*, **85**, 1979, pp. 141–57.

17. Sir Samuel Romilly, *Observations on the Criminal Law of England as it Relates to Capital Punishments and on the Mode in which it is Administered*, London, 1810, p. 4.

18. M. Madan, *Thoughts on Executive Justice, with respect to our criminal laws particularly on the circuits*, London, 1785, pp. 98–9.

19. *News from Fleetstreet. Or, the last speech and confession of two persons hanged there for murther on Friday the 22 of October 1675*, London, 1675, p. 5.

20. *Workes of William Paley DD*, ed. J. Paxton, 5 vols, London, 1838, vol. 2, pp. 424–5.

21. Madan, *Thoughts on Executive Justice*, op. cit., p. 37; Fielding, *An Enquiry into the Causes of the Late Increase of Robbers, &c with some proposals for remedying this growing evil*, London, 1751, p. 166.

22. The literature on the medieval English law is very extensive. Two good introductions to the formative period of the law as it existed in the timespan covered by this book are D. M. Stenton, *English Justice Beween the Norman Conquest and the Great Charter 1066–1215*, Allen & Unwin, 1965; and W. L. Warren, *Henry II*, Eyre Methuen, 1973, ch. 9, 'Royal justice'. F. Pollock and F. W. Maitland, *The History of English Law Before the Time of Edward I*, 2 vols (2nd edn), Cambridge UP, 1968, remains standard.

23. J. B. Given, *Society and Homicide in Thirteenth-century England*, Stanford UP, 1977, p. 40. Cf. Carl I. Hammer, Jr, 'Patterns of homicide in a medieval university town: fourteenth-century Oxford', *Past and Present*, **78**, 1978, pp. 3–23.

24. This seems to emerge, albeit somewhat shakily, from P. E. H. Hair, 'Deaths from violence in Britain: a tentative secular survey', *Population Studies*, **25**, 1971, pp. 5–24. Beattie, 'Pattern of crime', op. cit., p. 61, traces a 'real decline' in murder and manslaughter between 1660 and 1800.

25. A. Macfarlane, *The Justice and the Mare's Ale: law and disorder in seventeenth-century England*, Basil Blackwell, 1981, especially 'Conclusion: English violence in context'.

26. Cf. the comments of K. Wrightson, *English Society 1580–1680*, Hutchinson, 1982, pp. 159–162.

27. Hanawalt, *Crime and Conflict*, op. cit., p. 114.

28. G. Leveson-Gower, 'Note Book of a Surrey Justice', *Surrey Archaeological Collections*, **9**, 1888, p. 168.

29. Gatrell, 'Decline of theft and violence', op. cit., especially pp. 261–6, 334–6.

30. David Philips, *Crime and Authority in Victorian England: the Black Country 1835–1860*, London, 1977, p. 287.

31. Quoted in W. S. Holdsworth, *A History of English Law*, eds A. L. Goodhart and H. E. Hanbury, 17 vols, Methuen and Sweet & Maxwell, 1903–72, vol. 11, p. 534.

32. P. Linebaugh, 'Tyburn: a study of crime and the labouring poor in London during the first half of the eighteenth century', Warwick

University Ph.D. thesis, 1975, table X, p. 330; PRO, ASSI 23/5–6; ASSI 33/1.

33.   Marchant, *The Church Under the Law*, op. cit., p. 71; PRO, CHES 21/2, f.46v; *Quarter Sessions Records for the County of Somerset, vol. 1: James I*, ed. E. H. Bates, Somerset Record Society, **23**, 1907, p. 11; *Middlesex County Records*, new series, ed. William le Hardy, 4 vols, 1933–41, vol. 4, p. 168; Guth, 'Enforcing late-medieval law' op. cit., p. 90.

34.   M. J. Ingram, 'Communities and courts: law and disorder in early seventeenth-century Wiltshire', in *Crime in England 1550–1800*, ed. J. S. Cockburn, Methuen, 1977, pp. 125–7; J. A. Sharpe, 'Litigation and human relations in early modern England – ecclesiastical defamation suits at York', *Past and Present*, Society conference, 1980.

35.   *Some Annals of the Borough of Devizes, 1555–1791*, ed. B. Howard Cunningham, Devizes, 1925, p. 17; *The Book of John Fisher, Town Clerk and Deputy Recorder of Warwick, 1580–1588*, ed. T. Kemp, Warwick, 1900, pp. 12, 120; G. Leveson-Gower, 'Note Book of a Surrey Justice', *Surrey Archaeological Collections*, **9**, 1888, p. 174.

36.   *Buckinghamshire Sessions Records*, ed. W. le Hardy, 3 vols, Aylesbury, 1933–9, vol. 2, p. 445.

37.   G. Rusche and O. Kirchheimer, *Punishment and Social Structure*, New York, 1939, pp. 5, 40.

38.   It is hoped that work in progress by Joanna Innes will help remedy this situation.

39.   H. Fielding, *An Enquiry*, op. cit., p. 97. On the other hand, the house might have been a more effective institution in the earlier stages of its history. The Somerset JP Edward Hext reported in 1598 that when he sent 'dyvers wandrynge suspycyous persons' to the house of correction 'all in general wold beseche me with bytter teares to send them rather to the gayle', and some would even confess to felonies 'to thend they wold not be sent to the howse of correccion where they shold be ynforced to worke': *Tudor Economic Documents*, eds R. H. Tawney and E. Power, 3 vols, Longmans, London, 1924, vol. 2, p. 430.

40.   E.g. *Calendar of Assize Records: Sussex indictments James I*, ed. J. S. Cockburn, HMSO, 1974, pp. 71–3.

41.   These calendars are preserved in Essex Record Office, Q/SR 399–429, *passim*.

42.   Sir Edward Moore, *Liverpool in Charles the Second's Time*, ed. William Ferguson Irvine, Liverpool, 1899, p.33.

43.   Melossi and Pavarini, *The Prison and the Factory*, op. cit., p. 188. Cf. Weisser's observation that 'when stripped to its barest essentials – brutality, anonymity, industry – the prison incorporated those same hallmarks that were the hallmarks of the factory system': *Crime and Punishment*, op. cit., p. 170.

44.   Michel Foucalt, *Discipline and Punish: the birth of the prison*, Allen Lane, 1977.

45.   Melossi and Pavarini, *The prison and the Factory*, op cit., p.16.

46,   J.P. Kenyon, *The Stuart Constitution*, Cambridge UP; 1966, p.501.

47.   T. Nourse, *Campania Foelix: or, a discourse of the benefits and improvements of husbandry*, London, 1700, p.234.

48. Bernard de Mandeville, *An Enquiry into the Causes of the Frequent Executions at Tyburn: and a proposal for some regulations concerning felons in prison, and the good effects to be expected from them*, London, 1725, p.16.

49. Commons debates 1621, eds Notestein, Relf, and Simpson, op.cit., vol. 7, p. 54.

50. D. Hay, 'Property, authority and the criminal law,' in *Albion's Fatal Tree*, eds D. Hay *et al.*, Allen Lane, 1975, pp.40–9.

51. E.A. Wrigley and R.S. Schofield, *The Population History of England, 1541–1871: a reconstruction*, Arnold, 1981, especially ch. 6, 'Secular trends: some basic patterns'.

52. To discuss fluctuations in the value of real wages is to enter an historiographical minefield, and it is emphasized that this statement is made very tentatively. For an attempt to provide a framework for long-term changes in the value of real wages, however, see E. E. Phelps Brown and Sheila V. Hopkins, 'Seven centuries of building wages', *Economica*, new series, **22**, August 1955, pp. 195–206.

53. C. S. L. Davies, 'Slavery and Protector Somerset: the Vagrancy Act of 1547', *Economic History Review*, 2nd series, **19**' 1966, pp.533–49.

54. More work needs to be done on attitudes to the poor in the late seventeenth and eighteenth centuries. For an initial discussion, see Charles Wilson, 'The other face of mercantilism', *Transactions of the Royal Historical Soiciety*, 5th series, **9**, 1959, pp.81–101. The standard work on poverty in this later period is D. Marshall, *The English Poor in the Eighteenth Century*, Routledge, 1926. The problem is expertly put in a wider context by C. Lis and H. Soly, *Poverty and Capitalism in Pre-Industrial Europe*, Harvester, 1979.

55. Hanawalt; *Crime and Conflict* op.cit., p. 20.

56. Fielding; *An Enquiry*, op.cit., p. 2; *Tudor Economic Documents*, eds Tawney and Power, op.cit., vol. 2, pp. 339–46; *William Lambarde and Local Government*, ed. Conyers Read, pp. 110–11, 129–31, 134–5, 143–4, 169.

57. Theodore K. Rabb, *The Struggle for Stability in Europe*, Oxford UP, 1975, p. 4.

58. J. H. Plumb, *The Growth of Political Stability in England 1675–1725*, Macmillan; 1967, p.xviii.

59. V.A.C. Gatrell, The decline of theft and violence, op.cit., p. 255.

60. Ibid., p. 241. Dr Gatrell's investigations make some interesting points of contrast and comparison with Howard Zehr, *Crime and the Development of Modern Society: patterns of criminality in nineteenth-century Germany and France*, Croom Helm, 1976.

BIBLIOGRAPHICAL NOTE

As I have provided fairly full notes, I feel to a large extent exonerated from providing an exhaustive bibliography. Nevertheless, I feel that a bibliographical note of this type will be of considerable use to the reader, not least because it can be used to incorporate a brief recapitulation of some of the critical points made in the text.

By far the fullest introduction to the bibliographical background to the history of the crime in early modern England, although limited, perforce, to works published before about 1975, is L. A. Knafla, 'Crime and criminal justice: a critical bibliography', in *Crime in England 1550–1800*, ed. J. S. Cockburn, Methuen, 1977. This is updated by J. A. Sharpe, 'Ongoing research and recent publications', *International Association for the History of Crime and Criminal Justice Newsletter*, 1, 1979, pp. 22–33. Review articles in learned journals provide useful information on new publications and new interpretations. Three useful ones are: Victor Bailey, 'Bibliographical essay: crime, criminal justice and authority in England', *Bulletin of the Society for the Study of Labour History*, 40, Spring 198. pp. 36–46; E. W. Ives, 'English law and English society', *History*, 61, 1981, pp. 50–60; and J. A. Sharpe, 'The history of crime in late medieval and early modern England: a review of the field', *Social History*, 7, 1982, pp. 187–203.

Those attempting to grasp the interpretative and methodological issues involved should then turn to the collections of essays that have been printed on these. The earliest of them was *Albion's Fatal Tree: crime and society in eighteenth century England*, eds Douglas Hay, Peter Linebaugh, John G. Rule, E. P. Thompson, and Cal Winslow, Allen Lane, 1975. This is a little late in its chronological focus, and is also concerned overwhelmingly with social crime, but it contains much of a more general relevance: in particular, Douglas Hay's essay on 'Property, authority and the criminal law' should be read by anyone interested in the subject. Other, and more varied, collections are: *Crime in England 1550–1800*, ed. J. S. Cockburn, Methuen, 1977; *An Ungovernable People: the English and their law in the seventeenth and eighteenth centuries*, eds John Brewer and John Styles, Hutchinson, 1980; and the various articles in *The Journal of Social History*, 8, 1975. *Crime and the Law: the social history of crime in western Europe since 1500*, eds V. A. C. Gatrell, Bruce Lenman, and Geoffrey Parker, Europa Publications, 1980, contains two essays of immediate relevance to this present book: Bruce Lenman and Geoffrey Parker, 'The state, the community, and the criminal law in early modern Europe', a courageous attempt at a broad interpretative essay; and J. A. Sharpe, 'Enforcing the law in the seventeenth-century English village'. Mention should be made of a yearly publication dealing with the history of crime, *Criminal Justice History: an International Annual*, John Jay Press. The first issue of this, 1980, included three very relevant articles: Alfred Soman, 'Deviance and criminal justice in western Europe, 1300–1800: An essay in structure'; Tim Curtis, 'Explaining crime in early modern England'; and Terry Chapman, 'Crime in eighteenth-century England: E. P. Thompson and the conflict theory of crime.'

Detailed monographs are few. Regional studies are virtually restricted to Essex, with Joel Samaha, *Law and Order in Historical Perspective: the case of Elizabethan Essex*, Academic Press, 1974; and J. A. Sharpe, *Crime in Seventeenth-Century England: a county study*, Cambridge UP/Past and Present Publications, 1983, J. S. Cockburn's 'companion volume' to his *Calendar of Assize Records* is in the press as I write, and will probably contain invaluable information not only on the administration of the assizes, but also on crime and law enforcement in the Home Counties, 1558–1625. Reports also reach me that John Beattie's book on crime in Surrey and Sussex, 1660–1800, is in an advanced stage of preparation: those wishing for a foretaste should read his 'The pattern of crime in England, 1660–1800', *Past and Present*, 72, 1974, pp. 47–95. The findings of two recently-completed doctoral thesis will doubtlessly add much to our knowledge: Cynthia B. Herrup, 'The common peace: legal structure and legal substance in East Sussex 1594–1640', Northwestern University Ph.D. thesis, 1982; and P. G. Lawson, 'Crime and the administration of criminal justice in Hertfordshire, 1590–1625', Oxford University D. Phil. thesis, 1983. E. P. Thompson, *Whigs and Hunters: the origin of the Black Act*, Allen Lane, 1975, although more narrowly focused, has, like most work emanating from that particular historian, some very wide implications. Lastly, three monographs offer wide-ranging interpretations of crime and punishment in early modern Europe as a whole: George Rusche and Otto Kirchheimer, *Punishment and Social Structure*, New York, 1939; Michael R. Weisser, *Crime and Punishment in Early Modern Europe*, Harvester, 1979; and Dario Melossi and Massimo Pavarini, *The Prison and the Factory: origins of the penitentiary system*, Macmillan, 1981. All three should by treated with caution, despite their raising a number of important questions, not least those surrounding crime and punishment and wider socio-economic developments. Good monographs on individual offences include: C. L. Ewen, *Witch Hunting and Witch Trials. The indictments for witchcraft from the records of 1373 assizes held for the Home circuit AD 1559–1736*, London, 1929; Alan Macfarlane, *Witchcraft in Tudor and Stuart England: a regional and comparative history*, Routledge & Kegan Paul, 1970; and Peter C. Hoffer and N. E. H. Hull, *Mudering Mothers: infanticide in England and New England, 1558–1803*, New York UP, 1981.

Many may shy away from its technicalities, but legal history remains an essential tool for the historian of crime. The standard work of reference is still W. S. Holdsworth, *A History of English Law*, eds A. L. Goodhart and H. G. Hanbury, 17 vols, Methuen and Sweet & Maxwell, 1903–72, although this work is, as might be expected, constantly being subjected to minor correction. The general reader will find Alan Harding, *A Social History of English Law*, Penguin, 1966, a concise introduction, and might then like to graduate to J. H.

225

Baker, *An Introduction to English Legal History*, Butterworths, 1971. Some essays dealing with the interactions between law and society are to be found in *Legal Records and the Historian: papers presented to the Cambridge Legal History Conference, 7–10 July 1975, and in Lincoln's Inn Old Hall on 3 July 1974*, ed. J. H. Baker, Royal Historical Society, 1978. Some of the wider implications of the relationship between law and society will be discussed in *Disputes and Settlements*, ed. John Bossy, Cambridge UP/Past and Present Publications, 1983.

Those wishing to work on archival sources will need a basic grasp on Latin, a sound grasp of palaeography, good eyesight and a stout heart. Given these, they will find much to interest them in the quarter sessions records, and the records of the ecclesiastical courts, which are held in most county record offices. Quarter sessions records, in particular, have been printed for many counties: several of the better collections are mentioned in the notes of this book, while a useful, but by no means comprehensive, list can be found in Carl Bridenbaugh, *Vexed and Troubled Englishmen*, 1590–1642, Oxford UP, 1968, pp. xvii–xviii. Assize records, held at the Public Record Office in London, still contain many undiscovered secrets about serious crime. The records of the Home circuit have been heavily investigated, but much remains to be done; in particular, unusually rich regional studies could be based on the indictment files and deposition of the Northern circuit (PRO ASSI 44, ASSI 45, respectively) for the fifty years after 1650, while the gaol books of the Western circuit (PRO ASSI 23) permit a statistical analysis of serious crime and punishment in the late seventeenth and early eighteenth centuries. Other counties enjoy records of an assize type, apart from those listed in the PRO as Clerks of Assize records. The Bishop of Ely enjoyed right of gaol delivery, and records of his court survive, albeit in what is at times is a very broken series, in the Cambridge University Library. We have seen, in chapter 3 of this present work, how useful the records of the Court of Great Sessions at Chester might be: the PRO catalogue dealing with the Palatinate of Chester suggests that the county enjoys a virtually unbroken series of gaol files for the 500 years before 1840, a body of source material which calls out for investigation. Those wishing to work on Welsh materials will also find much to occupy them. The *Public Record Office List and Indexes, 40: List of the records of the Palatinates of Chester, Durham & Lancaster, the Honour of Peveril, and the Principality of Wales preserved in the Public Record Office*, suggests that indictment files similar to those generated by the English assizes exist for eight Welsh counties. These records, now preserved in the National Library of Wales, likewise demand urgent attention.

Those without the opportunity or the taste for archival research might like to gain a first-hand impression of early modern crime, or at least images of it, from reprints of contemporary literature. *The Elizabethan Underworld*, ed. A. V Judges, 1930, and *Cony-catchers and bawdy baskets*, ed. Gamini Salgado Penguin 1977, are collections of Elizabethan and Jacobean rogue pamphlets. These make lively reading, but how far they reflect the reality of the crime of the period is debatable. Numerous criminal biographies, more detailed from the late seventeenth century onwards, can be found in *The Complete Newgate Calendar*, eds J. L. Rayner and G. T. Crook, 5 vols, London, 1926.

INDEX

adultery, 5-6, 92
alehouses, unlicensed, 6, 104-5
arbitration, 45, 178-9
arson, 24, 49, 54-6, 66, 170
assault, 6, 22, 26, 46, 50, 51, 52, 84
assizes, 23-4, 31, 36, 37, 39, 53, 128, 134
   in Durham, 158
   in Essex, 49
   Home circuit, 10, 37, 53
   Northern circuit, 53, 57, 98, 108
   Oxford circuit, 53
   Western circuit, 53
assize sermons, 159-60

Bacon, Sir Francis, 126
bailiffs, 31-2
Bangor, diocese of, 178
Barnes, T.G., 22, 35
Beier, A.L., 116
Beattie, J.M., 10, 41, 59, 60, 62, 68
Baccaria, Cesare, 18
benefit of clergy, 67, 147
bestiality, 54
bigamy, 54, 66
binding over, 36, 48, 90
Black Death, 173
Black, J.B., 1, 8
Blackstone, Sir William, 13, 45-6, 125,
   126, 177
bloodshed see assault
Bohemia, 68
Book of Orders, 25, 84, 147, 181
Bradshaw, William, 161
Brewer, John, 142
Bridewell, 116, 179
Buckinghamshire, quarter sessions in, 50,
   179
buggery, 49
   see also bestiality, sodomy

burglary, 24, 49, 54, 66
   see also property offences

capital statutes, 63, 148-50, 182
Capone, A1, 120, 122
Castiglione, Baldassare, 96
certiorari, writ of, 22
Chancery, court of, 45
charivari, 77, 90
Chaucer, Geoffrey, 8
Cheshire, 50, 54, 65, 170, 171, 182
Chester, Court of Great Sessions at, 6, 8,
   54-70, 118, 153, 178
churchwardens, 86
Civil Wars, 18, 44, 57, 67, 96, 133, 134,
   152, 167, 176
Clark, Sir George, 1
class consciousness, 135
clerk of the peace, 35, 38
Cockburn, J.S., 4, 10, 37, 62, 71
coining, 12, 57, 66, 106, 111, 118, 140, 141,
   170
Colquhoun, Patrick, 44, 124, 184
Common Pleas, court of, 6, 32, 145
conspiracy, 23
constables
   high, 33-4
   petty (or parish), 34, 39, 76-7, 91
Cornwall, 19, 55, 95, 170
coroner, 33-4
crime
   patterns of, 49-62. 170-2
   problem of definition, 4-7, 44, 49-52,
     187
   'social', 12-13, 121-31, 133, 139-42
criminal class, 94-5, 117-20, 165-6
Cromwell, Oliver, 144, 161
Cumberland, 57, 119
Cumbria, Kirkby Lonsdale in, 11

227

cursing, 87-8
Curtis, T.C., 10

'dark figure', 42, 47, 48, 70
defamation, 6, 27, 33, 88, 93
Defoe, Daniel, 161
depositions, 35-6
Derbyshire, 31, 106, 107
Devon, 55, 57-8, 64, 65, 67, 68, 153, 170, 182
Exeter in, 95
Disney, John, 114
Dorset, Blandford in, 161
drink offences, 50
drunkenness, 27, 111, 154
duelling, 96-7
Dunton, John, 114
Durham, city, 158
Durham, county, 89
Auckland in, 89
Denton in, 89
Wearmouth in, 150
diocese of, 155

East Anglia, 19, 133
ecclesiastical courts, 7, 26-7, 35, 39, 50, 85-7, 88, 92
Elton, G.R., 4, 5, 17
embezzlement, 124, 149
Essex, 5, 16, 25, 49, 55, 57, 59, 62, 64, 67, 70, 78, 81, 89, 107, 110, 118, 123, 128, 129, 131, 170, 171
Barking in, 180
Burnham-on-Crouch in, 76
Chelmsford in, 88
Colchester in, 135-8
Earls Colne in, 11, 80
Kelvedon in, 11, 50, 76, 80
Romford in, 109
Terling in, 11, 52-3, 75, 76, 93, 153, 172
Ewen, C.L., 9

Ferguson, Catherine M.F., 56-7
Ferrers, Laurence Shirley, fourth earl, 96
Fielding, Sir Henry, 18, 111, 113, 114, 159, 161, 174, 180, 184
Fielding, Sir John, 104, 144
Fletcher, Anthony, 29
forgery, 177-8
Fortescue, Sir John, 143
Foucault, Michel, 181
France, 66, 74, 97, 134, 177
fraud, 56, 169

game laws *see* poaching
gaol, 32-3, 181-2

Gatrell, V.A.C., 186
gleaning, 123
Gloucestershire, 47, 107, 123
Cheltenham in, 101
Goodcole, Henry, 115, 152
Gordon Riots, 131
Gough, Richard, 47

Hale, Sir Matthew, 143, 151
Hampshire, 25
Southampton in, 101
Hanawalt, Barbara, 170
Harman, Thomas, 102, 103
Hay, Douglas, 12-13, 43-4, 62, 68-70, 127, 128-9, 130, 145, 148, 149, 150, 182, 187
Hertfordshire, 55, 57, 62, 108, 123, 170
Hexhamshire, 156-8
Hext, Edward, 44, 45, 184
Hexter, J.H., 14
Hibbert, Christopher, 132
highway robbery, 49, 54, 66, 107-8
see also property offences
Hobbes, Thomas, 185
Hobsbawm, E.J., 140, 189
Hogarth, William, 2, 164
Holt, Sir John, CJQB, 156
homicide, 24, 49, 54-6, 60-2, 66, 122
see also violence
horse-theft, 106-7
Hoskins, W.G., 72, 76

housebreaking *see* burglary
house of correction, 48, 90, 116-17, 179-81, 184, 186, 222 n39
Huntingdonshire, King's Ripton in, 172

indictment, 8, 36-7, 38, 49, 71-2, 78, 128
Industrial Revolution, 17
infanticide, 49, 54-6, 60-2, 66, 109, 170
see also violence

Jeaffreson, J.C., 9
Johnson, Dr Samuel, 146
jury
charges to, 158-9
grand, 37
leet, 83-4
petty, 37
service on juries, 76
justices of the peace, 16, 28-30, 39, 75, 89-90, 91, 93, 156, 172, 176

Kent, 30, 82, 102, 106, 158-9
Canterbury in, 82
Eltham in, 102
Rochester in, 82